Joe Dungan knows the multiple personalities of this town like no other.

—Charles Phoenix, Los Angeles "histo-tainer"

An unapologetic, funny, and unusual travel guide to a city that keeps therapists working overtime.

—Peter Greenberg, Travel Editor,
NBC's *The Today Show*

Joe has a jaundiced eye and an artful way with just a few words. L.A. can be treacherous and heartbreaking. And you won't find a better guide than Joe.

—D.J. Waldie, author,
Holy Land: A Suburban Memoir

Hilarious snapshots of the wildly eccentric in Los Angeles.

—Joan Wai, co-author,
Newcomer's Handbook for Los Angeles

This is more than just a rant against everything wrong with the most flawed city in America. It is part unassailable rhetoric, part impassioned plea, offered up by a lifelong resident who has both a stake in its future and a grip on its past. For all its laugh-out-loud moments—imagine David Sedaris or Augusten Burroughs stuck in Los Angeles—it is far too substantial to be considered merely a humor book.

—Tad Daley, J.D., Ph.D.
Writing Fellow, International Physicians for the Prevention of Nuclear War (Nobel Peace Laureate Organization)
Author, *Apocalypse Never: Forging the Path to a Nuclear Weapon-Free World*
(Forthcoming from Rutgers University Press)

L.A. Nuts

L.A. Nuts

A collection of the cult-hit columns

Joe Dungan

TRINCO PUBLISHING
LOS ANGELES, CA

First edition

Trinco Publishing, Valley Village, Calif.

Cataloging-in-Publication Data

Dungan, Joe.
L.A. nuts: a collection of the cult-hit
columns / Joe Dungan.
xii, 268 p. : ill ; 23 cm.
ISBN 9780982034569
1. Los Angeles (Calif.)—Humor.
I. Title.
813./54--dc 22
2008908373

First printing: November 2008
Second printing: June 2009

TABLE OF CONTENTS

Acknowledgments

First thanks goes to Russell Brown and Tim Grierson, the editors at www.thesimon.com, who first saw the potential for a column in a short-lived blog about a guy complaining about his neighbor.

Thanks to Yonga Smith for an elegant book layout and Kalman Apple for his fantastic and inventive book cover. Also to Ani Boyadjian and Bob Tome for additional help.

Thanks also to the many people who've provided encouragement and input over the years, notably Max Koch, Missy Krehbiel, Amy Wolfram, Russ Woody, and Ken the landlord. Special thanks to Nicole Montgomery for her support, good ideas, and pushing me to finish.

And to Mom, for a lot.

And to all the people who've shared their stories with me.

Home, Home on the Alluvial Plain

MEET CLYDE LANGTRY, PART ONE

In the four years Clyde Langtry has been my neighbor, I've had an awful lot of conversations with him and made careful observations. I've distilled the evolution of Clyde's insanity to the following: Mother nut met father nut. They had Clyde.

One day, he was explaining to me that his cats run away. That's right, cats, plural, run away, on a regular basis, proving that animals have an intuitive intelligence that humans can't begin to approach. Ergo, Clyde took to hiring a cat psychic to tell him where his cats ran to so Clyde could go find them. Clyde told me that the psychic had divined the location of the latest runaway to a neighborhood about a mile southeast of our apartment building, and he had to find a time soon to go look for it.

Where do you start with news like that? Good question, and I needed a good answer at that time because it was the very first conversation I ever had with Clyde. This is how he introduced himself to me back in 2001. Since then, he's been undoing that first impression by reinforcing it.

Furthermore, Clyde likes to talk. If I make the egregious error of walking out to my car while Clyde is around, I'm bound to get stopped and lectured on auto mechanics or nutri-biotics or whatever else is shorting out his hard-wiring that day. Being a polite guy, I try to listen, giving him the benefit of the doubt every time that what he's about to say is going to lead to something remotely relevant. Doubt has long been erased. Now I just listen to him for the material.

He's a fan of old stereo parts, which he proudly buys on eBay, all for a grand home entertainment system he's building. He likes chatting about his cats, how he "trains" them to fear street traffic, how his orange cat is the reincarnation of his previous cat of the same name. He proudly refers to the lemon tree in back as "his," though he doesn't water or prune it. He also used to skydive. No word on whether or not the chutes opened a little late sometimes, if you know what I mean.

And oh yeah, he's a Scientologist. Texts from his boy, L. Ron, as Clyde refers to him, have taught him much about human nature. I know this because, on lucky occasion, Clyde delivers impromptu lectures on human nature. One particular subtopic warm to his heart is how most people don't come close to maximizing their potential. I'm tempted to explain to Clyde either that L. Ron is L. Wrong, or that Clyde's maximized potential equates to spending his autumn years in a one-bedroom apartment and driving a trashed Ford Taurus.

Clyde occasionally criticizes President Bush. Not about his politics or the Iraq war or anything like that. He criticizes Bush's mind and soul, prattling on about Bush's eyes or aura or something. "I'm very good at reading people," Clyde likes to say during such conversations. He can't figure out why he has no friends, but he's very good at reading people.

The creepy irony is that Clyde is nearly the spitting image of George W. Bush. If he combed his hair and put on a suit, they could almost be twins. But Bush talks like a smug Texan and walks with a matching swagger. Clyde talks like he's constipated and strides like he just graduated from debutante school. Plus, I doubt Clyde owns a suit.

Sometimes the details of my chats with Clyde are a bit sketchy. The man just talks so much, I don't have the capacity to memorize every word. This is compounded by the phenomenon that sometimes when Clyde's talking to me, I tune out and think about women or beer or how serene the world must be to deaf people.

This leads to the issue of trying to end a conversation with Clyde. I've tried oblique approaches but they don't work. As soon as we reach something resembling a lull, I might invite him in to join me for six or seven tequila shooters, knowing he doesn't drink. He responds by telling me again that he doesn't drink, bragging about how few drinks he's had in the last thirty-odd years—and drones on about the evils of dissipation. When I try to go for a wrap with something more off-putting, such as, "Well, I gotta hit the toilet. My diarrhea's about to explode on me again," Clyde lectures me about my diet.

Clyde's fascinating to me because I can't figure out how he got this way, above-mentioned theory notwithstanding. Believe it or not, though, I have figured out why his cats run away.

Some time ago, Clyde and his wife, Priscilla, who is not outwardly nuts except for her choice in husbands, were going out of town for several days and asked our landlord, Ken, to feed the cats. All the food was in the refrigerator, in little dishes, each covered with plastic wrap, each labeled for each cat. All Ken had to do was uncover and set out each dish on each day. Slam-dunk, right?

That's what Ken thought until he opened their fridge and found little dishes of vegetables. Clyde neglected to tell Ken that he thinks cats shouldn't eat meat, especially that processed stuff made by pet food companies. Ken, however, embraced his humanity by going to the store for cans of Fancy Feast and tossing the vegetables. By the time Clyde and Priscilla came home from their trip, all the veggie bowls were empty and all traces of the meat were gone.

A few days later, Clyde thanked Ken and asked, in amazement, what Ken did to make the cats so happy and energetic.

That's enough about Clyde for now. And this on a day when I read in Deepak Chopra's *The Seven Spiritual Laws of Success* that one should train oneself to reserve all judgments about other people. Clearly, Deepak Chopra has never lived in an apartment building in Los Angeles.

This Is Our Air

Good news, everyone. Good news. The American Lung Association just released its annual air pollution ranking and we're on top again. The good news is that it didn't make much of a splash in the papers this week. The other good news is that we overtook Bakersfield in the dogfight for dirtiest air in the country, meaning we can now scrap our "Hey, at least we're not Bakersfield!" slogan we'd been tossing around.

People like to bag on L.A.'s cars and industry for our air pollution. While those are the chief culprits, our geography actually doomed our air from the start. Los Angeles was called "Valley of Smoke" by the region's Native Americans long before white land prospectors made it out here to advertise it to Midwesterners as the place to cure their respiratory ailments.

The geography at issue is the mountains. All our smog gets pushed into it by the onshore flow, then stops because it can't go above the mountains. The reason it can't go above the mountains is because it is trapped by our inversion layer. Our inversion layer is a meteorological phenomenon marked by a layer of dense, cooler air stuck beneath warmer, lighter air. Actually, phenomenon probably isn't the right word. It's more like an affliction. The dense layer below is the layer that contains all the smog, and it doesn't rise up and disperse the smog into the rest of the atmosphere. The only difference between today and back in the days of the Tongva and the Chumash tribes is that it comes from industry instead of campfires.

Anyone who's ever flown in or out of Los Angeles knows that our inversion layer is best viewed from an airplane. You don't even need to be a meteorologist to see it. Several hundred feet above the ground, one can see a distinct line: blue above it, brown below it. The only consolation is that you're likely to forget that you're breathing air in a commercial airplane. Sure, our air causes cancer, emphysema, asthma, and other nice things, but no one has ever spent two hours breathing L.A. smog and caught a cold.

Upon trapping all that smog, the sun beats down on it all day, chemically converting it into ozone. Twenty miles up, we need ozone to keep the sun from frying us to death. But we've been destroying it ever since we learned how to make Styrofoam coffee cups. Down here, inhaling it causes edema. And we make it by the truckload every day.

Over the centuries, the severity of the air pollution has fluctuated, but the smog has never gone away. It was actually worse in the 1940s than it is today. One day in 1943, the smog had grown so thick and noxious that visibility downtown was reduced to three blocks. City leaders were so alarmed that they thought it was a chemical attack staged by the Japanese. Turned out to be a chemical being produced by The Gas Company's downtown plant.

Things have gotten better since then. Industry began to get regulated so as to prevent episodes like "gas attack day" from ever occurring again. We kept raising the bar so that the air would stop causing headaches and nausea and other sensations better left to the entertainment industry. And Los Angeles hasn't had a stage three smog alert since 1974. (In response to that unfortunate day, Governor Ronald Reagan urged locals to drive slower to reduce car emissions.) That didn't occur in L.A., but in Upland, a city out in what we blithely call the Inland Empire, our literal and figurative dumping ground to the east of us that gets all of our day-old smog because there are few mountains to prevent it from blowing out there. That was, in fact, the last stage three smog alert in U.S. history, but I doubt anyone in Upland brags about it.

Still, there remained rare occasions when things were substantially bad. There were a handful of days in my San Fernando Valley childhood where the air was so toxic that we were ordered to breathe as little as possible during recess and lunch. We were not allowed to take handballs and kickballs out, and playground supervisors ordered us not to run. Twice a day, we sat around in little clusters, occasionally getting up to walk over to some other cluster to see their version of doing nothing. Looking back, it was probably good practice for office life.

The only time the smog blows away is when the Santa Anas or some other strong wind kicks up. (By "away," of course, I mean to the Inland Empire.) These winds are powerful enough to eliminate the inversion layer entirely for a time, thus blowing nice, clean Pacific Ocean air over us. After those winds, when there's trash all over everyone's front yard, the air is beautiful. The only thing to worry about then is sunburn. The smog is so dirty and so evenly spread out that it acts as a nice ultraviolet ray protector. I call it our industrial sunscreen. When it's here, it can cause eye irritation in the uninitiated. When it's gone, it's so bright outside that the sunlight actually hurts my eyes.

The most effective way we regulate smog is with regulations. The Air Quality Management District has a Web site devoted to the subject. Anyone who wants to start a business that pollutes has to go through the AQMD for the proper permits and comprehension of the rules. I'd explain the rules but they're so involved that I was afraid that I'd die of old age if I actually tried to read them all. Maybe all those rules have led to confusion, because last time I checked, the air still looked like vomit in gas form.

Then again, maybe the AQMD just doesn't work so well. They've incurred million-dollar fines twice.

Whether you're running a polluting business or not, you probably own a car, which means you have to get a smog certificate for it. Los Angeles may be the place that made "smog" into a verb. Everyone's had to smog their car at one time or another, a lifeless, biennial ritual in which you pay someone 30 bucks (plus an $8.25 "certificate fee") to spend 15 minutes running your engine so that a machine can measure tailpipe exhaust. I haven't done a scientific survey, but I've never heard of anyone failing a smog test. Frankly, I'd like to know how much less pollution would be in the air if we didn't have to go pay someone $38.25 every two years to run our engines for 15 minutes.

If this seems arbitrary, consider the owners of cars that are six or fewer years old. They do not have to get smog checks because their cars are so new, and, presumably, their engines burn cleaner. Therefore, instead of $38.25 every two years, these owners only have to pay the California Department of Motor Vehicles $12 every year because a bureaucracy isn't a bureaucracy if it isn't gouging everyone for something.

For all that smelly bureaucracy, however, the DMV does encourage the use of cleaner-burning cars. Electric and hybrid cars are not subject to smogging at all. And drivers of most such cars qualify for access to carpool lanes on the freeway even when they're the sole occupant of the car. All they have to do is send a form to the DMV—and eight dollars to cover costs surrounding the sticker.

Last time I checked, the DMV had run out of stickers—and is unable to print more unless the state assembly raises the ceiling on how many can be issued.

In *The Control of Nature*, John McPhee writes of man's efforts to peacefully coexist with a few of Earth's more gargantuan natural forces. Despite our tirelessness and intelligence, any successes are transitory. The smog in Los Angeles might well have been a chapter in his book. Try as we might, we keep finding ourselves breathing the worst air in the nation. Regulations keep getting tighter, inducements keep increasing, consciousness keeps getting raised. But the geography and the comfortable climate it induces, like so many other things out here in the land of dreams, are killing us. Because, in the end, for all our tirelessness and intelligence, no amount of passionate progressive ideology will move mountains.

Meet Spencer Paltz:
Jack-of-All-Tough-Rackets

I had the hardest time writing this column. Maybe it was because the subject matter hit too close to home: not-rich writer, alleged nut, potential for full social retardation. Maybe it was because he's sad, awkward, or utterly harmless. More likely, it was because he's sad, awkward, *and* utterly harmless. There's so much to say about Spencer Paltz that one hardly knows where to start.

I always figured Spencer was in his late 30s or early 40s, but Ken the landlord says he's more like 55, which I find remarkable because he has the black, non-receding hair of a college kid and the soft, creakless voice to match. I usually see him moping from the apartment he shares with his mother to her car to fetch the groceries she buys on a seemingly daily basis. I can always tell when he's on a grocery schlep because he makes a slow, painful walk as if he's using up his daily hour of exercise time at Pelican Bay. When he's heading back to the parking lot to get in his car to actually go somewhere, he walks through the courtyard with more alacrity, but not much more.

In truth, he's actually very sweet, a quality he shares with his mother. Back in December he came by to ask if I could drive his mother to the hospital the next morning for scheduled minor surgery, as he would be unavailable. The two of them stood at my door and looked at me like they were asking for donations on behalf of the local orphanage. I drove her to the hospital the next morning. For the next few weeks, they thanked me every time they saw me, about a dozen times in all—and mailed me a Christmas card.

Apparently, Spencer has a background in technical writing, screenwriting, and other kinds of writing. I've never actually seen any of this writing. I'm not sure I've ever seen Spencer go to work, in fact. I do hear him talk of interviews and applications and jobs he used to have and how tough it is out there now. Of course, we're talking about a guy who can't get a civil service job because, he claims, of inherent racism against white males in the civil service industry.

Right or wrong, you'd think he'd consider a different career path. But I suspect this is part of Spencer's pattern of demonizing every industry he's ever attempted. One story has it that Spencer pissed himself out of a high-paying technical writing job because he complained that the orders he was given wouldn't result in clear writing. Anyone who knows anything about technical writing knows that clarity isn't the highest priority. Spencer was replaced. Now he complains that technical writing is a tough racket.

And according to Ken the landlord, a major studio once offered Spencer six figures for a screenplay he wrote. They told him flat out that they would change most of it and put someone else's name on it. Spencer turned them down because he wanted the movie to be shot exactly the way he wrote it. Anyone who knows anything about the screenwriting business knows that artistic vision isn't the highest priority. Spencer was rejected. Now he complains that screenwriting is a tough racket.

And so on.

If some writers make woeful conversationalists, then let's just say Spencer must be some writer. The confounding part is that he's usually eager to talk, even when logistics are against him and he has nothing to say. For instance, he'll see me walking in the parking area in back sometimes and he's compelled to do more than wave. He quickly puts down the window and turns his head way over his shoulder to address me. He seems to think that he might miss me completely if he spends the extra two seconds needed to roll the window down all the way. So he only rolls the window down far enough for me to hear him shout. Meanwhile, I've come to a complete stop because I see him cranking the window so frantically that I think he's got something urgent to tell me. Instead I get this:

"Hey, Joe, how's it going?"

Me, from about 15 feet away, "Fine."

"That's good."

Pause.

Me: "I gotta get going."

Spencer: "Okay. I'll catch you later."

These chats are even shorter when his engine is running.

When he's not strapped into his Tercel, our conversations tend to spread their wings a little. Take this impromptu visit to my door a couple of months back:

"Hey, Joe. I'm just seeing how it's going." He's so earnest you'd think I was fighting bronchitis or something.

"Oh, it's going fine."

Spencer: "Yeah."

Spencer says "yeah" a lot, but not as a question to induce details ("Yeah? How so?"), nor as encouragement ("Yeah. That's good news."). He uses it as a stalling tactic until he thinks of something else to say.

Spencer: "How's the writing?"

Me: "Oh, it's going fine."

Spencer: "Good. Keep writing. It's good for you."

Fiber is good for you. Writing is a curse.

I gestured back at my computer. "I'm kinda' in the middle of something." Maybe I was, maybe I wasn't. I don't remember.

"Oh, okay. I'll catch you later."

As soon as Spencer thinks you're late, busy, or carrying perishable groceries, he's apologetic and the conversation promptly ends. I wonder if he asks himself why I always appear to be late, busy, or carrying perishable groceries.

Spencer is also another example of a bothersome phenomenon in this town: The less success people have had in the entertainment industry, the more they like to volunteer how much they know about it. A couple of weeks ago, I mentioned that I was rewriting a screenplay, whereupon Spencer delivered a lengthy speech to me about the realities of the screenwriting business. One thing he warned me about was the possibility of having a studio interested in your script but telling you that they'll change most of it and put someone else's name on it—the very thing that allegedly happened to Spencer. He went on about it like it was a truly horrible fate for a writer. I get the feeling Spencer Paltz doesn't hang out with many starving artists.

"But what if they offer the writer enough money in exchange?" I asked. "Wouldn't it be worth it then?"

"I don't know. That's never happened to me."

I related that to Ken the landlord, who replied, "When he told me that story, I told him he was an idiot for turning down all that money, so he probably lied to you because now he doesn't want anyone to know about it."

Last night in the parking lot, Clyde was chatting me up about his abilities to perceive evil, so I asked him, "Say, Clyde, are any of our neighbors evil? I mean, like, way, way worse than just heinous B.O. kind of evil?"

He thought about it and said, "No, nobody here is really evil, at least not evil enough to fuck with any of the neighbors or anything. But you know who has real problems is Spencer. That guy's got so much mental mass weighing him down, almost to the point of insanity."

Clyde paused. Then he looked right at me and said this:

"I should talk, huh?"

Where do I start?

This Is What It's Like to Smoke Here

Picture the smoker who flies to Los Angeles for the first time. It all starts with him on a smoke-free flight that's several hours long, which is probably several hours longer than he usually goes without a cigarette. He goes to his hotel to unwind with a smoke or two, only to discover that he reserved a nonsmoking room. He goes down to the hotel restaurant and asks for a seat in the smoking section. The hostess explains that the nearest place he can smoke and eat at the same time in Los Angeles is in his rental car.

Now reaching high anxiety, he figures to hell with food and goes to the first bar he can find so he can get toasted. He asks the bartender for a match because he couldn't take his lighter on the plane. The bartender tells him he can't smoke inside—and he can't take his drink outside. He doesn't want to smoke outside, either, because the neighborhood around the airport isn't exactly Mayberry. So he jumps in his car and lights up. He drives to the beach and, in between tokes, yells at the ocean. This gets the attention of a nearby police officer, who comes over and writes him up for smoking on the beach.

The above story is made up, but the circumstances are entirely true. Smoking is outlawed in every enclosed public building in California. And yes, that includes bars. I remember when the law was first passed in 1998, bartenders complained that they'd go out of business if people weren't able to light up while drinking. I suppose they were afraid that smoker-drinkers were going to stay home and drink alone every night just so they could exercise their freedom to smoke. If they did do that, they didn't do it much. They still drink at bars, then go outside and congregate on benches and in tents to smoke. Last time I checked, no bars have gone out of business.

Before tents and benches became commonplace, bar patrons defied the ordinance. One night, years ago, a friend of mine asked for an ashtray so she could smoke at the bar. The bartender made her say "I insist" before he'd give it to her. This, he claimed, was to relieve him of liability should undercover police officers start handing out citations. Ken the landlord told me he once saw a bunch of cops come into a smoke-filled bar and try to write everyone up. Trouble was, the smokers were crafty enough to leave their cigarettes in the ashtrays and only touch them when they wanted a drag. Since the police only saw two or three people actually smoking, they were only able to give two or three tickets.

Ken pointed out an overarching absurdity that seemed lost on everyone else. "The law is designed to protect employees. All the bartenders at that place smoked."

If you think the state's smoking restrictions are extreme, just take a look at what some local cities around here are doing. A few years ago, West Hollywood passed an ordinance allowing renters to file complaints if a neighboring tenant's cigarette smoke drifted into their home. Santa Monica is considering banning smoking on the open-air Third Street Promenade. Most of our beaches are smoke-free. And Calabasas recently banned smoking outdoors entirely: restaurant patios, sidewalks, parking lots, everywhere. I wonder how many people are running around complaining that the city of Calabasas will go out of business.

Not that smokers look cool, but they at least manage to look dignified. However, smokers who are forced by law to walk off someplace to light up can't help but look sad in some way. Years ago, Dodger Stadium management banned smoking in the seating part of the stadium. So they painted rectangles on the ground in distant corners of each level. No doors. No walls. Just lines. I still have vivid memories of seeing smokers standing in imaginary rabbit warrens far from the seats, puffing away in these dim patches of cement, isolated and avoided. Some looked out at the sliver of the playing field they could see from that distance. Some looked up at the TV monitors that management had so thoughtfully installed for them. Some looked at nothing. They looked like an unsold Edward Hopper painting.

When I recently went back to the stadium for the first time in years, there was a nice courtyard setting inside the gates but still outside the stadium. I figured this was the new smoking area for the hundred or so remaining tobacco-using fans of the Dodgers. They wouldn't have to stand in the corner like penitent schoolchildren anymore. How nice. But I was wrong. I visited the Dodgers' official Web site, where I found out their smoking policy: Smokers have to be signed out by security personnel so they can go smoke in the parking lot. They used to get sections. Now they get discharged.

I took a class at Valley College in the spring and was surprised to see the school had co-opted the Dodgers' rabbit warren idea. Smokers couldn't just step outside for a light. They had to sit in *very* small rectangles, literally in the middle of open areas between buildings. You couldn't not stare at them when you walked out of a building. I suppose school management figured that if they could force students to go outside to smoke, they might as well try to humiliate them while they're at it.

The embarrassment factor must be working. Ken the landlord, a lifelong smoker, says he's reluctant to reveal his habit too soon to people. When he does reveal it, he says, people react as if he were a drug addict or a member of the wrong political party. A friend of mine who works at a school tells me that the few smokers who work with her are very careful not to get caught smoking at school events and such. In a recent article in *The Los Angeles Times*, the writer was going around asking smokers about the smoking ban at the beach. The article stated that many smokers either didn't want to go on record or were too embarrassed to be interviewed.

When you're a child, you notice and remember a lot. When I was a kid, my dad lived in Northern California, in Concord, which is in the suburbs east of Oakland. He was in the restaurant business. Along with two other guys, he ran three stores, and used to take me along to them, where I met dozens of my dad's coworkers. What I noticed about them was that nearly all of them smoked. One of the other owners, his wife, and a manager were the only three who didn't smoke. All the others, all the waitresses, all the cooks, all the busboys, would smoke up in the break room.

I don't think it was ever that prevalent in Los Angeles. Not even in film noir.

Northern California was also the only place I ever had a run-in with a smoker—and it was with a pseudo-relative. When we were kids, my brother and I went to one of our dad's restaurants with our stepmother. Unbeknownst to her, my brother and I requested a nonsmoking table. When she saw the table we were given, she was so offended that she got up and left us there to walk home. I've never known a smoker to be so self-absorbed. Then again, if my dad was to be believed after the divorce, she was something of a bitch to begin with.

The relatively few smokers here are generally polite about their habit. They only smoke where it's legal, and even then they try to keep it away from other people. And the scofflaws usually do it out of ignorance more than defiance. I've seen a couple of people light up in public places over the years and when I explained to them the laws here, they were quick to take their cigarettes outside. This doesn't illustrate smokers' politeness as much as it does their rarity. It's literally been years since I've seen anyone light up in a public enclosed space around here. Although, about a month ago, I saw a guy smoking at a gas station, proving that some of us are, in fact, truly insane. But if all of our laws restricting tobacco use means that all of us are nuts, then put tin foil on our heads and radio a message to smoke-filled cities nationwide: Welcome to Los Angeles. Please don't smoke here. Or here. Or here. Or here....

Meet Our Pedestrians: Both of Us

A few months ago in a local magazine, a writer articulated locals' new outlook on gridlock. She compared it to places that at least had discernible climate changes, but weather still unpleasant enough to make people wish they were elsewhere.

With our gridlock reaching pestilential proportions, we're not even "elsewhere" anymore. People who live *here* wonder about moving to *those other places* where the weather sucks but at least the commute doesn't take an hour and a half. Even though some of us move to those cities, you'd never know it, either by the traffic or the cost of living. Both remain staggering. Even more staggering is that so many of us remain locked in an endless staring contest; more and more of us work *there*, but we want to live *way out here*, and if only some of those other people on the freeway would move elsewhere instead of doing the same thing we're doing, they could make our lives much easier.

But not enough of them move away or change their commuting patterns, and the population here continues to grow—and with it, the tension that accompanies commuting. As a result, our lives have been substantially affected. The writer of the recent article cited several examples of people compromising their social lives because it's too hard to get to places and people that are no further away than they were five years ago.

What kills me is that people are so insistent on living in the communities they want to live in, but they don't walk around in them. Even with the trend towards compromising our social lives because gridlock compels us to stick close to home, we still don't walk around our own communities. These are the same communities we insist on living in rather than live someplace closer to our workplaces, presumably because every community between home and work is so expensive that we can't afford it or so crap-ass that we wouldn't be caught dead walking around in it.

It's easy for me to encourage living closer to your workplace now that I work from home. Not so much when I worked in Commerce, a city southeast of downtown that's about as pastoral as it sounds. I worked there because it was the home of the best job I could find at the time. And, as fate would have it, I was between apartments just as I got the job. Active despiser of commuting that I was, I looked for apartments roughly in that direction, but ended up back in my home, the Valley—in an apartment a couple of miles *farther* from Commerce than my previous place. Then when the chance to become a freelancer presented itself, I jumped at it, in no small part because the stress of the commute was shaving years off my life.

I walk around my Valley Village community plenty, and what I lose by not driving I gain by walking. One of the most important things I gain by walking occurs when I visit the nearby post office. The first thing I gain is a near-unobstructed use of the sidewalk. I go a good three miles per hour each way, any hour of the day—including rush hour. The second thing is that I don't have to fight traffic to get there. Magnolia Boulevard is just one lane in each direction at the post office and traffic is often heavy. Third, I don't have to look for parking. Parking around there is so difficult that sometimes the closest parking spot is the one behind my building where I keep my car.

But the biggest joy is the adventure of crossing the street. Since crosswalks have proven to be the sites of the majority of pedestrian injuries and deaths— not to mention a potential black hole of lawsuits against the cities that present them as safe places to cross streets—cities have been eliminating crosswalks nationwide. But they haven't been eliminating those pesky jaywalking laws. This distills my choices to: obeying the law with a slight risk to my life; jaywalking, which trades a slight chance of a ticket for a slight statistical decrease in risk of physical safety; or driving to a place that I can walk to in less time than it would take me to drive there. I usually jaywalk, just because when there's a rare break in traffic, I'm not usually at the crosswalk. In other words, I'm turning into a New Yorker.

Two days ago, I did the crosswalk thing to the post office. On this day, a critical mass of pedestrians formed spontaneously, so I figured all of us walking together would make the cross that much safer. At the double-yellow line, our herd, of one mind, waited for an SUV to go flying through before we finished crossing. Then the driver slammed on the brakes and stopped halfway through the crosswalk, close enough for him to apologize to us without shouting. You'd think a critical mass of pedestrians would prevent such near misses. Then again, our critical mass consisted of two people.

Since the number of pedestrians is lacking, the sense of community is lacking. As an amateur community redevelopment maven, my suggestion is the same one that club owners have been using since forever: Get more women out there, because they attract men. You get enough women walking up and down the street, then men show up, then suddenly my community sidewalks are the hottest places in town. The fatal flaw in that plan is the "get more women out there" part. I know too many women who think our streets, deserted of everything but speeding cars, are scary, even during the daytime.

My friend Tina, who lives around the corner from me, told me recently that she doesn't feel a sense of community outside of her apartment building. (The fact that we had that conversation by Instant Messenger wasn't lost on me.) The only time Tina said she felt anything resembling a sense of community was when she was dog-sitting and was forced to walk up and down the block every day with someone else's dog. Even then she tried to stay under the radar because our community is, in her purview, creepy. If you think you're surrounded by creeps, the only thing that might discourage that notion is an excess of walking. But that's a hard activity to take up when you think everyone else is a creep.

The idea of not walking here is not new. People have been not walking in L.A. for decades. Walking in Los Angeles is such a curious activity that law enforcement officers consider it suspicious. D.J. Waldie, a local city official and author who doesn't drive and is as buttoned-down in dress and demeanor as a guy can get, was once stopped and interrogated by a sheriff for walking down a suburban sidewalk in the daytime. Ray Bradbury, another renowned nondriver, was also once stopped by police, so suspicious did he appear for walking. Can you imagine what that would sound like during an arraignment? "Your honor, the arresting officer witnessed the defendant walking." The idea.

It's such a novelty that not only does one person have a Web site devoted to city walks he's taken, but when I did an Internet search for "Los Angeles" and "walking," his site came up fourth.

But the classic joke is in Missing Persons' song about it. There are plenty of activities that nobody does in other cities—or, more to the point, things we could presume based on our perceptions of those cities. I'd guess, for example, that since pop music acts, comedians, and garish circus shows are the most popular entertainments in Las Vegas, people could go around saying, "nobody goes to the opera in Las Vegas." Since Washington D.C. is so full of politicians and their sycophants, "nobody tells the truth in Washington D.C." could have become an old adage by now. Since Minnesota is a notoriously nice state, people might say, "nobody says 'fuck off' in Minneapolis." No songs about those. But put "nobody walks in L.A." to music and it becomes a hit. Either it was a catchy tune, or it was damn true even a generation ago when the song was released.

People here, particularly transplants, particularly single ones, complain that it's hard to meet people here. With debilitating traffic crippling our social options, and pedestrianism perceived as dangerous, is it any wonder that, in our self-imposed isolation, we think of everyone around us as an undesirable? As my humble megalopolis grows, however, we will become—are already becoming—Manhattanized. Population density and impracticality of driving will force us to adopt more walking, and we'll be forced to find out firsthand just how creepy our neighbors are.

And if that prospect frightens you, please move away now and take your grid-lock-inducing cars with you so the rest of us can get back to more driving.

This Is What It's Like to Park Your Car Here

In *Crash*, Don Cheadle's character opens the film noting that, unlike in "real" cities where you're forced into other people's personal spaces, everyone in L.A. is insulated in their cars. That impersonal nature of interaction, he tells us, is what gives rise to the urge for Angelenos to feel things. And in a city where traffic is mind-boggling and parking is at a premium, it's also what gives many of us the potential to go batshit with fear or fury every time we get behind the wheel. We think we're safe boxed into our metal and glass, and we neither know much nor care much about the people around us boxed into their metal and glass. Ignorance and apathy won't get us to our favorite restaurants any faster, but neither will wisdom and compassion.

Two weekends ago, when I went to a club to see a singer-guitarist friend play a set, I arrived early and nabbed a good parking spot. A car whizzed by, and a woman riding shotgun stuck her head out the window and yelled something at me. I thought it was a joke, but I wasn't sure. Were they friends who recognized me from afar, or were they drunk teenagers, circling the block, waiting to slash my tires—or me? When the car parked down the street and its riders came walking by, I saw that they were friends of mine who had recognized me and were just giving me a hard time. But the fact that I had to see them walk by and confirm it goes to show you my fear of incurring tizzyfits from strangers over a parking spot.

And I'm hardly alone. The concept of road rage is very real in this town. Okay, fine, we're not all peace-lovers out here, but the circumstances try anyone's patience. Heavy traffic merely exacerbates the truly infuriating things: acts of bad driving, be they deliberate or careless. It's hard not to get mad as hell at the army of dumbasses who keep inventing new ways of operating cars poorly. Now imagine all that frustration culminating in that grand moment when the driver is about to park and doesn't get the parking spot he was eyeballing. He's not mad that he'll have to walk farther to get to his ultimate destination as much as he is that he has to keep driving.

You can express your feelings to the offending driver, but you risk the offender being some maniac who expresses his feelings by busting a cap in yo' ass. Fortunately, many drivers in L.A. wear giant signs to indicate how menacing they are. These signs are in the form of heavily tinted windows, loud stereos playing bad music, and an excess of shiny chrome and similarly tacky pimped-out accoutrements. Then again, Ted Bundy drove a nondescript VW Bug, so you're really not safe assuming anything about a person by his car.

People move to L.A. with dreams of stardom in the entertainment industry, or amassing immeasurable wealth in the entertainment industry, or screwing every MAW (model, actress, whatever) in the entertainment industry. Or all three. My dream is to have the guts to confront an astonishingly rude driver, preferably of a large truck or SUV, by getting out of my car—in traffic—and exploding into a rage so fearsome that he's compelled to remove his balls and return them to God at once. If I can get him to shit his leather seat, that would be gravy. I have loftier dreams, really.

Fast forward to Wednesday of last week. I walk out of my therapist's office and head to my car, the culmination of that grand moment when I get to leave the Santa Clarita Valley. I discover that a Ford pick-up truck on hormones is parked in a spot perpendicular to mine. The rear of the truck sticks out. Far. Very far.

It sticks out so far that it blocks me in.

First, I write a note that I plan to leave on his windshield. Then I come to my senses. I try to see if I can inch my car out first *before* leaving the note. No luck. Not enough room. Then I get proactive about it. I write down his license number with the intent of going door to door in search of the owner. I've seen the kind of people who drive these cars. Some of them are not the sorts who like being given orders. No telling what I'd be up against. But my tolerance for rude, thoughtless people continues to reach record lows. At last, I thought, this might be my chance to tear some asshole a new asshole.

Just then, a skinny guy, no older than 30, yakking away on a cell phone strolls up. My one shining moment. My dream realized. He looks unthreatening. Gutless, even. I fly into action.

My dream went like this:

"Excuse me. Is this your truck?"

"Yeah."

"You blocked me in."

"Oh." He looks at my car, realizes the situation with genuine surprise.

"How am I supposed to get out? You put this big thing in a compact parking spot. How am I supposed to get my car out?" I sound about as intimidating as Andy Rooney.

"I'm sorry."

"I was about to go knocking on doors looking for the owner."

"I'm sorry, I didn't know."

He gets in his truck and drives away.

That was it.

Looking back on that moment outside my therapist's office, I don't regret it. I handled it pretty calmly, not unlike someone who's gone through a lot of therapy. And I got the owner of a testosterone truck to apologize twice in 20 seconds—no easy trick in the domestic-violence capital of California.

More importantly, I defused a situation that could have turned ugly. I didn't know his temperament, nor he mine. That unknown, that wondering what lies on the other side of someone's look or tone of voice or heavily tinted windows, is what keeps people—especially in L.A.—from risking fights in the first place, their urge to feel things be damned.

Five minutes later, I'm in the drive-through of In-N-Out Burger. The person who takes my order isn't there. He's just an electric box surrounded by parked cars.

"Hi, how are you today?" the electric box asked.

"Eh, I'm okay. Some asshole parked his Ford F-150 in a compact parking spot and the back of his car stuck out so much that he blocked me in. I couldn't get my goddamn car out. So I'm sitting there like an idiot. I don't know what to do. It's in this big complex. I don't know where this guy is. Finally, he comes walking up and he's, like, retarded. He doesn't even realize what he did. I say, 'Hey, dude. You blocked me in. Helloooooo.' He says, 'Oh. Sorry.' He doesn't even care. I mean, what the hell is wrong with people? Jesus, you can't even park in a parking lot anymore without some asshole blocking you in."

There was a pause. The poor bastard stuck with headset duty that day probably couldn't tell if I was joking or what.

"I'm sorry to hear that."

"How are you?"

Meet Milt Dorfman: The Man Who Says Hi, Sometimes.

As a freelance writer, part of my work involves looking for work. One thing I do all day is to get on the phone and call companies asking them about their occasional or ongoing need for freelance copywriting. It can be a drain, sitting here, by myself, calling up strangers, achieving a conversion rate that even junk mailers would scoff at. Sometimes I need to take a break to do the other things writers do: Look for material.

Like many of the others here, Milt Dorfman has been living in this complex since the Pleistocene. He's about six-two and really bulky, particularly where a man doesn't want to be bulky. Ken the landlord says Milt used to be trim as a greyhound when he was a serious bicyclist. Now the man is shaped like a giant pear and walks as if he's about to have a stroke.

Still, I wouldn't call him oafish except for the expression he wears on his face, a combination of confusion and exhaustion tempered by an oddly piercing gaze. His eyelids look like they're about to give up, and he talks with a matching lack of energy. He sounds like he doesn't have enough wind to blow out a match. I'd try to offer a comparison of some TV personality who talks so weakly, but people who look and sound like Milt don't appear on television.

When I mentioned Milt to my neighbor, The Confidante, the other day, she asked, "Is he retarded?" I doubt it, but the man's social skills are severely stunted. My early conversations with Milt went like this:

Me: "Hi, Milt."

Milt: "Hi." He'd force the word out like it took half his energy.

Long pause. His eyes would bore into me, emphasis on bore. This included the eye that doesn't work.

That was basically it. He'd keep walking, I'd keep walking, but he'd keep looking at me for a long time, like I owed him a lengthy answer to some deep question he'd asked.

I mentioned this phenomenon to Ken the landlord. Ken said, "He's waiting for you to tell him that you're gay."

I figure the only reason someone could want this is because he himself is gay, even though a guy who dresses like a frat boy who just woke up probably isn't gay. That said, the prevailing theories remain: My neighbor Milt is either retarded or gay—or both, but quite possibly neither. There's nothing wrong with being retarded or gay. I just never thought I'd be actively wondering such things about Milt.

Once, a while back, Milt took my laundry out of one of the complex's two washing machines, no more than a few minutes after it was done, and dumped it in a dryer. He did this despite the fact that the other washer was available. When I questioned why he did this, he said, "Someone cut in front of me."

Several months ago, Milt's cable went out. Naturally, he knocked on my door.

"My cable just went out," said Milt wanly, like a man whose cable just went out. "Is your cable out?"

"I don't have cable."

"Oh. You don't have cable?"

"No."

"I thought you had cable."

"Nope."

Silence.

"My cable's out."

He just stood there and kept looking at me like I was the landlord. Lucky for me, Ken the landlord, who really is the landlord, happened to walk by and took care of it for me.

"Yeah, I think the city's doing some street work and that's interfering with it," Ken said.

I'm sure it was a lie. Ken has mastered what to say to people to get rid of them. Milt wandered off.

It wasn't the first time Milt had mistaken me for the landlord. Once, while I was unlocking my door, I heard this from Milt's apartment:

"Ken?"

It was Milt. He was looking right at me from his window about 20 feet away. Ken lives in another apartment not adjacent to mine, and we don't look alike. I figured Milt would piece this together immediately.

Milt: "Ken? Ken? Hey, Ken?"

Me: "I'm not Ken."

Milt: "Oh. I need Ken to come over and fix my screen."

This is indicative of his inability to focus on more than one thing. No matter what you say to him or what your agenda might be, he's out to talk about one thing and is incapable of adapting to any other subject. Take this a few months ago outside the laundry room:

"Hi, Milt."

"Do you need a kettle?" He routinely skips the "hi" part.

"What?"

"I have two kettles. I just wanna know if you want one."

It occurred to me recently that I've never had a lengthy, substantial conversation with him. Ever. Okay, some have been longer than others, but all of them have been lacking in substance. Curiosity is catching up with me. *What is the deal with Milt? Does he do things like bang his car into the wall next to his parking spot and let his socks bunch up around his ankles because he's retarded? Are his stunted conversational skills the result of latent homosexuality?*

I've become compelled to talk to him more. I fight against the instinct to walk the other way when I see him coming. I linger more so as to "accidentally" bump into him somewhere.

Last weekend, he wandered through the courtyard and said to me and another neighbor, *"Guten tag."* I replied in kind.

Later that afternoon, I saw him in the parking lot.

Me: *"Guten tag."*

Milt: "I lost my cell phone."

Tuesday morning, in between phone calls to prospects, I saw him coming back from his P.O. box. This was the second time I'd seen him that day. Or was it the first? It was becoming a blur. Milt-mania.

"Hi, Milt."

"Hi."

"What's n—"

"Nice day, isn't it?"

"Yes, it is."

"Not too hot." Milt wears shorts almost all the time, even when it's too cold.

"Yeah, we're lucky to have such nice weather."

"I get all these magazines," Milt said, flipping through his magazines. "I don't know where they come from."

"What have you got?"

"Oh, *Vanity Fair, Good Housekeeping....* I don't know how I got them. They look good on the coffee table, though."

I was about to ask him what he did all day since he apparently has no job. Instead he said, "Well, I'll see ya' later" and lurched off.

Tuesday night, I'm keeping my blinds open so I can see his car come up the driveway. Around 8:15, here it comes. I race out, pretending to look for something in my car.

Knowing that Milt takes an eternity to park his car, I slow my gait. Slower. I'm downright moseying now. I get to my car. I open the door. I have nothing to look for. Finally, Milt heaves himself out of his car. Then I close my car door and walk towards him as he does likewise.

"Hi, Milt."

"Here. Shake my hand."

I shake his hand. I figure he's about to tell me he just had another grand-nephew or something. Instead, he says nothing and looks at me as if he's waiting for me to tell him that I'm gay.

"Where you headed?" he asks.

"I was just looking for something in my car."

"You walking this way?"

"Sure."

We head back towards the apartments.

"What do you do?" I ask. "Did I hear you say once that you do day-trading on the computer?"

"Oh, yeah. I get up around 5:30 and check the overseas markets. I'll have about five screens going on my computer at once."

"You do all right with that?"

"Yeah, I'm doing all right. I used to be a broker. I just love this stuff."

He goes on about day-trading and studying the markets for another minute. The whole time, I'm thinking that no gay retarded man could talk like this.

Silence. Now he looks at me like the conversation has gone on too long. He lists towards his stairs.

"Well, I'll see ya' later."

Wednesday morning, I hear what sounds like his old rattle-trap car speed by my window. I go out to my car again to look for a misplaced prescription from my gastroenterologist if anyone asks. Sure enough, it was Milt.

"Hi, Milt."

"Hi. I just went to the gym. I didn't push myself that hard but, oh well." Then his cell phone goes off. I guess he didn't lose it.

After the call, he said, "That was Paul. We're going to go have coffee." This was the perfect pregnant pause for him to invite me. Will this be my chance to find out the meaning of Milt?

Instead he says this: "I wanna talk to you about your P.R. business."

"Sure. What do you need?"

"Oh, I don't know yet. I just might have a couple of things going on."

My God. Milt is a prospect. Who knew?

And yesterday morning. I catch him again, this time as he heads to his P.O. box. We talk about a bunch of things. Most notable was Milt's take on Christmas: "I hate it. I can't stand having people putting a gun to my head, telling me to love my fellow man." This is much funnier when you remember that he talks with the passion of your average economics professor.

I ask him about his possible need for a copywriter. I figure he'd forgotten about it. Instead, he says, "Oh, I talked to my brother [who works in marketing for the wine industry] this morning and asked him if he needed a creative writer. He says he doesn't need anyone right now. He and his partner do all the writing. But you never know. I know some people in the finance industry too. I'll talk to them."

This man is not retarded. Maybe he smoked a lot of grass in his 20s, but he's not retarded. And if he's gay, he certainly hasn't hit on me. I think he's straight. (And there's nothing wrong with being straight, either.)

Then just as I was deciding all this, he ends the conversation by inviting me to come up and see his apartment sometime, not unlike a man who might be gay.

Also not unlike a slightly weird guy who's only trying to be neighborly.

This Is Our Noise

It rained a few days ago, which I bring up only because it's news. This is shaping up to be the driest rain season since we began measuring such things, so nowadays when it rains, it's especially welcome. We don't just need the water, but I believe we need the sound. I know of no one who doesn't like the sound of rain, and I suspect that it helps a city full of stress cases calm down a little. It's also a nice sound because it drowns out all the other noise in the city.

The noise in Los Angeles is constant. There is usually traffic, on every street, most of the time. Sometimes, a car comes by blasting music that always seems to be the most unappealing music ever recorded. (Just once I'd like to hear someone driving by blasting a Rachmaninoff piano concerto.) Sometimes, it thoughtfully peels out nearby. Even cars that aren't in use are noisy here; Los Angeles is the international capital of paranoiacs who get car alarms that go off when no one is breaking into the car. This happens either because the car owner hasn't figured out the sequence of turning off the alarm before entering the car, or because a flea flaps its wings next to it. But I have never heard a car alarm go off because a thief broke into the vehicle. No one has. Ever. It's too crazy an idea even to be an urban legend.

We have plenty of helicopters here, many of which like to fly as close to the ground as the FAA will allow. On occasion, they'll fly in circles over one's neighborhood—at night, if you're lucky—to catch some asshole who was rude enough to commit a crime, then dumb enough to flee just as the cops arrived. The helicopters are in a noise contest with the muffler-free motorcyclists, who outnumber them and are closer to the ground. We have more construction workers than in other cities because every building here needs to be rebuilt because they're not expensive enough already. People honk horns because no one's invented a car that yells, "Watch where you're going, asshole." Dogs bark more here because, in this town, everyone wants attention.

There is also no shortage of sirens, because we have no shortage of crimes or seriously injured people—including heart attack victims due to the shock of all the sudden and loud noises.

The past decade has seen the rise of a fantastic form of noise pollution: cell phones. Other people's cell phone conversations have the uncanny quality of blending into the din of any room at the same time they are clashing with it. They would be amusing if they weren't so infuriating. It begins when someone's crotch starts playing "Dontcha" or "Mambo Number Five" or "Darth Vader's Theme" because people aren't thoughtful enough to keep their cell phones on vibrate. Then they proceed to have a conversation that is, without exception, long, loud, and outwardly pointless. (The only people polite enough to take their conversations outside, I've noticed, are people who actually have interesting conversations on their cell phones. The boring chats are shared in front of everyone.) It even happens in movie theaters, where you would think people would be too polite to do such things. Nope. Lights down, quiet, everyone involved in the movie, then, sure as shit, some asshole's cell phone goes off. There is no law against it, and the few stewards of public places who have bothered to enact policies against cell phone use are slow or reluctant to enforce them. God forbid any customer go an entire evening without easy access to mundane conversation.

Even in the dead of night, when everyone's asleep because there are only about eight places in town that are open after two in the morning, the city makes noise. I can best describe it as a long sigh.

While some of this may resemble the hustle and bustle of a big city, for some reason in L.A., it adds up not to a collective noise, but just the sum of noise parts. New York City has the noise of a metropolis, but it is the kind of noise that energizes a person, the buzz of an empire in constant action. L.A. sounds like an overworked machine, its efficiency needle in the red. The only hustle we have is done by people in showbiz. There is no bustle. There is lurching, staggering, screeching, stomping, grinding, shouting, stalling, and underneath it all, a wail in the form of man's search for meaning. And searching for meaning in Los Angeles is like looking for diamonds in a landfill.

Believe it or not, there are times when we don't want to hear all that noise. Sidestepping the impracticality of going hundreds of miles away every time, we opt for something simpler: drowning out others' noise with our own noise. Therefore, a person such as myself might be living his life in his quiet Valley flat, trying to ignore the surround sound system of my upstairs neighbor, while both of us are trying to tune out the perpetual quilting bee on the balcony across the driveway. This is on the same balcony where someone has one of those cell phones that doubles as a walkie-talkie, so on occasion we get to hear an extra conversation as well as an electronic chirp every time the other person talks. (As I write this, outside the same building, some twit is yelling up at a balcony to someone. I keep hearing "Judit" over and over. Finally she explains to someone else sticking their head out of their balcony that she got locked out and didn't have a key. The explanation was so loud that I didn't have to open my window to hear it.) And none of us are any match for the periodic plane taking off from Bob Hope Airport, one of the busiest commercial airports in the country. The good news is that with all that noise going on, I don't have to hear my neighbor's parrot.

As for legal recourse, it does happen. Police do pull over loud cars and show up at noisy parties, but rigid enforcement is pretty futile in a city with a perpetual shortage of police officers. Besides, many of the definitions of noise violations appear to involve judgment calls. But the city noise ordinance has a section about leaf blowers that's amazingly clear-cut. I did a double-take when I read it: "No gas-powered blower shall be used within 500 feet of a residence at anytime."

Okay, judgment calls I can understand. But why don't police enforce such a clearly written law in the gardener capital of the world? I called the North Hollywood Police Station. First, I wanted to make sure that noise law enforcement wasn't just a theory, since I've never actually seen anyone get a ticket for being loud. A very nice officer informed me that patrol officers do, in fact, cite noise polluters when they can.

"What about the ordinance against gas-powered leaf blowers?" I asked.

"I don't think there is an ordinance against gas-powered leaf blowers."

"Yes, there is. It's on the noise enforcement team's Web site."

"For LAPD?"

"Yes."

"Oh, in that case, it's probably because of the drought. The city doesn't want to encourage people to use hoses to clean off driveways. As I understand it, they're going to repeal the leaf blower law."

"Which is why the police don't bother to enforce it."

"Yes."

In other words, we're noisier than we need to be because it doesn't rain enough.

THIS IS HOW WE TALK

A few months ago, I got into a discussion about which segment of the country speaks English correctly. I'd just assumed it was Los Angeles. Some of us don't enunciate that well, but the majority of us have the inflections down properly. I always knew how to make the "a" sound, as in "cat," until it occurred to me in this conversation that I may have been mispronouncing "cat" my whole life.

Around the same time, I was on the phone with someone who lives in Las Vegas. She pointed out my accent. I insisted that I didn't have one. She insisted that I did: a Los Angeles accent. And it's not like this woman lived in the Bronx or something.

I know a Los Angeles accent exists, but I always thought it was present only in a minority of our residents. And I always thought it was represented not by an accent but by an overuse of "like" (as in, "I'm, like, uffended"), "totally" (as in, "I'm, like, totally uffended"), and "all" (as in, "He's all, 'You don't have to be, like, totally uffended'").

But it is also marked by a laziness in inflection. One native friend of mine, for example, rarely says the word "butt." She says "buh," sort of clipping off the very end of it so that it sounds like she's about to interrupt herself. The best way I can spell it is B-U-dash. "Bu—." She also does it with other words that end with T. "Not" often comes out "no—." "I am no— happy with the size of my bu—."

Despite these regional quirks, it's never occurred to me—or anyone else in Los Angeles with whom I've talked about this—that we have any kind of accent. This myopia about language may be a sign of a greater self-absorption that permeates Los Angeles, but more likely it's because our TV representatives have become the self-appointed arbiters of what English is supposed to sound like.

You may have noticed the curious lack of accents—or widespread application of the Los Angeles accent—among characters on television shows. How often do you hear anyone on *ER* flatten the "A" in "Chi-CAH-go?" Which characters on *Friends* besides Joey sounded like a New Yawker? They all sounded like people from Los Angeles. Heck, Phoebe sounded vaguely like a Valley Girl. (Actually, I went and looked it up. Lisa Kudrow, who played Phoebe, is from Encino.)

There are either many reasons for this homogenization or one giant circuitous one. For starters, most of the shows on TV are made here, so they star people who live here. The actors from here already have the Los Angeles accent, and the ones who move here develop it after years of commingling with us. If they don't lose their regional accent, they have agents and managers who tell them to do it or else they won't get cast in anything. (Directors and producers look at so many actors for each role that they will find any reason to pare down their lists of candidates. If an actor has a slight drawl, that might be enough reason to eliminate them from contention for a role.) While this practice may increase an actor's chance of getting work, it also reinforces the homogenization of the local accent.

As for trying to replicate an accent for shows that take place in a particular region of the country, that's usually too much of a bother. It's hard enough to find the right actors for a TV show. But to find actors who have the right accent or train the right ones to speak in the regional tongue is more trouble than it's worth. Also, the convention of every TV show having the same accent is so entrenched that any deviation from it—especially since TV audiences are already used to hearing the "Angelized" accent—would detract from any realism it might add. Besides, who watches TV for the realism?

The only exception is for shows that take place in the South. For all our tacit insistence that everyone sound the same, we here in TV land can't ignore the Southern drawl. But that's where our sense of realism ends. While residents in the South can no doubt distinguish variations on the Southern twang, residents of Los Angeles can't—or won't. Characters that feature Southern accents all seem to use the same one. It's the thickest of the thick, obvious to the point of comical, and so absurd that it defines their characters. It sounds like a cross between Georgia and Mars.

As a result, since we hear the Los Angeles accent all around us, whether on TV or off, we assume that we speak with the correct accent. The irony of it all is that Los Angeles's source of this homogenization is the rest of the country. We're a mess of transplants, most of whom come with our home region's tongue. The only reason we can't hear Minnesota, or Oklahoma, or West Virginia in our accent is because it's drowned out by New York, Rhode Island, Texas, Alabama, and all the other accents that have blended with it.

If our non-accent accent doesn't distinguish the Los Angeles dialect, our subject matter might. We talk about a lot of the same things everyone else does (the weather, the war, who's going to win on *Dancing with the Stars*), but we do dwell on subjects that aren't as common elsewhere. Since a premium is placed on appearances, subjects related to that come up a lot. The one I hear about most often is gyms, probably because people complain about them so much. I don't think I've ever heard anyone mention how great their gym is. But I've heard an awful lot of people share how much they don't like their gym.

We're also big on cars, a topic close to our hearts because it combines two of our greatest obsessions: appearances and spending time in traffic.

Oddly enough, religion is a recurring topic. There seems to be more of a search for faith here, possibly because we have less of it than anywhere else. I hear—and get drawn into—conversations about other religions. And these are with people who aren't even proselytizing. I think there's more of a genuine interest in discussing—not arguing—the topic here.

Maybe it's just the company I keep, but the entertainment industry might be tops on the topic du jour list. Show me any restaurant with more than 12 people in it and I'll show you at least one table that has someone talking about an agent or a script. Sure, this is an industry town. But I'd be willing to bet that they don't sit around in bars in Pittsburgh all day and talk about smelting.

I remember reading a Q and A column once where a reader asked the columnist what segment of the United States spoke English properly, since our country has so many distinct accents. The columnist replied that Midwesterners spoke it correctly—or more close to correctly than anyone else in the country. If this is true, then why don't any Midwesterners that I meet insist that they speak it right?

Because, like the rest of us, they watch more TV than read Q and A columns.

MEET CLYDE LANGTRY, PART TWO

Wednesday, out in the parking lot, I headed to my car as Clyde was digging something out of his trunk. He looked up at me and said, "Enjoy your hamburger."

I wasn't going to get a hamburger. We hadn't been talking about hamburgers. I don't think we've ever discussed hamburgers. I have no idea why he told me to go enjoy my hamburger. After careful consideration, the best I can determine is that he meant to say "hi" and it accidentally came out "enjoy your hamburger." It's not much of a theory, I admit.

Because of this elegantly bizarre moment, however, I'm inspired to propose that "enjoying the hamburger" become an expression meaning, "using crazy people for entertainment purposes." For instance, "I was jogging in the park, then slowed down to enjoy some hamburger near the drinking fountain." Or, "You missed some great hamburger on the subway this morning." Or, "Joe's got quite a variety of hamburger living in his apartment complex."

In Clyde's honor, I'd like to share other noteworthy conversations I've had with him in recent months. Enjoy your hamburger.

May 23

I was walking through the courtyard to go inside to eat my take-out dinner when I heard, "Hi, Joe!" It was Clyde. His apartment door was open but I couldn't see him. Glare from outside and he had no lights on inside. Plus, his wife has a well-watered set of bushes and trees out front. Goddamn Amazon jungle growing on their porch.

I finally spotted him. He was dead-assed on his couch, Bermuda shorts (with a brown belt), and a yellow, short-sleeve, button-front shirt. It was unbuttoned now that the weather's hot, making Clyde look something like Lee Strasberg pulling his gangster number in *The Godfather, Part Two*, making this the only time I would ever, ever consider putting Lee Strasberg and Clyde Langtry in the same sentence.

I held up my dinner bag and said cheerfully, "Got me a burrito!" This led to talk of dietary habits, and, from there, the alimentary canal. Next thing I know, I hear something like this:

"You're not getting anywhere until it comes out black. Like car-tire black."

He was talking about feces. His own feces. Clyde's feces.

"I had one that came out about that long," he said. I swear to God, he put his hands at least a foot apart.

"You had one what? Are we talking about...?"

"The colon."

So not only was he going on about his own turds the same way the guy at the next barstool might brag about the catfish he pulled out of Lake Mead over the weekend, but I now have to live with the fact that Clyde Langtry craps bigger than me.

Clyde: "You ever hear of polyps?"

Me: "Uh-huh."

Clyde: "I had one of those come out. I could tell by the shape."

I was overwhelmed with questions. Don't polyps have to be surgically removed? Did they teach him this in Scientology classes? How does a man who examines his own poop manage to remain married this long?

Then he prattled away about a powdered drink or something that one could use to clean out the lower tract, but I don't remember what it was. Just as well. I don't take dietary advice from anyone who buys nutritional supplements from infomercials.

May 28

Came home today to find Clyde working on his old Ford Taurus, 167,000 miles of hell on wheels. I can't tell if it was originally painted powder blue or if it's just sunbleached.

"Say, Clyde, what are these things on the front bumper?" I pointed at the two little, black, bullet-shaped projectiles, his latest additions.

"They're supposed to whistle at deer to warn 'em that you're coming," he said. "I can handle anything: windy roads, other drivers, rain, snow, ice—" Instinctively, I took a look at a front tire: balder than Dick Cheney. "—but I can't handle deer."

"Tell me again. What's the deal with that?" I pointed at the hole he cut in the middle of the hood some time ago, a rectangle about four inches long and eight inches across, hinged back in place and controlled by a lever next to the steering wheel.

"Oh, that was to relieve high temperatures," he said. Last time he told me about it, he used the term "vapor lock." I was hoping he'd use it again only because it sounds funny when he says it. He makes it sound like psoriasis or dry rot or some other modern annoyance. It's also funny because Ken the landlord, who knows plenty about cars, told me that it's impossible for Ford Tauruses to get vapor lock.

He continued. "But I measured the temperature when it was open and again when it was closed and it didn't make much difference. That was a dumb idea."

Clyde's developing humility. Amazing. Naturally, I had to fuck with him.

"You know, Thomas Edison had a thousand dumb ideas before coming up with the light bulb."

Clyde smiled the gappiest, I-don't-trust-dentists smile I've ever seen.

July 7

Clyde: "As a spirit I'm able to perceive evil, even when my body is someplace else. I can't do it visually—not yet, anyway, but I'll be able to soon.... But you can just tell when someone's evil. You can see it in their eyes. They're just not there."

I get that look in my eyes all the time when I talk to Clyde.

July 12

Clyde knocked on my door a little while ago. He asked me to keep an eye out for a package delivery in a few days, and if I was home, would I be so kind as to sign for it. Naturally, this led to a 20-minute conversation about a bunch of other crap.

"I'm glad I'm just a visitor on this planet," he said. "It's a nice place to visit, but I wouldn't want to live here."

Clyde described a life scale of some sort: "L.A. is down around covert hostility.... Then you get to monotony. That's barely above zero. But it won't get you very far. The next steps are around one, one-point-five, two, two-point-five.... Eventually, you get to action, which is around 30, but that's as far as you want to go because the next level is 40 and there, you're not human. You're a spirit." He smirked. "But there's something to be said for being at 40."

After mundane chit-chat, he got to more substantial stuff again. "This course I'm going to take defines everything in the dictionary. Have you ever looked up the word 'to' in the dictionary? T-O? There's, like, 50 definitions. And the course spells these out visually so you understand what you're reading. Because if you don't understand the previous sentence, you won't understand the next one. Before long, you're not making any sense at all."

Imagine Clyde accusing someone of not making sense.

August 4

"Hi, Clyde. What's new?"

"Give me a hundred dollars, I'll tell you a hundred stories."

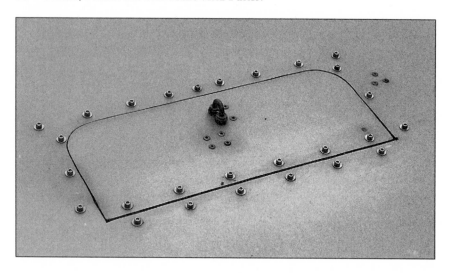

Since he found out I write for a living, he's developed an interest in my finances, namely how to part me from them. I can understand his temptation. He rarely works.

"I have all kinds of stories going back my whole lifetimes," he said.

"Lifetimes?"

"Sure, I've lived lots of lives. Don't you know about your past lives?" He was nearly gloating.

He prattled away about how he can get in touch with his past lives, the usual claptrap that he trots out about him being a higher life form than the average person, blah blah blah. The best nugget of that conversation was this:

"When I was in fifth grade, I read about the Spartans, this group of warriors in ancient Greece. And this book was really vivid. It made me feel like I was there. And to be honest, I'd be surprised if I *wasn't* there."

August 24

Today, Clyde told me again of his certainty that his orange cat, Marmalade, is the reincarnation of his previous orange cat, Marmalade.

Me: "How can you tell?"

Clyde: "How can I tell? There's a thousand ways. When it's time to eat, he comes up to me, he meows, leads me into the kitchen, and jumps up on Priscilla's desk, just like how Marmalade used to. I can also tell by looking at his face. He makes the same facial expressions. I can just tell that he's thinking the same thoughts as Marmalade did."

He spent the rest of the conversation shoving his hands down the front of his shorts and playing with his nuts. He played with his nuts for about 10 minutes before he bothered to explain that his hernia belt had broken.

Clyde on alternative fuel technologies: "This technology's been around forever. Flying saucers have been using it for centuries. Flying saucers visit us all the time."

"Really?"

"Why don't you look it up on the Internet? Look up Golf Breeze, Florida. A whole city saw a whole bunch of flying saucers all over the sky. Golf Breeze, Florida. I knew a guy on an aircraft carrier, saw one floating above him, the mother ship, big cigar-shaped thing. You couldn't miss it on the radar screen."

"Golf Breeze, Florida. I'll look it up right now." I later looked it up. It was actually Gulf Breeze, not Golf Breeze. Clyde just talks funny sometimes.

"They're partial to California. They visit the California desert a lot. Those stories of cow mutilations you hear about? No human could do that. That's a technology that we don't have.... Why do you think astronauts found remnants of ships on the moon?"

"Wait a minute. If they saw flying saucers on the moon, don't you think they would have said something to reporters about it?"

"Use some common sense. Why do you think it is that we can only see one side of the moon?"

"I've never thought about it."

Clyde then rambled away about the universe's beginnings, how "they" made Earth only for the purposes of being a prison, finally getting to his point: The moon was used by "them" as a lookout and "they" didn't want us to see all the equipment, lookout towers, and so on that "they" store on the side of the moon that doesn't face Earth.

"Clyde, I gotta tell you. I consider myself a smart guy, and I doubt I could have used common sense to reach that conclusion."

"You think it's a coincidence that it rotates around us but it never spins, not the tiniest bit, so we can't see what's on the dark side?"

I couldn't make this shit up if I took drugs.

WELL, THAT'S OVER

MEET MY SHITTY EX-LANDLORDS

I must admit that I sometimes get cheesed off with my current landlord, Ken. The poor man is more than a bit of a burnout case, so some chores around here go undone. But I try to be grateful for what he does do, since he is all peach fuzz compared to my previous landlords.

Several years ago, I lived in a guesthouse a few miles from here. It wasn't really a guesthouse. In technical real estate parlance, it was a shithole. I've decided that it must have been constructed by thumbless blind men. And upkeep was merely a theory. Thin, crappy brown carpet, ticky-tack walls, plaster peeling off—indoors—a huge gap above the door, through which piles of dust blew in and climate-controlled air wafted away. And that's just the stuff I could see. No telling what kind of toxins were seeping out of the paint.

The rest of the property wasn't any better. In front was a two-bedroom house that was occupied by a nice family of four who deserved better but couldn't afford more. The few times I was in there, I found it drafty, dark, and generally depressing. The roof was so shot that, legend has it, an employee from the Health Department happened to be driving by, saw the roof, and pulled over to ask the tenants who the landlord was just so he could nail him for a code violation.

Four guest shitholes, three of which were about 20' × 20', were crammed into the backyard—which would flood nearly to the point of impassibility during heavy rains, by the way. There was a building with two side-by-side units. A Latino couple that liked to have lots of company over when they weren't bickering and their new baby who liked to scream occupied one unit. The other unit was so uninhabitably tiny that it went unoccupied for the last several months I was there.

The other building had an upstairs unit and a downstairs unit. Upstairs was a heavy metal fanatic who used pot and alcohol so liberally that he once liberated himself into County for 21 days for repeated drunk-driving offenses. Downstairs was a depressed, broke, wannabe writer whose window was five feet away from the noisy Latino couple and their screaming baby. That was me.

One day in 1999, the owner's brother, Scott, and Scott's lover, Austin, knocked at my door. I'd met Scott before, a short Armenian man with a raspy voice and large eyes. He was always absurdly happy to see me. I think he had a little crush on me. That, however, would change. Austin was humorless, passive-aggressive, beady-eyed, and generally shlubby. He never changed.

They were dropping by to tell me that they'd taken over management of the property from Scott's brother three weeks ago, and, therefore, my rent check was three weeks late. When I told them I'd paid Scott's brother on the first like I always had, they replied that he'd never received it and that I owed them the money. I called Scott's brother and he confirmed that the check never showed up. I assumed it had been lost in the mail and he said he'd tear it up if it arrived. I promptly wrote a check to Scott—right after which Scott's brother mysteriously found my first check and deposited it, thus double-billing me for one month's rent. When I called all of them on it, they insisted it was an accident and didn't apologize for the inconvenience. It wouldn't be the first time they wouldn't apologize for something.

Not long after that promising start to their tenure, Austin went around and gave everyone a form to fill out on which they could air their grievances and list things we felt needed fixing. We sent him back long lists of problems: peeling paint, insect infestations, leaky roofs, poor insulation, pretty much everything you can think of. At last, I thought, this place was going to get a makeover.

Austin responded by putting brand new screens on the windows. And doing nothing else.

All utilities were grandfathered in from the main house, which meant the landlords were responsible for the utility bills. Scott and Austin, like Scott's brother before them, were fond of paying them late. They were particularly fond of not paying the gas bill, which led to the occasional red notice posted by the Gas Company, letting the occupants know that if the overdue balance wasn't paid by such and such a date, the gas would be turned off. These notices appeared so regularly that one could mark the changing of the seasons by their arrival. Scott's brother missed the shutoff date once, a mistake so thoughtless and egregious that I was sure that Scott and Austin wouldn't possibly repeat it. Wrong again.

On the day after Christmas, 2000, after another boring day at my boring, low-paying dotcom job with stock options, I came home only wanting to turn on the heater and make some kind of warm dinner. I could do neither because Scott and Austin let the gas bill lapse one too many warnings too long. I called them and left two nasty messages—they never picked up their phone—and a few hours later, Austin called back to explain that it wasn't his fault. He and Scott accidentally had sent the wrong checks to the wrong utility companies.

The gas got turned on that night, but I had had enough of Scott and Austin. The fact that this place was a dump wasn't a secret; I didn't expect it to get better. But if these two fools weren't even decent enough to keep the heat on during winter, they deserved no favor. The next day, I reported them to the city's Department of Housing. When I gave their names and my address to a department case manager, he looked them up on his computer and informed me that Scott and Austin had never registered with the department as the legal property managers and were therefore subject to triple the normal registration fees.

Then I wrote Scott and Austin a page-and-a-half letter, single-spaced, listing everything I could think of that was wrong with the place. By submitting the grievances in writing, they had 30 days to do something about them. To make sure they received them, I sent them by certified mail with a return postcard that required a signature. I'd already figured that they could simply ignore some certified letter and simply not sign for it, so to be sure they'd sign for it, I put my January rent check inside it also.

I was right. They were afraid to sign for it. And they knew full well that it contained my rent check because I always paid on time. Finally, after nearly two weeks of them trying to figure out how to get my rent check out of their post office without signing for the envelope it came in, Scott called me, confused as to why he hadn't received the rent yet.

"Gee," I said, playing along. "You should have received it by now. I sent it by certified mail."

"Oh, is that what that envelope is. Why did you do that?"

"Because there's something in it that I wanted to make sure you got."

A couple of days later, I got my signature card. They received my grievances. Austin sent me back a letter explaining that most of my complaints weren't their fault, weren't their responsibility, or weren't things they could do anything about. Furthermore, sending the rent checks by certified mail was, and I quote, "not allowed." These shits must have been miserable to play sandlot baseball with.

One thing I was entitled to by law was a deadbolt lock on my main door of entry. I'd never had one, but I didn't need one. There was no crime in our backyard; the guesthouses were so goddamn small, no one knew they were back there. Still, I felt Scott and Austin deserved a little something, so after 31 days with no new lock, I opened up the phone directory and called the first locksmith I could find. I had him put in a double-deadbolt just to make it fancy. Then I deducted the cost from March's rent and sent Scott and Austin the receipt. All perfectly legal.

They didn't take it well. On the last day of March, 2001, there was a knock at my door in the early evening.

"Who is it?" No answer. "Who is it?"

"It's Austin."

I opened the door and Austin handed me an envelope. "Joe, I have to give you this." And he walked away.

It was an eviction notice. Or it was something that was trying to be an eviction notice. It didn't give any of the legally allowable reasons a landlord can evict a tenant in Los Angeles. It actually didn't give any reason. The letter wasn't even dated. Scott and Austin had merely decided that the one guy who consistently paid his rent on time was costing them too much money and he had to be out in 30 days.

Even though the eviction wasn't legally valid, I was kind of shocked. I'd been served an eviction notice by a slumlord. *A slumlord!* It was like being slapped by a midget. I wasn't sure whether to laugh or chase him to his car and... and... yell mean things at him. Since I'd just secured a new, higher-paying job that could afford me a new, nicer apartment, I issued my own 30-day notice and left 29 days later.

Naturally, they jerked me around in returning my deposit. It took me two months of waiting and me threatening legal action before a check arrived—for the full amount. These two knuckleheads were so scared I'd sue them or something that they didn't even bother to deduct a cleaning fee. So, on a Friday at 5:00 in the afternoon, I raced out to the bank to cash it before Scott and Austin put a stop payment on it or paid some other overdue bill with my money. When the teller at the bank handed me my cash, I just stood there and looked at it.

Scott and Austin broke up not long after that, I found out later. Since they were living in Austin's house, Scott was the one who had to leave. The man hated parting with money so much that rather than check into a motel, he crashed for a while in one of his own shitholes. The only one available was the uninhabitably tiny one that no one wanted. I wish I'd known. I would have made a special trip over there to point and laugh.

MEET OUR INTERNET DATERS

I was an Internet dater off and on—mostly off (way off)—for years. In a city with so many colorful characters, it's remarkable how many Internet dates ended with the assessment, "Nice person, no chemistry." It's especially unbelievable when you consider that a person's photo and profile may seem attractive, their emails and/or phone calls substantiate the attraction, and when you meet them in person, you don't have enough chemistry between the two of you to melt an ice cube. Over and over and over again. This not only makes for a demoralizing personal life, but if you're a writer, it's damned hard to find material.

Undaunted, however, I have a few tales.

In the old days, the late 90s, AOL had a dating site that was free. You didn't even need to have a profile up to contact people on the site. I got a glimpse of how small Los Angeles was when, on a date with one woman I met on AOL Personals, she politely informed me that on the same day I had sent an introductory email to her, I'd sent a similar one to a girlfriend of hers. After two dates, she told me that she'd decided to work things out with her ex-boyfriend. I regret not asking her to put in a good word for me with her girlfriend.

Possibly the worst date I ever went on was an AOL date. Things were already pretty tepid when my date's pager went off in the middle of dinner. "Chad?" she said. "Why's he paging me?"

And she whipped out her cell phone right there at the table and called him. She told him how excited she was to hear from him, but would have to call him back because she was in the middle of dinner. Then she hung up and told me how thrilled she was to hear from him, seeing as how it had been so long since they'd seen each other. I'd like to say that it was the AOL Personals' commune-like sensibility that encouraged her to be so flighty in the middle of the dinner I was buying her, but more likely, she was just a twit.

I eventually upgraded to a real dating site, whereupon my experiences became more unreal. Take the attractive, funny, single, childless woman in her early 30s who asked to meet me for a drink a couple of years ago. We met and hit it off right away, whereupon she admitted that she was not single and childless, but, in fact, separated with a toddler. She had married young, found out recently that her husband had cheated on her, and was now playing the field because she didn't have the chance to do so when she was younger, but wasn't sure if she was going to leave her husband or not. She added that she wasn't going to sleep with me because she had integrity.

On another Internet date around the same time, a woman met me for drinks at 7:00 one night. When she got her bailout call—the call you set up with a friend whereupon receiving it, you can use it to concoct an excuse to leave early—at 7:10, she pretended to be surprised that her cell phone was ringing. She continued with the date, during which she made introductory chitchat by asking me how well endowed I was. When I called her a few days later and happened to mention her overt interest in sex, she was confused as to why I would make such a presumption.

I take solace that I'm not alone in these misadventures. In fact, some of them can have a dark side. One friend of mine began Internet dating last year by striking up a phone and email relationship with guy from Utah who'd contacted her. To her, he was just a man to talk to as she found her Internet dating sea legs, even though he tried to get her to come out there for an in-person meeting. After a couple of months, during which time she started real dating with men here, "Utah McDaddy" emailed her one day to say that he may be going away for a year to a year and a half. When she called him to ask what he meant, he confessed that he'd actually done time for statutory rape and had recently violated parole by crossing state lines. She doesn't talk to him anymore.

My friend Sally, the magnet for celebrities, met a former child TV star on the Internet. She said they've become pals because he's a nice guy, in spite of the fact that he occasionally calls her to ask her to go away with him for a weekend bacchanalia.

A septuagenarian woman I know who's been Internet dating for a while had a discouraging episode with a sixtysomething man. He waited until their third date to tell her that he was not only HIV-positive but also gay, and he was wondering if she could help him convert to heterosexuality.

One guy said he went on an Internet date and the woman showed up with her therapist. (The man told the story to another woman on an Internet date, who then told it to me on an Internet date.)

But, again, it is the overwhelming dullness that is perhaps the most amazing thing about Internet dating. When I went around soliciting others' stories, the ones above weren't just the best ones; they were the only ones. The rest of their stories were nonstories: nice person, no chemistry. And in the great Ponzi scheme that is Los Angeles, you never get the sense that you'll never find the right person here. It is a never-ending casting session where no one seems right for the part. After looking at the profile pages for a little while, everyone looks the same. The more coffee dates you have, the less you want to have them. But since there is no deadline, the only thing stopping you from continuing to look is your tolerance for boredom.

Or your quota for material.

Meet Howard Berman:
The Congressman
Who Wasn't There

In 1985, the late George Plimpton wrote a well-researched feature for *Sports Illustrated* about an eccentric pitching prospect at the New York Mets' spring training camp. Among other readable details, Plimpton related that this guy, Siddhartha "Sidd" Finch, could throw a fastball 168 mph, more than 60 mph faster than the fastest fastball any human had ever thrown. I was a teenage subscriber to *SI* back then, and I not only read the Sidd Finch story, but, as a baseball fan, I devoured it. What was this going to do to baseball? What happens when Pedro Guerrero or Andre Dawson faces this guy? Will the commissioner change the rules or something?

Two weeks later, Plimpton and *Sports Illustrated* revealed that the story was a clever April Fool's Day hoax. (The issue in which it was printed was dated April 1, among other clues.)

On paper, it says that Howard Berman has been my congressman since he took the oath in 1983. In reality, I've never seen this man except for a picture on his Web site. There *is* a voting record for a guy named Howard Berman, but I can't get him on the phone. George Plimpton isn't around to fess up to any possible fraud. And as absurd as this may sound, I can't believe my congressman really exists because, unlike other area representatives, I've never seen him on television.

He could be Sidd Finch.

L.A. is a politically left-leaning town, and we are expressive about our left leanings. We attend anti-war rallies. We have lots of anti-Bush bumper stickers on our otherwise pristine cars. It is considered *de rigueur* in L.A. to align with other lefties to bitch and moan about how shitty life is. Some of us can't throw away a beer bottle at a party without hunting down the hosts to ask if they recycle.

I'm a proud rider of that bitch 'n bottle bandwagon, and I've decided the über-cause of our times is the impeachment of the president. To that end, I contacted my congressman, Howard Berman, Democrat, this summer, to see if he could impeach the president, please. The man has been my congressman for over 20 years and I've never asked him for anything. I figure he can do something about this one request. Seems fair, no?

I sent an email to Mr. Berman asking him to impeach the president, please. He responded right away. I mean, within minutes. I was thrilled. Oh, boy. My congressman's gonna impeach my president. I opened the email. It read:

> *Thank you for your message to Congressman Howard Berman. To ensure delivery, if you did not include your name and address in the email, please resend the message with this information. Congressman Berman will get back to you shortly. Thanks again for sharing your thoughts.*

I sent him two more emails expressing the same sentiment. I got back the same message. A goddamn auto-reply. A mechanical answer from a person who may not even exist.

So I called his Washington, D.C. office once. That got me an intern thanking me for my call—and telling me that no one, to his knowledge, had called to request that Mr. Berman impeach the president, please. Then again, he did say, "But I'm new here."

Finally, about two months ago, I got a more personal response from Howard Berman—or someone claiming to be Howard Berman. It was another email, a nice, bland, harmless, politically hedged email, explaining why he can't impeach the president. He rattled off the reasons I expected, namely how it was impossible since Republicans control everything in Congress. He added that restructuring Iraq, homeland security measures, and fighting the Bush tax cuts "require all of our attention now." Maybe he meant it requires everyone else's attention because on his Web site, he congratulates himself for securing money for local projects and he trumpets his appointment as chief liaison to the entertainment industry. There's even a picture of him with our mayor.

At this point, I gave up. I figured the only way to get through to him would be to meet him in person, and according to his Web site, the only way to meet him in person is to be the mayor of Los Angeles. If it weren't for that picture, I'd be 100% sure that he didn't exist. I mean this guy is *never* on television.

Every week, as the news gets worse for George W. Bush and the political climate keeps leaning to the left, the more tempted I am to ask Representative Berman if his feelings have changed. But still I refrain. I know he's not going to jump on the impeachment horse unless the Democrats gain control of the house in 2006, and I have no other requests for him. Not even to ask if he could use his show business liaison gig to get my latest screenplay to Paul Giamatti's people.

Fast forward to Tuesday, our state's special election. I waltzed up Laurel Canyon Boulevard towards the neighborhood convalescent home after parking almost a block away. As I passed Shakey's Pizza, a guy was coming at me the other direction. I slowed down and gawked. That white hair and gentle face reminded me of someone. Despite the nondescript dress shirt and tie, he wasn't just some day trader who'd dashed in to vote after a day of trafficking in mutual funds. He wasn't a celebrity. He didn't remind me of a friend's dad or former coworker.

He didn't slow down. He didn't look at me. He walked past me and turned towards the parking lot between the convalescent home and Shakey's Pizza, down that too-narrow driveway.

It was him. My congressman. The guy on the Web site.

I ran back after him. "Excuse me?"

He turned around.

"Are you Howard Berman?"

"Yes."

I raced up to him and we shook hands.

"Hi. Joe Dungan. I'm one of your constituents."

"Thank you for voting. I'm very curious to see what happens today."

I didn't even have my "I Voted" sticker on yet. What is this guy? A mind-reader?

"I'm the guy who keeps sending you the letters asking you to impeach President Bush. I mean, I know you can't, really, because Republicans control everything, but I just want you to know I want that guy out of there."

"I tell you, I think he's overreaching."

"Thank you for being a loyal Democrat and just know that when it's time to impeach the president, you have the support of many people out here."

"You're welcome."

That's all of the conversation I can reconstruct. I remember him talking plenty more, but strangely enough, I don't remember much of it. I don't even remember if he said goodbye. That wasn't some actor pulling off a ruse in public. Nobody but a politician could improvise such forgettable chitchat so eloquently.

Jesus, he exists. At least, the man I ran into matches the picture on his Web site. *I have a congressman!*

In my fit of disbelief—you'd think I'd met Paul McCartney or something—I neglected to hand him a business card. I didn't even bother to send him a follow-up email until the next morning. I made clear in the header of the email that I was the guy who ran into him in the Shakey's parking lot. He can't possibly run into too many people at Shakey's. He'd have to remember it was me. In the email, I reminded him who I was, that it was a pleasure to meet him finally, reiterated my distaste for the president, and asked if he has a speaking schedule or something for his in-town visits.

True, that was only 48 hours ago, but I haven't received an answer.

Not even one of his instantaneous auto-replies.

Meet Rose and Her Incredibly Unstable Friend Marnie

Rose was—and probably still is—walking sunshine. She can get anything she wants just by asking. It was not uncommon for her to call me with the news that her roommate, an unmarried, childless woman in her 50s who owned a house, was gone and that she was going to barbecue something tasty out by the pool and that all I need to do is show up with a six-pack. Or for me to pick her up at the mechanic while her car was being serviced. Or for me to help her update her résumé with the latest plays or short films she'd acted in. I always said yes. After all, she was Rose.

But we'd been drifting apart, even if we hadn't said it. We talked less and less frequently. Our annual Christmas gift exchange didn't happen until March, and we'd made no plans to see each other again.

Then in May, she called me. In tears. Her friend of several months and roommate of one week, Marnie, was going undisputedly apeshit and wanted Rose out immediately. Rose didn't know what to do.

I'd met Marnie on several occasions. The times I'd talked to her, she seemed to carry an air of a wild past. I'd never seen but only heard about her more tempestuous episodes from Rose, who'd complained more than once about Marnie's instability. I wasn't entirely sure that Marnie was guilty of being nuts, but Rose's repeated complaints had given me suspicion nearly beyond a reasonable doubt.

Surprised—and disappointed—as I was that Rose had made the gross error in judgment to move in with such an unstable person, I decided I couldn't let

Rose twist in the wind. I dropped what I was doing, rented a truck at 5:00 in the afternoon, and raced to their apartment in Koreatown to get her out.

Rose was throwing items into what few boxes she had. Per her request, I'd bought more when I rented the truck. Marnie, for her part, was not doing her part. While Rose was packing boxes that I hauled to the truck, Marnie alternately dumped some of Rose's items in the hallway and sat on her bed and watched a DVD.

Marnie had hidden Rose's video camera and swore she wouldn't return it until every last one of Rose's items was out. When we finally reached that point, Marnie refused to surrender it. I was in the hallway when I heard some arguing and scuffling. Moments later, Rose emerged with the camera. It was time to leave at last.

Except that Rose couldn't find her car keys. Marnie had hidden those too.

Rose was beside herself with frustration. "You see how crazy this makes a person?!"

I saw.

A moment later, I stood out in the hallway while Rose and Marnie yelled at each other. Marnie was doing what can best be described as a grab-push: She would grab Rose's arm or whatever appendage she could find and shove her towards the hallway. Rose wasn't backing down.

Rose turned to me and shouted, "Stop her!"

As they fought, I seriously weighed the difference between chivalry and assault. Marnie was clearly out of her goddamn mind, but this wasn't my battle. And I certainly didn't want to make an enemy out of someone so psychotic. No telling what kind of revenge she'd seek. But she had no good reason for such rudeness. She was arbitrarily being a psychotwat about things, and I'd already upended my whole evening for this bullshit and was hardly in the mood for any more. But I didn't want to hit a woman, for crissakes. I can live with a lot of things. But I really don't want to spend the rest of my life having people whisper behind my back, "There goes the guy who cold-cocked a dame in Koreatown."

I did nothing because I'm not a violent sort at all. Having never been in a fist-fight, no telling how much repressed suburbanite rage might have come gushing out had I taken a swing at the bitch. I could have ended up with six months in Vacaville. I decided long ago that if I ever do hard time, it'll be for something cool like robbing Vegas casinos, and not for something as lame as breaking up a spat between two chicks.

Rose chased Marnie back inside and closed the door. For a good minute or so, I heard shouting and screaming, along with the occasional banging around. I stood alone in the hallway, admiring the freshly polished banister.

The door flew open. Rose came out and said, "Let's go."

"Do you have the keys?"

"She threw them out the window."

We ended up in the garden courtyard behind the building, stomping around some dense brush, looking for car keys. I asked two Latinos who were sweeping up if they saw a set of keys arcing out the second-floor window. They didn't understand English. It was getting dark.

I asked Rose if Marnie merely tossed them out the window or chucked them for distance or what. She didn't know, but didn't seem too worried that it would take long to find them. "She's done this before," Rose said.

She's done this before!?

I think this was when it hit me. I was no longer mad at Marnie as much as I was mad at Rose. Marnie might not be able to control her insanity. But Rose can control who she spends time with. She'd known Marnie a good eight months at this point, knew she was as unhinged as Tupperware, and chose to move in with her?

Marnie, in her helpful way, came down to bitch us out for leaving empty boxes in her apartment. Rose popped up with the keys. "Let's go."

"Gimme those!" I yelled. I shoved the keys in my pocket. I didn't want to risk having Marnie yank them out of Rose's hand and hide them in her vagina or something.

We headed down the hallway and out the front door. Marnie was finally behind us.

Rose got in her car, I got in the truck, and we drove to the Rite Aid near my place in the Valley. I had to get a jumbo-sized padlock for the truck. We locked the truck and parked it around the corner. The lock came with two keys. I held one and gave her one.

She—and her new dog—spent the night on my foldout couch and I spent the night in my bed, steamed.

The next day, upon figuring out what to do with her stuff, she told me to meet her at her previous place, the house she'd moved out of a week earlier. We unloaded her stuff, I returned the truck, she reimbursed me for all the expenditures, and she gave me a ride home. In the previous 24 hours, she'd thanked me countless times. I didn't hear a word of it. All I wanted was to wash my hands of this whole episode, which, by that afternoon, I had. Except that I'd accidentally walked off with one of the keys to her padlock.

I waited a week before doing what I had to do. I called her. The beginning-of-conversation niceties lasted a minute or two.

"I'm never doing that for you again," I said. "If you get yourself into such a fix again on purpose, don't call me, because I will not help you. Do you understand me?" My God, the woman is 34 years old.

"Okay, and all I can say is I'm sorry. And if you hadn't come, I would have had to figure out something else."

"Also, Marnie is insane, okay? The woman is out of her fucking mind. You hang out with whoever you want, but I want absolutely nothing to do with that woman ever again for any reason. If you have the world's biggest party, don't even bother inviting me if she's going to be there, okay? It's your life. Keep company with anyone you want, but keep me away from her, understand?"

I was hoping to hear that she'd decided that Marnie's behavior had crossed a line of some sort, that she'd finally had enough of Marnie. Instead, Rose justified her feelings by explaining that in her family, no matter how crazy a person was, their bad behavior was always overlooked in favor of their good qualities, and that Marnie had plenty of good qualities.

I left it at that. I didn't bother explaining to Rose that you can have people in your life who had both good qualities and emotional stability. Nor did I ask if she was still talking to Marnie. Rose thanked me again and told me she wanted to buy me a nice dinner. Sure, I said. Let's set a date.

A week later, there was a message on my voicemail. It was Rose. She thanked me again. Told me again she wanted to buy me dinner. And would I like to adopt a kitten? It seems a stray had given birth to five kittens—behind Marnie's apartment building.

That was four months ago. No dinner. Actually, we haven't spoken at all. I suspect she's been busy with other friends who are more inclined to indulge her neediness and I suspect I've been busy avoiding needy people. I occasionally think about how she went from being so important in my life to someone I only occasionally think about.

This, in spite of the fact that, every day, in my bedroom, I see the extra key to her padlock.

This Was One of
Our Elections

A couple of weeks ago, we hosted the Oscars again, a contest that has virtually no impact on any of our lives, and for which relatively few of us get to vote. Tuesday, we had an election in which the entire city had a chance to change the course of the woefully bloated and oft-maligned Los Angeles Unified School District. Take a guess which contest got more attention.

Let us back up a moment.

Up for grabs in this election were four of seven LAUSD Board of Education seats. This is important because a regime change in the board is a major step toward school reforms that Mayor Antonio Villaraigosa has been pushing since before he was elected. This is important because the LAUSD has been so constipated and incompetent for so long that most people have more or less given up on the idea of ever changing it. Then this opportunity presented itself.

As obvious as it seemed, I wanted to make sure that voting for the challenger—who, in my district, was a criminal prosecutor named Tamar Galatzan—was, in fact, the right thing to do. So I went around soliciting opinions. About half the people I asked didn't even know we were having an election. Some knew, but didn't know what it was about. One guy thought he knew, but didn't recall getting a sample ballot. One guy found out about it the same way we find out about a new Chinese restaurant in the neighborhood: junk mail.

Ah, the junk mail. It began a few weeks ago, and it was largely pro-Galatzan. I don't remember seeing this much junk mail in any election, ever. Fliers, foldouts, letters, one-sheets, and on and on. It conveyed pretty much the same two things: Galatzan was a proud parent and prosecutor who had the backing of the mayor; and the incumbent, Jon Lauritzen, was a failure in every way. Galatzan's camp even sent out a "report card" on him, citing low marks in a number of "subjects." (They gave him a D in Trimming Bureaucracy.)

Seeking more constructive commentary, I sought out two people I know who have worked with the LAUSD. The first friend I called told me that while the teachers' union was supporting the incumbent, the consensus among teachers was that the incumbent was dead weight. The conversation with the other friend— which actually took place after the election—proved a little more cryptic.

"Should we care about who we vote for?" I asked.

"We should care," she said dispassionately.

"I should have picked Galatzan because that might change the makeup of the board and lead to changes in the LAUSD, right?"

"Right." A moment later. "I'd like to find out how many people voted. I don't care who won."

"Wait a minute. You just said I should vote for Galatzan, right?"

"Right."

"So we *should* care, right?"

"Right. We should care. But I don't care."

"You just said we should care."

"You're right, you're right. I retract my last statement."

Just as I was about to wonder if this kind of absurdity is endemic to the school system, she confessed that she'd been in the car all day and the glass of wine she just finished had gotten to her.

Monday, the day before the election, Galatzan turned up the heat on the propaganda, sending me more junk mail from one candidate in any election than I can ever remember. If I counted correctly, it was five different pieces. One pointed out that Lauritzen spent $95 million on a computer system that doesn't work, and now he wants a pay raise. It showed a toilet with money either flowing out or stuffed in, I couldn't tell which. Either way, it didn't flatter the guy. Another mailer also trumpeted Lauritzen's support for a pay raise for himself, this time with a picture of a guy in a boater and a bow tie, trying to resemble some old-time huckster politician. It didn't make me think Jon Lauritzen was a huckster. It made me wonder how much a print model makes these days for grinning like an idiot while wearing a boater and a bow tie.

In the same day's mail, I got a letter from the city's Police Command Officers Association. I'd never heard of it. I figured it was some organization hitting me up for a donation. Instead, it was a letter endorsing Tamar Galatzan. Six pieces in one day, and enough overall to fill a throw pillow, but I couldn't find my sample ballot.

I don't recall getting much mail from Jon Lauritzen. In fact, I didn't know much of anything about him, but in my mind, he had plenty going against him.

He was on the board of a school district that has been on the slow track down the shitter for decades. I couldn't find any evidence to dispute all the things Galatzan's junk mail was accusing him of. Plus, as long as elected officials keep enjoying long rides on voter apathy, I'm going to keep going around voting against every incumbent I can find. And I saw Lauritzen in a television interview. He didn't seem like a very engaging guy. Imagine Donald Sutherland on downers.

The nice thing about off-year elections is that it doesn't take long to vote. There aren't many races on the ballot, and voters have a tendency to take a powder. When I arrived at about 3:00 on Tuesday, it was about a dozen volunteers and me—and I was still summoned to the wrong goddamn table to sign in.

For a city full of judgmental, opinionated people, we gave an amazingly small amount of shit about the election. While disappointing, this is no surprise. Our last *mayoral* election had only a 33 percent turnout. This election, which would determine the future of our extremely broken public education system—not to mention some city council seats—turned out a whopping 7 percent of the electorate. But the school board and city council shouldn't take all the blame. There were also four community college board of trustees seats at stake that contributed to the voter apathy.

Galatzan finished first, garnering nearly 13,000 votes in district three. According to one news source, Mayor Villaraigosa's campaign committee gave over a million dollars to help finance Galatzan's junk mail blitz. This translates to a cost of roughly $90 for every vote she got. Let's hope this isn't a sign of her spending habits when she gets on the board.

But I am being premature. Since a third candidate prevented her from attaining a plurality, there is going to be a runoff election.

Author's footnote: Galatzan won the runoff election. According to my friend who works in the LAUSD since before and now months after the election, she can't tell a damn bit of difference. Then again, she said she wasn't even sure the new board members had taken office yet.

MEET LOCAL NUTS PAST

Yesterday, a good friend of mine woke up to a disturbing discovery on her front door. Someone had placed fliers around the neighborhood telling everyone that there was a halfway house nearby. The point of the flier was, in short, that the person behind the flier doesn't want the halfway house in the neighborhood and wanted others to feel the same. He thoughtfully provided the phone numbers of the local councilman, assemblyman, and state senator for complaining purposes.

My friend has been sober for 14 years and has become a healthy and productive member of society, thanks in part to her stay in a halfway house as she got over her addiction. With that background, you can imagine her outrage at such inflammatory fearmongering. As for me, my first reaction was puzzlement since the fearmonger didn't actually accuse anyone in the halfway house of anything. I was also confused because there is a halfway house near my apartment building and I've never had a problem with anyone there.

As for people in other nearby places, that's a different story.

I can only point out what I've seen and substantiated, and there are some substantially tweaked people around here. Some live here, some don't. But they all have qualities that are at the very least, curious, and at worst, felonious.

We have a dogwalker who likes to have cell phone conversations in our courtyard from time to time. We have a bum. Short, bald, dirty guy. Visits the post office regularly. I think he has his own P.O. box. We have a guy who shows up outside the post office to play what looks like a homemade banjo. He also sells CDs of his banjo songs. I always swear that I'm going to buy one someday.

I never do, but I did chat with him once. He lives in Orange County and drives all the way out here at least once a month to play the banjo outside the post office. Either he's got a bad agent, or there isn't much of a banjo music scene in Orange County.

But it's the nuts of the past who stay with me, like pretty places stay with writers of sappy songs. I remember not long after I moved into my apartment, a squat little man and his two boys were out by our pool. I didn't think that much of it, figuring they might have been guests of a tenant. A little while later I saw them walk from the pool, through the courtyard to the sidewalk. I followed them. They walked to the building next door and went in, presumably because they lived there. Our pool is nicer than theirs, but still.

Another time, just as I pulled out of my driveway, a white Cadillac Escalade sidled over to the curb, right in front of my driveway. The driver and her two kids were about to visit someone next door, I would find out later. I figured she was going to reverse into the available parking spot next to the driveway. I came back a while later, and I was wrong. She parked right in front of our driveway. I called a tow truck and this giant flatbed showed up, pulled the SUV aboard, and drove away with it.

About an hour later, the twit with her two little children wandered around our courtyard sticking her head in open windows. "Where is the manager? I need my car back." Like we fucking valeted it for her.

I also hear of nuts past from elders who are still alive to tell the tales. Ken the landlord has been here long enough to qualify for historian (or historic) status, and can attest that the most extreme nuts came and went before I moved in. For instance, about 10 years ago, some disgruntled tenant—again in the building next door—was making Molotov cocktails in his apartment. The fumes ignited a spark from the refrigerator motor and it incinerated the guy and his apartment instantly. Fire officials said the flames were so intense that the guy didn't have time to fall over before being burned to death. Investigators later found these homemade gas bombs planted under cars in the downstairs garage. If they'd gone off, that building would have been history, along with part of this one, I'm sure.

And oh yeah: The guy who killed Bill Cosby's son used to live in the building next door.

The apartment building next to that, according to Ken, once housed some or all of the Red Hot Chili Peppers before they made it big. Possible litigation prevents me from repeating what Ken alleges they did to their apartment before they moved out. Let's just say that Ken wouldn't have wanted the Red Hot Chili Peppers as tenants.

Then, of course, there is this building. Some years back, Ken showed an empty apartment to a woman, who promptly said she'd take it. When she moved in the next day, she informed Ken that the bedroom carpet was gone. Ken fol-lowed the trail of stray carpet fibers—and goo of a slug that had gotten squashed and smeared underneath the rolled-up carpet—to an apartment across the way, occupied by a guy who'd happened to mention that he wanted to reupholster his van. Sure enough, Ken caught the guy with hacked-up pieces of bedroom carpet all over the floor of his van. Within hours, Ken and the building's owner had compelled the guy to move out. (Ken, incidentally, replaced that stolen carpet with more carpet. That apartment, incidentally, eventually became my apartment. Too bad the van guy wasn't living across the way the day before I moved in so he could have taken that carpet too. It was so shot when I moved in that it has given me a new appreciation for linoleum.)

Over the years, we've had our share of deadbeats, druggies, and general do-badders. Fortunately (for me, anyway), most of them came and went before I got here. The worst one was actually referred by the building's owner. Let's call this tenant Garrett. When Garrett moved in, he explained to Ken that after a lifetime of heavy drinking and going to bars to pick fights with guys just to see how badly he could cripple them, he finally had his shit together in life. Well, as it turned out, Garrett didn't really have his shit together. He didn't exactly have all his marbles. He was actually still criminally dangerous, as evidenced by the night he threatened a couple of other tenants with a gun. Next thing Garrett knew, the cops had surrounded his place, helicopter overhead and everything. Ken got on the phone with Garrett to explain to him that he was going to get shot to death unless he came out with his hands up and without heavy clothes that could conceal a weapon. So Garrett the genius came out with his hands in the pockets of a jacket. He didn't get shot, but he ate a nice helping of manure when the cops threw him down on the freshly fertilized lawn.

I'm no psychologist, but it sounded like Garrett could have used some help. The kind of help one finds, say, at a halfway house. The kind of halfway house that might, say, get smeared in fliers that get passed around by a neighbor. The kind of neighbor that is so gripped with fear that he might do something far worse than anything the average halfway house resident would do. But I told my friend to try not to worry about it. Seriously, what kind of a neighborhood has residents that are stranger or more dangerous than people in the local halfway house?

This Was Our Hollywood Peace March

Los Angeles is not an easy place to protest a war. For starters, it requires walking, which makes us more uncomfortable than trying a new restaurant without a recommendation. It also requires us to go against the stereotype of allegiance to flakiness and self-absorption. Not that there's peer pressure, but when you tell people that one of the things you did over the weekend was protest a war, they don't exactly respond as if you'd treated yourself to a spa day. Even saying that you hit a karaoke bar elicits a more animated response. War protesting may be admirable, but it isn't considered cool, even to people who share your politics.

My friends Patty and John, who are neither flaky nor self-absorbed, invited me to go war protesting with them last Saturday. I'm against the Iraq War, and I believe that masses taking to the streets do have an effect. But I wasn't going to commit to attending until I knew where it was going to be held. Turned out that it was not only in nearby Hollywood, but it was going to start and end at conveniently located subway stops. Los Angeles may be the only city in the United States where practicing the First Amendment right to peaceably assemble is a function of the traffic and parking situation.

The instant we came up the escalator at the Red Line station at Hollywood & Vine, the entire movement was in my face. Every ethnicity and class from my city was milling about amongst street vendors, police officers, volunteers passing out fliers for their sub-movements, scores of signs on poles sticking up above the heads. But what jumped out at me immediately was across the street on the

Pantages Theatre's marquee, in big black letters: *Cats*. No matter what symbolic meaning you find in that, it can't possibly be flattering.

Now well after noon and with lots of sounds from the pavement, the three of us headed toward the front of the demonstration. While waiting for the march to start, Patty and John looked up at a building that was being converted into condominiums and discussed the possibility of moving into one of them. Los Angeles may also be the only place in America where you can browse for real estate while marching for peace and no one will accuse you of betraying the cause.

This being Los Angeles, our march had celebrities. We got within 50 feet of the front, right where a horde of reporters surrounded Martin Sheen and Maria Bello. I don't know if the march was early or the interviewing started late, but the truck driver leading the procession honked at them to get out of the way so they could start. I didn't think that was very peaceful of him.

We lurched down Hollywood Boulevard at a heel-toe pace comparable to that of your average wino. It was not unlike driving down Hollywood Boulevard, except that it seemed faster. I looked over and saw that *Walk the Line* was playing at a discount movie theater, then noticed that I happened to be walking on the double yellow line in the middle of the street. For all the meaning and profundity of a war protest, there isn't actually much to do.

I don't know if it was because of the cause or the city, but we have some creative activists here. One sign had the caption "Bush's Exit Strategy" next to a drawing of a man bending over so far that his head was up his own ass. A sign on the back of somebody's jacket read "Will someone give this guy a blow job so we can impeach him?" Another group carried an umbrella decorated with peaches and branches listing the President's malfeasances. It was, of course, the impeach tree.

Another demonstrator held a small sign: "Rome fell." He was walking against the flow of the other marchers.

For part of the march, we ended up in front—and I mean *right in front*—of a group of about 30 angry young people. They were dressed in all black, most with bandannas over their faces. One kid had a gas mask on. Real anarchist-looking types. Their chants were your typical anti-war slogans, until they got stupid about it and chanted an epithet aimed at the police, about a dozen of whom were on bicycles on the sidewalk just a few feet away. The officers never said a word or tried to quiet them, but for the rest of the march, every time I looked over, they were riding parallel to the kids in black.

During the march, I spied Mike Farrell of *M*A*S*H* fame heading back the other way as if he were looking for someone. Here's a guy who's using his power of influence to speak out for a worthy cause, I thought, a cause that still remains unpopular with a substantial segment of the country, which no doubt jeopardizes his career as an actor. I considered racing over to thank him for his integrity, but it felt too akin to starfucking. Starfucking has its place in this town, but starfucking during a peace march just seems tacky, even in Hollywood.

The march ended at Hollywood and Highland, right in front of the Kodak Theatre. The last leg of the march, in fact, was the exact stretch that Oscar invitees walk every year from their limos to the show. I doubt the protest organizers were trying to tack on a subtle layer of self-importance. I think they just wanted the keynote speeches to be delivered in a high-profile part of the city. Either way, I've decided that, no matter the cause, it's better to start a march in front of *Cats* and end up at the Kodak Theatre than the other way around.

Since the march stopped moving here, my activist companions and I decided the marching part must be over. We decided it would be a good idea to eat, so we ducked into Hamburger Hamlet and watched the masses from our booth by the window. Tactically, it turned out to be a smart move to be at the front of the march; we beat nearly everyone else to the restaurants. However, if we were really thinking, we would have had lunch at the restaurant next door. It was closer to the stage where people were speaking, and they had a second-floor dining room for better street viewing than the Hamlet. The fact that the restaurant next door was Hooters had nothing to do with my regret.

That was about it. We couldn't hear the speakers, and the colorful characters were making too many crosses in front of our window, as if they'd run out of people to talk to at a party. By the time we were done with lunch, the speakers were done talking. Just as well. We were tired. All that one-mile-per-hour marching is exhausting when you have to do it the day after St. Patrick's Day. We walked to the Red Line station down the block and rode back to the Valley.

The next time anyone accuses us Angelenos of having shallow priorities or not walking anywhere, I would point out that thousands of us do care about important things and thousands of us walk. And if we can do them simultaneously so as to save time for other stuff, like spa days and karaoke, all the better.

REALLY?
COME ON NOW.

This Is Our Nontraditional Historical Landmark

Los Angeles has a rich history, one that we've paved over with offices, apartment buildings, mini-malls, and lots of other useful crap that we need. It's not that we don't value our history. It's just that there is more value in destroying it and building new stuff on top of it. Since the value-niks outnumber the preservationists in both quantity and capital in this town, the commercial buildings outnumber the historical ones by a mile.

For all of our apparent disdain for our own history, L.A. was actually at the forefront of city preservationist movements. In 1962, when it occurred to enough people that urban overgrowth was swallowing our past, Los Angeles enacted the Cultural Heritage Ordinance. It was one of the first of its kind enacted in any major urban center, even predating a similar ordinance in New York by three years. Under our city's ordinance, the Cultural Heritage Commission, a five-member panel of mayor-appointed citizens, was created to review and recommend sites for landmark status, a designation that over 700 of them have since received.

In one instance, preservationists even managed to relocate our history. In 1969, a group of prominent citizens teamed up with the help of the city's Cultural Heritage Board to create Heritage Square, a sanctuary that now consists of eight historic buildings—and a recently acquired boxcar. The square is on some unused acreage at the end of a cul-de-sac in a Highland Park neighborhood where urban overgrowth appears unlikely to encroach. In one way,

Heritage Square is encouraging. We revere our history so much that we make the effort to find a compromise with the commerce that threatens it. When looked at another way, however, it's kind of sad that we think so little of our history that, rather than let it be, we shove some of it in a vacant lot in the barrio.

But generally, our history, unlike the rest of our city, remains hidden and unflashy—and, except for rare instances like Heritage Square, not freeway-close. If the average tourist came up to the average L.A. resident and asked him where a guy could go to look at historical landmarks, the average L.A. resident would be stuck for an answer. Some people would suggest downtown, but few would be able to name more than Union Station and Olvera Street. Some people might suggest visiting the missions, even though most of us don't know where they are—or even how many we have. There was a time, not that long ago, that if any tourist asked me where to find historical landmarks, I would have suggested Boston.

I've since been somewhat enlightened. I would suggest tourists—and locals—find a copy of *Landmark L.A.* Nearly 500 pages of photos and multiple cross-referenced indexes make this the definitive guide to our city's historic and cultural landmarks. Anyone who thinks we are nothing but a bunch of money-grubbers need only look at the 700 sites listed in *Landmark L.A.* Why, we have century-old Victorians. Frank Lloyd Wright residences. Sleek postwar buildings.

And pallets.

When I first got this book, I went straight to the section on San Fernando Valley landmarks. What were the cool old things in my valley that I must know about? The Van Nuys City Hall is in the book. Cool. I've been there. The La Reina Theater on Ventura Boulevard is in the book. I saw movies there before it was turned into a Gap outlet. There are a bunch of other places I've never even heard of, some of which I've driven by and never noticed. I must visit these places, I thought.

Then on page 243 was something called "Tower of Wooden Pallets." It was located in Sherman Oaks, halfway down the part of Magnolia Boulevard that dead-ends at the San Diego Freeway. Maybe I don't have an artistic eye, but in the picture, it looked like a five-foot-tall woodpile in an empty lot. A couple of years ago, I did a drive-by of this "monument" just to see what it was all about. There was a chain-link fence around the property, there was a bunch of brush growing over everything, and near the street was a pile of wood that vaguely resembled the photo in the book. I don't think I even turned my engine off. I just made a U-turn and got on with life.

But perusing the book again compelled me to dig deeper this week, so I did a little legwork about the pallets. In 1951, a man named Daniel Van Meter lived on the property, and he was known largely for being eccentric. Among other things, he was once convicted of failing to register as a subversive during World War II. One day, he heard that the Schlitz Brewery was going to discard 2,000 wooden beer pallets. So he schlepped up to Schlitz and took them back to his property, where he built them in a stack around, he claimed, the burial site of a child who died in 1869. In 1977, when the fire department said it was a hazard and threatened to demolish it, Van Meter sought refuge via historic and cultural landmark status from the Cultural Heritage Commission. The next year, he got it. As Jeffrey Herr, Arts Manager of the city's Cultural Affairs Department, writes in the preface to *Landmark L.A.*, the list is "peppered with some nontraditional landmarks that help define the character of Los Angeles." Then again, as one commission member later said of their decision, "Maybe we were drunk."

Since Van Meter died in 2000, his family has been seeking to undo the commission's decision so they can sell the property, a 1.43-acre lot valued at $7 million by one estimate. The present plan is for a developer to build an apartment complex on the site, a move that would fulfill a jeremiad that Van Meter wrote nearly 30 years ago: "In a few years, this piece of the good earth may be covered by apartments for the storing of surplus people."

I found out something else: It wasn't a five-foot-high pile of wood. It was a 22-foot-tall room, a cavern with a staircase spiraling around the outside and a plumb line hanging from the roof. I even found a picture of Van Meter standing inside it, holding a chicken. Why doesn't it look like that in the picture? Why didn't I see this thing on my drive-by a couple of years ago? How can you miss a 22-foot-tall building made of beer pallets? Wait—did I read on another Web site that it was sagging, or had been partially demolished, thus the five-foot-high pile? Now I had to see it. Wednesday afternoon, I dropped what I was doing and raced down Magnolia Boulevard to get what may be a last look.

I found a parking spot across the street from the lot, which looked bigger than when I last remembered it. Something else was different too: The gate was open. I wandered in and found a photographer, a genial fellow who had been contracted by a historian to take pictures of the thing. Take pictures of what, I couldn't tell. It was an abandoned lot filled with weeds, brush, trees, and, as I discovered, junk, including a bus and at least two cars. I followed him deeper into the lot.

Then I saw it. *Landmark L.A.* got the wrong photo. This thing was for real. It may have been sagging, but it was still 22 feet high, or thereabouts. It was an igloo-shaped thing, an overgrown beehive clearly laid out with thought and care. The photographer told me I could go in if I wanted. A narrow entrance had been built into the side. I went in. It was dirty and grubby and had empty bottles on the dirt floor, but the plumb line was still there, a cement anchor hanging from a beam across the top of the open-air roof. Hundreds of prismatic views of the outdoors could be seen in every direction through the pallets. God, it was quiet inside. It may have once been a glorious sanctuary, the kind of place that a convicted unregistered subversive probably enjoyed building and sitting in during his spare time.

The photographer referred me to a freelance historian who was overseeing the photography as part of a survey of the property. She explained that before

demolition of a designated city landmark could be authorized, a historical documentation of the structure and the land around it had to be conducted. But it was largely a formality, she said. The apartment complex isn't a done deal, but it looks like the developer is going to get his way.

A determination of the artistic merits of the pallets has been playing out since Van Meter's death. A 2004 environmental impact report included an analysis of the tower from an artistic and historic perspective. The analysis deemed it historically insignificant and artistically uninventive. The historian I met said that, on occasion, museums and galleries raise funds to disassemble, transport, and reconstruct large pieces such as this at their venues. To date, no such facility has stepped up to do this. Except for a 2005 *Los Angeles Times* article about it, there has been little mention in the media about the tower's threatened destruction. Unlike other historic monuments that are faced with demolition, no outraged preservationists, prominent scholars, or concerned citizens appear to be doing anything to save the pallets.

It would appear that, at the moment, the pallets' only hope is me.

I don't know when art should trump commerce, and the more I think about it, the more uncomfortable I am with the idea of arbitrating such things. Lacking the ability and the desire to assign a dollar value to the pallets, I'm left with a default view: As much as I loathe the trend toward expensive ticky-tack rental property overtaking the city, I'm all for individual liberty. I see no reason why the owners shouldn't be as free to sell this property to a developer as the previous owner was to use it for a giant fort that his goats could pee on.

But as long as I'm here, if you or someone you know has the wherewithal to rescue this tower and properly move it to Heritage Square or elsewhere for preservation, well, that would be nice. What's a city full of nontraditional people without a peppering of nontraditional landmarks?

Author's footnote: At press time, the tower had been razed, and a giant apartment complex for the storing of surplus people was being built on the lot.

Meet Clyde Langtry, Part Three

Never has a chat with Clyde Langtry so resembled *Waiting for Godot* than the one I had with him some weeks back, a dialogue so bankrupt of meaningful content that it's still hard to imagine, looking back, that I wasn't overcome with gout. *Waiting for Godot* can be an entertaining play, but only when done well, and only maybe if you've never seen it before. Maybe. Allow me to describe it for you. There are no spoilers ahead because it has no plot. It's about these two losers in the middle of nowhere who talk about nothing while waiting for someone who never shows up. The play ends when they run out of things to talk about, then it keeps going for another hour and forty-five minutes.

Now, imagine that condensed to twenty minutes. The two losers are Clyde and I. Late morning. The courtyard of our apartment building is abandoned. We hear traffic in the distance. And we're not waiting for anything in particular.

I enter from the back, carrying clean laundry. Clyde enters from his apartment, carrying a tied-up grocery bag (presumably trash) and a wooden picture frame. He also has a small aerosol can jammed into the pocket of his tattered flannel shirt. What follows are the highlights.

Clyde: "I've been working on my hi-fi notebooks."
Me: "Your what?"
Clyde: "Hi-fi notebooks. I work on 'em every day."
Me: "These are notebooks you fill with information on hi-fis?"

Clyde: "All kinds of information. Mono too." He goes on about the specifics of stereo versus mono, and record needles, wraps up with this: "Hearing the pure timbre of music on a mono recording is the greatest emotional joy I know of."

I never would have figured that that was his greatest emotional joy. In fact, I've never heard Clyde talk about emotional joy. I just assumed he was an automaton: *Must work on car. Must drink distilled water. Must talk to cat about state of the universe.*

Silence.

Clyde: "I gotta put new headlights on my car. The ones I have don't work very well."

Me: "New bulbs won't do it?"

Clyde: "The lights themselves are just too dim. Plus the plastic covers are all cracked."

Me: "Can't you just replace the covers with old ones from a car junkyard?"

Clyde: "Oh, I have a couple of those already. I polished them and they're already getting cloudy again. No, I got these little headlamps. I'm gonna mount 'em, and if they're not bright enough, I'm going to put a third one in the grill, like a Cyclops."

Me: "Isn't one of those two cars parked on the side of the driveway yours?"

Clyde: "Yeah, the Toyota. I gotta get that thing fixed. Needs some transmission work. And a new battery, probably."

Silence.

Clyde: "Women. They don't know how to take care of cars. Priscilla never changed the oil on that thing."

I've heard Clyde go off on plenty of other subjects, but never this. He even mocked his wife, doing a half-assed imitation of her voice, the way husbands everywhere do when they're irritated with their wives. I was actually relieved to see this side of him. They never fight, but in the four years I've lived here, I've never sensed the slightest bit of intimacy or affection between them either. At least there's occasional disgust.

Silence.

Clyde: "I was at the farmers' market in Hollywood yesterday and a woman stopped me. She said her oil light went off on the freeway. She kept driving. She didn't pull over. Well, it ruined her engine and something must have sheared off in her transmission because that wasn't working either. She said she shifted gears and nothing happened. Then a police officer gave her a ticket because she had it parked in the wrong spot. So she tells me all this and I gave her thirteen dollars to help her get her car fixed or towed or something." Cavemen telling stories around the campfire have nothing on Clyde.

Silence.

Clyde: "I got a new temperature gauge."

Me: "What was wrong with the old one?"

Clyde: "It was digital. Those things go haywire. I got one made in China, but it's good."

Silence.

Clyde: "You know, [our neighbor] Jezbo was a pilot. I admire that guy. He's done everything. If he wants to go do something, he goes for it. Now if we could only get him off the alcohol."

Me: "Oh, well. What can ya' do?"

Clyde: "Oh, I know what to do. But will he listen, is the question. Alcohol just ruins people."

Me: "Some of the most entertaining people I know are heavy drinkers."

Clyde: "But what would they be if they stopped drinking?"

Me: "Less entertaining."

Silence.

Clyde: "Alcohol and drugs have messed up so many artists. I was just listening to Miles Davis on the radio and I can't stand his music because you can tell that it's polluted with drugs. It's the most ass-fucking-backwards music."

Me: "Was he on drugs?"

Clyde: "Oh, yeah, all his life. Cocaine, alcohol. Heroin too, I think. And he died young because of it."

Silence.

Me: "Well, I'm gonna put my laundry away."

Clyde: "You do that. I'm going to go do my thing."

A garbage truck roars in front of our apartment building.

Clyde: "That's a tough job. You gotta cut through the grill to mount the headlight."

The garbage truck drives away. There's a lull in the street traffic. Long silence.

Clyde: "I had a drink about a year ago. I was at my parents-in-laws' place in Maryland and I just felt like a beer. So I said, 'Yeah, Bob, I think I'd like a beer.' So he gave me one. It was imported. And I drank it. And that was that."

Clyde smiles, totters up and down on the balls of his feet.

Clyde stops moving.

We do not move.

THESE ARE OUR AIRPORTS

Nothing strikes dread in—and draws groaning out of—Angelenos like being asked to drive someone to the airport. The dread happens instantly because people fear the requested airport might be Los Angeles International Airport, aka LAX—which we always articulate not by saying "lacks," but by spelling out as if to a listener in denial. The groaning happens when we find out it *is* LAX. Getting there and getting back is a pain in the ass. Like everything else here, the airport is conveniently located only to people who happen to live near it.

People in Los Angeles have strong feelings about taking someone to LAX, as well as about asking someone to take them to LAX, yet you can't tell much about these people by their attitudes on these subjects. Such people run the spectrum. I know one person, a very nice guy, who has proclaimed that he has a standing refusal to take anyone to any airport, ever. Then there's me, also a purportedly nice fellow, who seems to be schlepping to LAX every few months or so, because I have a number of good friends who think nothing of asking me for a ride, because, I guess, they think it's nothing. Yet I have a number of friends who *never* ask me to take them to LAX. They must think it's akin to asking someone for a kidney.

The airport itself is actually a remarkable achievement considering what a perceived mess it is. Driving through it for passenger pick-up and drop-off, while not enjoyable, is actually pretty painless. Getting through security is relatively easy unless one flies during a holiday weekend. LAX's percentage of on-time flights is among the highest in the country. And its *Jetsons*-inspired Theme

Building is an elegant example of city architecture, except for the fact that it will be closed indefinitely for structural repairs.

Los Angeles has to be the international air travel capital of the world. LAX is the busiest, or fourth-busiest, or fifth-busiest airport in the world, depending on which measure you're looking at. We have four outlying airports that are ranked in the top 20 percent in the nation in terms of volume. And Van Nuys Airport is the busiest general aviation airport in the world, by every measure, apparently. (The lengths people go to in order to avoid driving in this city, really.)

As our outlying areas keep growing in population, our outlying airports keep gaining in popularity. Of course, we can't leave things well enough alone in L.A. without the celebrity factor. There's a busy airport in Burbank that the locals call Burbank Airport because it seems logical, even though that's never been its official name. Then a few years ago it became Bob Hope Airport, because Bob Hope died that year and having a street named after him, having a public square named after him, and having deeds to who knows how many acres of the San Fernando Valley wasn't enough justice, apparently. The airport in Santa Ana was renamed after John Wayne in 1979 because he lived nearby—and died that year. That airport was in danger of going down a dark alley of shame when a thoughtful, hardworking member of the County Board of Supervisors wanted to rename the airport after *The O.C.*, the TV show, but he withdrew his suggestion after too many complaints.

Then there are the airports not named after famous people. The one in Long Beach is named Daugherty Airport, after the "famous" barnstorming pilot, Earl S. Daugherty. I guess there haven't been any major movie stars living in the area, ever. Oxnard Airport is just called Oxnard Airport. I guess their County Board of Supervisors has better things to do than go around asking local celebrities if they'd like the airport renamed in their honor. Ontario Airport, in the Inland Empire east of L.A., has actually been renamed LA/Ontario International Airport, so as to entice more people to fly there. I don't know how much of an enticement that could possibly be, but then again, if I were in charge of anything in the Inland Empire, I'd try whatever I could think of. Frankly, they'd probably have more luck naming it after one of their own regional celebrities. Wouldn't you fly to Jessica Alba Airport once just so you could say you landed on her?

The square mileage of greater L.A. is so absurd and traffic so congested that outlying airports offer flights to LAX. United Express offers daily flights, none more than 50 miles, between Santa Ana, Ontario, and Oxnard Airports and LAX. The idea of an L.A. resident flying to LAX is so appealing that more of us would be inclined to do it if driving to Santa Ana, Ontario, and Oxnard weren't so difficult. Still, I'd like to fly in from one of those airports to LAX someday— to pick someone up at the airport. That way, when they ask me where I parked, I could say, "Oxnard. We have to get to Terminal 8 quick so we can make the 8:20 flight." I'd do it just to see the look on their face.

And then, there's Palmdale Airport, in the desert about an hour north of L.A. If our airports were a litter of dogs, Palmdale Airport would surely be the runt. In 2005, its last full year with commercial service, it ranked 549th in the nation—out of 554 commercial airports. Three airlines have attempted commercial service out of Palmdale Airport. All failed. United Express is attempting to become the fourth. This month, it began commercial service to San Francisco. It's going balls to the wall with the enterprise, launching with not one, but two daily nonstops.

Furthermore, the airport is overshadowed by Edwards Air Force Base, where people drive from hundreds of miles away just to watch the space shuttle land. Such is the irony of air travel in Antelope Valley. It's either short commercial flights that few people want, or trips into outer space that few people can take.

But none of these airports is my favorite. My favorite airport is so far away from L.A. that it couldn't be considered an outlying airport, even if it offered commercial air service. About a half hour north of Palmdale Airport is Mojave Airport, where there is no commercial air service, yet dozens of commercial jets. Mojave Airport is known for its storage capacity. On any given day, one can drive out to this quiet patch of desert and see any number of planes from a variety of airlines all lined up, getting dusty. Pictures don't do it justice; they can't help but look Photoshopped. It is one of the most delightfully strange things I have ever seen.

Now *that's* an airport I'd be happy to drive someone to.

This Is How We
Drive Our Cars

It's easy to categorize drivers here as insane. The more open-minded among us, however, don't wish to make such generalizations. Only some are insane. The truth is, drivers here fall into one (sometimes two or three) of several categories. I've slowly been categorizing our city's drivers for some time now, but only as a way to keep myself occupied while I'm stuck in traffic. I never thought it would lead to anything until I recently discovered a potentially revolutionary new category.

The obvious category is what we cleverly call **The Asshole.** He also goes by The Dick, The Fuckin' Dick, The Cocksucker, The "God Damn, Did You See What That Guy Just Did?" and others. Every road belongs to him and he's constantly irritated that other people are using it. He makes dangerous lane changes, usually without signaling. He tailgates drivers even in the fast lane, no matter their speed. Sometimes he'll flash his high beams at them, or sometimes he'll go around them, even if he has to go all the way to the slow lane to do it.

Unfortunately, The Asshole has an influence on trends in city driving. One day about five years ago (reports vary), The Asshole decided to reinvent the right turn. Rather than come to the usual rolling stop of about three to five miles an hour, he takes the turn at about 15, swings into traffic, and figures out that whole space cushion thing later. He only yields if he is absolutely positive that he'll be in an accident. Not cause one. Be in one. The "Asshole Right" was born. Now you see it all the time.

The Madwoman. Her habits resemble those of The Asshole, but she's not aggressive or angry. She's only comfortable going her speed (fast), and is oblivious to subtleties like the centrifugal force that sends her belongings all over her car on sharp turns. She floors the gas, slams on the brakes, stops on the freeway before figuring out which off-ramp she wants, all with little regard to the law, the wear and tear on her car, or the heart rates of her passengers. I refer to her as female only because all known instances of The Madwoman happen to be the neurotic mothers of some of my friends.

There is also **The Dumbshit.** You name it, this guy does it, and every time you see him do something dumb, the conclusion you draw is always the same: He wants to die and doesn't care if others join him. The Dumbshit's latest trend is making unsafe left turns in front of oncoming cars. He doesn't even hurry. To accommodate The Dumbshit, the oncoming driver is forced to slow down, sometimes dramatically. A few months ago, a friend of mine who was in the oncoming-driver role had to brake hard and spin out to miss The Dumbshit's left turn by inches. Oh, and The Dumbshit seems to like breeding with other Dumbshits. There are more and more of them every day. I swear to God.

Sometimes you just get stuck behind a slow driver. He may have an old car with bad acceleration. Or he doesn't have insurance and he's paranoid about being pulled over for speeding or getting into an accident. Or he's visiting from some small town where the pace of life warrants slow driving and he hasn't adjusted to Los Angeles. Or his hand-eye coordination is so compromised that he's using every active brain cell just to go down the street in a straight line and he's afraid that if he goes one mile an hour faster he might skid off the road, flip his car, and be burned to death inside the wreckage after the inevitable explosion. I call this kind of driver **The Baker** because he drives like he has a wedding cake in the front seat.

One variation of The Baker is **The Cruiser.** This is a guy, always riding with a friend or two, who isn't merely a slow driver. He appears to be sightseeing on every street he drives. My theory about The Cruiser is that his journey *is* his destination. His home life is terrible, and he has nowhere to go, so he kills an evening by driving around. I'd feel sorry for him if he weren't so goddamn irritating.

Oh, and there's **The Normal Driver.** He blends into the flow of traffic. He neither flips off nor gets flipped off. He shows courtesy and safety all the time. No one knows how many of him there are because no one pays attention to him.

And then there is **The By-The-Book.** He usually appears to be a teenager, and he obeys every single traffic law to the letter. And he always has someone riding shotgun. This is the driving test administrator from the Department of Motor Vehicles. Within days of the DMV tester leaving the car, The By-The-Book turns into one of the other kinds of drivers, never to revert back except when he sees a police car in his mirror.

I remember reading an article years ago in a local magazine that analyzed the traffic patterns in Los Angeles. An expert came up with a way to decrease freeway accidents as well as stop the snake-like deceleration/acceleration cycle caused by armies of cars racing to interchanges. His suggestion? We all drive exactly 45 miles per hour on the freeways all the time. The backdrop of the theory is that if we all approach our destinations a bit slower, it would be substantially easier for everyone to make lane changes and slide through freeway interchanges without looking like the Three Stooges trying to get through a doorway. Unfortunately, his proposal would be a hard sell on Los Angeles drivers, if not entirely impossible. We'd much rather get around town like stooges.

The idea of us all driving the same speed is pure fantasy. The closest thing we have to an equalizer is rain. During rainstorms, all categories of drivers morph into just two: too fast and cautiously slow. Since the majority of drivers fall into the cautiously slow category during the rain, traffic is actually worse. The extra accidents the rain causes contributes too.

Oddly enough, driving slower on purpose is something that some people unwittingly choose all the time and they don't even realize it. They choose it every time they use a cell phone. Show me someone on the freeway in one of the middle lanes going about 10 mph slower than everyone else, and I'll show you someone on a cell phone.

Which leads me to the potentially revolutionary category of Los Angeles driver. He is a sad creation, the result of a number of sinister factors. It didn't occur to me that there is a new driver among us—one whose ranks are increasing, by the way—until I realized the newest trend in driving. It is thoroughly idiotic, raising the bar for absurdity everywhere: Some of us now remain stopped at green lights.

This is not because there are more ambulances going by. There are no extra red light runners to avoid. People are not stalled. There is no practical reason for it. As best as I can tell, it is because our cars are becoming the most pleasant places in our lives. Traffic has gotten so bad, and technology has gotten so good, that we have found more and more ways to keep ourselves entertained and distracted in the car. Combine that with the already high premium we place on car luxury, and it's no wonder we're looking for ways to drag out our car trips.

If you don't think this trend is teeming with potential, just envision what it will do to our city if it continues. These people will force all of us to spend more time in our cars, making traffic slower, freeing us up to do even more things while we drive, making traffic slower still, and so on. This would lead to two things. First, our cars would become such advanced, comfortable places that we will willingly spend more time in them than in our homes. This will lower the demand for houses, which will lower their prices to affordable levels.

The second thing it would do would be, at long last, to force us all to drive the same way, at the same speed, in effect putting us all in the same driver category. Once we'd all been "trained" to drive the same way, we could outlaw the most distracting car activities one by one, freeing our heretofore distracted minds up to drive at higher and higher speeds until we are all driving at 45 mph, the speed that would theoretically make all freeway traffic flow like the Los Angeles River (when it has water in it). Therefore, I have come up with a name for the driver who stops at green lights.

The Sane One.

These Are Our
Football Teams

In 1986, my old friend Bob, the college football fanatic and UCLA booster, flew from Los Angeles to Dallas, then drove with a friend 200 miles to Norman, Oklahoma to see his beloved football Bruins play the Oklahoma Sooners. "You're driving up the highway in the middle of nowhere," I remember him telling me after he got back, "and all of a sudden, it's a traffic jam. Everyone's going to the game." I don't know what else Norman, Oklahoma has going on, but it must be one hell of a college football town.

No college or game has that effect on Los Angeles. The closest Los Angeles gets to the kind of college-town atmosphere you see in Norman, Oklahoma is our annual UCLA-USC football game. And even describing that as a day of college-town unity is charitable. Its attendance and bluster simply exceed that of all other college athletic events in this city, which, to the city's many non-sports fans, is not unlike pointing out who was the tallest munchkin.

Because of the fragmentation that our city's disparity hath wrought, there is only so much capacity for any one thing, including college spirit. UCLA and USC are big, old, and rich enough to have more or less cornered the market on that particular capacity. The most sports press that the other regional four-year colleges get seems to happen when they upset UCLA or USC at something besides football. Never football. None of them have even played, much less beaten, UCLA or USC at football in years.

I went to California State University, Northridge, known colloquially as "C-Sun." Here in the Valley, population 1.6 million as of the year 2000, it is our only major four-year university. You'd think with one four-year college football team for that many people, the locals, particularly the alumni, would be all over it. Wrong. In fact, due to years of our fervent and loyal disinterest, CSUN was forced to scrap its football program in 2001. But it's not like we couldn't have seen it coming. When I mention to fellow CSUN alumni that we lost our football team a few years back, they usually reply that they never knew we had a football team in the first place.

The lords of college football need not take our city's apathy towards their sport personally. We care just as little about pro football too, as evidenced by the magic year of 1995, when we set a record that will likely never be broken by any city, ever. We had the most pro football franchises move out in the same off-season: two (Rams and Raiders). Nearly as remarkable is the fact that, to this day, local newscasts often lead off the Sunday football report with Rams and Raiders highlights, as if there's a large contingent of loyalists here who still give a shit about teams that buggered off a decade ago. This, to me, is the equivalent of getting weekly updates on some girl who dumped you in high school.

(The only thing sadder than fans of the former Los Angeles Raiders still getting excited about their former team—if anyone here even does that anymore—are current Oakland Raiders fans who were dumped by Al Davis when he moved the team to L.A. in 1982 before gimping back to Oakland 13 years later like a ne'er-do-well in some hackneyed country-western song. Then again, if I were a sports fan stuck in Oakland, I might take whatever I could get.)

As for L.A. fans feeling betrayed, the only real effect that losing two pro football teams at once has had on us is general happiness. With certain exceptions, league rules black out local TV coverage of nationally broadcast games in cities on days when the home team plays. When we had two teams, one of them was invariably playing at home, which invariably limited our viewing options. Since we no longer have any NFL franchise, football fans here get to watch an extra game on Sundays. If you're thinking we're so pathetic that we'd rather watch other teams on TV than have one of our own to root for, consider that most of the football fans I know (a very crude survey sample, I admit—of a somewhat crude bunch, they'd admit) brought their team loyalty with them from another city, or adopted another city's team as their own. I know multiple Cowboys, Eagles, and Steelers fans. I know of no Raiders fans, and exactly one Rams fan, and I occasionally make fun of him for it.

Since then, we periodically hear rumors and innuendo to the effect of landing another franchise. The closest these ever came to fruition was in 1999 when the NFL did everything short of buying our city council members vacations to Aruba to get them to promise enough taxpayer money for a new stadium. Fortunately, Houston, smarting from the departure of their also-ran Oilers franchise to

Tennessee, places such a premium on football that the city cheerfully coughed up the dough, and we were left to spend our money on trifles like education and road repair.

I would argue that our city's diversity is so broad and its hugeness so hopeless that it cannot foment citywide loyalty to a team (in any sport), even when that city lets its residents choose between two teams and allows them to channel their loyalty into what is essentially a one-day-a-year rivalry. I would also argue that one measure of a city is loyalty to a team—or in our case, two teams. I hardly care who wins. But I admit that I find it comforting that the Bruins and the Trojans, while individually unable to come close to uniting the city the way the Sooners do in Norman, Oklahoma, collectively make an effort to unite us better than any other teams in town can, even professional teams. It is worth noting that, unlike pro sports franchises, the Bruins and Trojans neither blew in from someplace else nor have any chance of moving someplace else.

And yet, as much as I romanticize college towns, the thought of living anyplace where the whole city shuts down for any event rather disturbs me. Maybe it comes from living in a place where such unity only occurs during an earthquake or a race riot. More likely, it comes from a reality of our megalopolis that we rely on to validate our individuality but rarely articulate: We are more comfortable with our diversity than with our commonality. We're free to give a crap about whatever we want in Los Angeles, because no other event will ever be so large that it will usurp that right. Comforted as I am by signs of unity that are not caused by terror-inducing events, I take even more comfort knowing that conformity will never win out. Thus the purpose of the Bruin-Trojan game: It makes us a college town for only a day, and only for those of us who want to live in it.

And even then, we'll stop watching at halftime if it's a blowout.

This Is What It's Like
to Buy Houses—
or Not Buy Them

Picture it: A young married couple is looking to get out of their North Hollywood apartment and buy their first house. They find a nice middle-class house in a decent neighborhood in Van Nuys with two bedrooms, a den, one-and-a-half bathrooms, and a detached garage.

They offer $27,000 for it. And their bid is accepted.

This is what happened to my parents in Van Nuys in 1967, before they divorced, before that part of Van Nuys became a bit dodgy, and before real estate increased about 2,200% in value. If you still think nostalgia is for assholes, then you have no soul.

I bring this up only because the cost of housing is something we used to bring up all the damn time here. But it comes up in conversation less and less these days, probably because it is as much of a reality of life here as the traffic. And the reality is a beautiful one for people who own a place and a hideous one for those who don't.

At this point, you may be wondering what I'm saying that isn't true about the rest of the country. First of all, it's not true about the rest of the country. In some cities, housing prices are as stagnant as fashion trends of a cattle rancher. (Ever hear anyone telling you to get in on a great real estate deal in Detroit?)

Second of all, prices are more exaggerated here than in other "hot" markets. Sixteen of the 100 most expensive zip codes are in our county. The median home price is $545,000, putting Los Angeles fourth in the nation. One study cited Los Angeles as the least affordable housing market in the nation, stating that a grand total of 2 percent of the homes are affordable for residents making median incomes.

There is one figure that astonishes me most. Consider that, depending on the personal finance expert you talk to, one should spend 25 to 33 percent of one's income on one's mortgage. In Los Angeles, the average is 62 percent, putting it far ahead of that of any other city.

In the twisted world of real estate, the demand that shot prices up also forced many of us out of the buying market. So in addition to a huge number of people racing to buy homes, another huge number of people took shelter in the rental market, driving up rents as well. Today, the 27 grand that my parents spent for ownership of an entire house in what was then a very decent neighborhood gets you a year's rent in a small apartment in a marginal neighborhood.

So not only are pre-2000 buyers basking in the good fortune of buying something that doubled in value in five years, but even renters of the era are considered lucky. I was fortunate enough to get into a nice apartment in 2001 that was run by a guy who didn't realize just how much he could be asking for his vacant units. As the years go on, people register more and more astonishment when I tell them just how little I'm paying for my place, and how rent-control laws will forever dampen my annual rent increases. Despite the purported illogic of renting, I'm very reluctant to give up my inexpensive flat unless I'm absolutely certain I won't be returning. Nice apartments this cheap are nearly as extinct as $27,000 houses in Van Nuys.

I'd gone my whole adult life not looking at open houses because I never felt I could afford one. Seemed like a waste of time, like test-driving a car I had no intention of buying. But one Sunday last year, when I went for a jog at a nearby high school track, I gave it a shot. A Realtor was setting up little flags outside a modest house across the street just as I arrived. More than an hour later when I headed back to my car, I saw her standing by the living room window, gazing out longingly for anyone to come in and look at the place. I had a job back then, so in the back of my mind, I felt I wasn't completely wasting her time, since, theoretically, I might have qualified in some way for a loan to buy the place. Plus, the Realtor was pretty.

She was a very nice woman who led me on a walk-through of what I would call a small tragedy. The previous occupants were renters who'd been there for about 30 years and had done nothing to the place but wear down the carpet. The décor was straight out of a 1970s catalog. The add-on den was a dank hole that looked best suited for people to crash on the floor and get high. The backyard was the size of a beach towel. And it was all across the street from a high school. Despite all these inducements, the owners were eager to unload it, so they were asking about $30,000 less than comparable houses in the area. They were asking $569,000. It took about two months, but it sold.

I haven't walked through an open house since.

I've concluded that there are three types of homebuyers (or non-homebuyers) here. People who got in before the boom are the ones literally sleeping in their cozy retirements. No one talks about them, and they don't have much to talk about except how sorry they feel for young people today.

People who got in more recently are alternately thanking their lucky stars that they did and wondering how the hell they're going to make the mortgage next month. They do both in private because the former is immodest and the latter is too personal a matter to discuss publicly—for the most part. On occasion, I hear such people freely admit that they couldn't possibly have afforded their house without their parents' help. One woman I know even shared that she and her husband had no business buying a house during the boom. They were both unemployed and had lousy credit. But at least it got them out of the townhouse they were renting for over two grand a month.

Speaking of rent, that brings us to the rest of us: renters—in which there are subcategories. Some renters are so resigned to renting for the foreseeable future that we don't bother to foresee any other future, so we don't talk about when or how we're going to buy anything more extravagant than concert tickets.

Some renters are getting closer every day to moving to other states (some of whose cities are already so filled with ex-Angelenos that it's either a joke or a nuisance). Generally speaking, for whatever reason, such people have a tendency to ponder such a move in private. Next thing you know, you're getting an email from them, telling you of their new address—in another state, where they bought a house for a price so low that you think they're lying about it.

But then there is another subcategory of renter: those of us who are waiting for the bubble to dispense with this slight leak bullshit and burst already. We're convinced it's possible, because it doesn't make sense, we keep telling ourselves, that prices not only got this high, but have stayed this high. We go around complaining that this is unfair, that we don't feel sorry for all the fools who are foreclosing on homes they could never afford in the first place because people like them drove up the cost of houses. We also excoriate flippers who only added to the demand, and are glad to see them bailing out on their investments.

And still, housing prices remain high, mainly because we're all locked in a staring contest, waiting for each other to leave so demand will drop. So we have all resorted to waiting for something that can cause a mass exodus, something that would induce a reduction in demand sharp enough to force a precipitous drop in home prices.

An earthquake.

We're not asking for anything bad. We simply wish a violent act of God would scare the shit out of a few hundred thousand of our neighbors and compel them to flee permanently. Never mind the death toll, which could reach into the thousands, or the property damage, which would likely be in the billions. We want a goddamn house and we don't care who has to die so we can afford it. And there is no discretion factor on this topic. If there's one thing that Los Angeles homebuyers agree on publicly, it's wishing a humongous natural disaster on ourselves.

Otherwise, we'd just have to rent for the rest of our lives. And that would be crazy.

Meet Clyde Langtry, Part Four

September

Clyde told me that he had a clean bill of health. Seems he had to go to a Scientologist-referred doctor for a physical in advance of his eventual move to Clearwater, Florida, so he can continue his work with the church there. Clyde's been threatening to move to Florida for years. All I want to know is when his apartment becomes available.

A mental analysis and a spiritual analysis were included in addition to his physical, all part of his recent interview to see just how fit he was to move to Florida. This took months because someone in Florida lost his file, then sent only part of it, all of which delayed his interview. Clyde explained that this was his fault. Scientology teaches that if anything goes wrong in your life, it is at least partly your fault no matter how culpable someone else is in the problem.

"Someone with my face in another galaxy must be a wanted man," Clyde said. "Hubbard—" (that's L. Ron, not Mother) "—told a story about how one of his little kids once snuck up on him and scared him. He said, 'I thought the intergalactic sheriffs had finally caught me.'"

Without the delivery, the full Clyde experience is lost.

We had another brief but loony conversation, this time about the appendix. "It's a natural detoxifier," he said. "Your body needs that to detoxify the body. The tonsils are too, but they got mine a long time ago. Fortunately, I still have my appendix."

One day this month, I saw a shirtless, tattooed guy with a trash bag and a stick racing through the courtyard. Clyde saw him too and, from my window, I saw them exchange what appeared to be polite words. I asked Clyde what they said.

"Oh, that was just a guy collecting cans. I'm always nice to those guys. I figure they're making an honest living and doing us a service by recycling."

"Oh, good," I said. "He looked pretty creepy. I just wanted to make sure he wasn't a criminal or something."

"No. I can tell who the criminals are just by looking at them. There was a guy driving up the driveway next door and he was a criminal. He was casing the joint, looking for cars to steal. I could just tell."

"There aren't criminals here, are there?"

"No. Not criminals. But we definitely have some crazy people here."

"We do?"

"I should sit down with you sometime and tell you about them. I have to get to the office now." I have no idea which office this is, seeing as how he doesn't have a job. "But there are so many crazy stories here that you could write a novel."

I was thinking of a column, actually.

Early November

Clyde knocked on my door. "Can you keep an eye on the place for a month or so? I'm going to San Francisco."

"What for? Petitioning?"

Clyde is a professional petitioner. He's one of those people who sits outside retail stores and pushes clipboards on people who just want to buy their diapers and yogurt and go the hell home. Apparently, it pays pretty well. After all, you have to be a special kind of person to sit outside a Wal-Mart all day.

"Yep. Priscilla goes out from time to time for a teaching job. Just keep an eye out for riff-raff or suspicious characters."

"Sure, no problem." Even dumb thieves must know that Clyde has nothing worth stealing, but that's no reason not to be neighborly. "When are you leaving?"

"In about 10 minutes."

Ten minutes later Blue Thunder bellowed down the driveway.

December 9

This afternoon, Clyde came home from his month up the coast. I heard that familiar rumble of a car that doesn't work very well, and sure enough, here came Blue Thunder past my window.

Out the window facing the courtyard, I saw Clyde bound through with his suitcase and his leather jacket that he's probably been wearing for decades. He stopped at his door and, for some reason, didn't go in. Perhaps he didn't have a key. But he was looking in, as if to see if his wife was home or something. I returned to my work.

A bit later—*and I mean seconds later*—I looked up and there he was outside my door. I opened it.

"Hi, Clyde."

"I just thought I'd come by and tell you I'm back."

The man hadn't seen his wife for a month, and I don't think he'd even kissed her hello, but he wanted to shake my hand. I'd be afraid of the guy if he weren't so harmless.

"Welcome back. How'd it go? Make lots of money?"

"Made great money. Worked outside the toughest store in San Francisco and still got signatures."

A moment later, Priscilla came out and brought him a cup of tea. At *my* doorstep.

"You want to say hello to your wife? I'll avert my eyes."

"I'll say hello to her, but I won't do it here in front of you."

That's the kindest gesture Clyde has ever made to me.

Ken the landlord, who's known Clyde and Priscilla since he became landlord over 20 years ago, said he's never seen any physical intimacy or affection between the two of them, ever. Know what? I believe him.

The next day, I saw Clyde playing with his new dashboard-mountable compass. He stood in the middle of the courtyard with it, making repeated 90-degree turns. He eventually stopped, facing his apartment door about 10 feet away. To any neighbor looking out their window, he looked like a guy who couldn't find his way to his apartment with a compass.

January 11

Clyde knocked on my door today.

"I'm leaving."

"Where are you going?"

"Clearwater, Florida."

"You moving?"

"No, just doing some work for Scientology."

"You going to look for houses? I know you want to move there."

"No, I won't have much time. Listen, I'm expecting a package of electronic parts, about like this."

He made a rectangular shape with his hands, roughly the size of a decent-sized box of worthless electronic parts. I told him I'd keep an eye out for it.

January 16

Today, I heard Clyde yell, "Hi, Joe" just before I made it into my apartment. Clyde is wont to do that sometimes, that is, hurriedly yell hello to me before I get out of earshot. The man really likes having conversations.

I turned around and was treated to the sight of Clyde stepping out of his door. He was wearing a striped button-front shirt and long underwear tucked into his socks. Brown socks.

When I asked him what was new, he told me that he had to fly back to L.A. this morning after getting nothing done. Then he talked in circles about how he went all the way to Clearwater, Florida for his work, which was supposed to be some sort of an audit of Clyde as administered by the church, and for reasons that aren't even clear to Clyde, he couldn't take the tests he needed to take. He kept using the word "betrayed," seeing as how he's given so much money to the church over the years. He also said that he shouldn't be complaining about all this because he'll be forced to divulge his indiscretion to the church later when they do an ethics audit of him.

"So what are you going to do?"

"Oh, take some more classes here for about a year. I tell you, I've taken so many classes and tests that they've got a stack of files this high on me." He held his hand out above his knee. Imagine anyone writing so much about Clyde Langtry.

After a good five minutes of this, he insisted that he race in to put on some pants.

Moments later, we got to talking about the hummingbirds around here. "They're cool as shit. Did you know—this is amazing—they can travel thousands and thousands of miles and return to the exact same spot?"

"Really?" I thought he was about to relate something he saw on TV.

"Yeah, and I'll tell you how I proved it. I saw one by my back window. He was sitting out there and just looking at me, like 'Where's the feed?'"

"How do you know it was a hummingbird that'd been here before?"

"He was communicating with me."

Moments later, Clyde was back to Scientology. "You know, you can't lie to them. They can read your thoughts."

"They can?"

"Sure. They can read thoughts that are registering below your conscious, thoughts you don't even know you're having."

"How do they do that? Like, with electrodes on your head?"

"No, they put these two cans in the palms of your hands."

"How do they work?"

"They run a little current through your body and when your brain registers certain thoughts, a little needle moves just a tiny bit. Sometimes, the needle makes a big jump."

"How do they test people who have no hands?"

"I don't know the answer to that."

Clyde also told me that before they made these fancy cylindrical devices, they used to build them out of asparagus cans. I didn't ask him if they took the asparagus out first.

A few minutes later, I was pounding all this out on the keyboard when there was a familiar weak tap at the door.

"Listen, I hope you're not going to write about all this."

"I hadn't planned on it."

"Good. We're not supposed to criticize the church to members of the press. Even though you're not a reporter, technically, I shouldn't be doing it. If you write about this and they find out, it could be a problem for both of us."

"You just told me a moment ago that when they do an ethics audit of you, they'll find out that you blabbed. Isn't that the case whether I write about this or not?"

"Yeah, yeah, I know."

Still, he had my curiosity peaked.

"What happens to journalists who write bad things about the church?"

"They do a very noisy investigation of them and, I tell you, they always find something bad in their past."

"Invariably? You mean like a felony or something that they did earlier in life?" I had to phrase it carefully. I didn't want Clyde to think I was asking about journalists' past lives.

"Yep, invariably. A felony or something like that. Every time."

In that case, I'll be sure to exercise discretion.

This Is How We Celebrate Christmas in Public

Los Angeles has no more Christmas spirit than it does any other kind of spirit. It's L.A.; there's room for so much that nothing gets enough attention. However, the many, many transplants here get a collective itch for holiday spirit this time of year—something akin to what they recall wherever they came from—and have no outlet for it. For starters, Christmas conjures up images of snow for many people. Our nearest snow is an hour or two away. We ski on it. There is also the unity that Christmas decorations and festivities brings to small towns across America, a coziness that Los Angeles hasn't had since the Spaniards ran it. Then there is the religious aspect of Christmas, which, in a secular town like ours, will be trumped by the commercial aspect every time. For all of our grandiosity and opulence, the most definitive Christmas tradition we have is the pageantry of a transplant asking someone to drive them to the airport so they can go home for Christmas.

That lack of Christmas spirit is alive and well in my apartment building. Tuesday, Ken the landlord and I happened to see Spencer cleaning up the handrail leading up to the apartment he shares with his 83-year-old mother, Ruth. Ruth needs to use the handrail to help her up and down the stairs, and Katie, who lives across the landing from Spencer and his mother, had wrapped garland around it. Spencer had removed all of it and was wiping off whatever sticky residue accompanied it. In his gentle, dispassionate voice, he explained with uncharacteristically foul language that he had better things to do with his time. (Ruth

told me that he'd slept in that very morning.) He did not atte
however, how sap could come from garland made of plastic.

It is worth noting that Spencer said "someone" had decorated tl
though Katie is the only other person who uses that set of stairs. It ...so worth
noting that Spencer harbors the delusion that Katie plays the accordion and
sometimes asks her how that's going. This isn't relevant. It's just really funny.

This year, I did my usual. I jammed my three plastic, jumbo-sized candy
canes in the dirt outside my porch. Not to sound all grinchy about things, but I
neglected to hang the battery-operated wreath on my door, drape the faux-gar-
land over my venetian blinds, or put out the stained-glass Christmas angel. I'm
not a girl, for God's sake.

The one holiday festivity I will partake in is in Studio City. Every year on
a Saturday evening in early December, along a stretch of Tujunga Avenue, the
street lights up and locals fill the sidewalks to pop in and out of stores, restaurants, and the local coffeehouse. I don't go for the parade as much as I do for the
sense of community. The parade itself isn't much of a parade. It consists of about
three floats. It makes several visits throughout the evening, during each of which
it stops about every hundred feet so as to extend the duration of the parade
another few minutes. Also, a bunch of high school girls in little holiday jailbait
outfits walk along and do synchronized dance routines to the songs, even though
"Let It Snow" isn't exactly hip-hop.

A few years ago, the big float, the one with the lights and carolers and loudspeakers blasting Christmas songs, had a power outage right there in front of
hundreds of revelers. Someone fixed it after several minutes—then it went out
again. This year, the parade was so late and the wind so cold that I gave up waiting for it and went home. Those who stayed long enough to tell the tale say it
eventually arrived and went back and forth about 30 times.

My recent fascination with Christmas is mainly a function of my friends'
longing for it. My friend Amy the writer, who is from eastern Pennsylvania and
has lived out here for more than a decade, may be the reigning queen of festivity
hunting. Among other quests, she's driven to Montrose to watch a Christmas
parade, which is remarkable only because (a), few people know where Montrose
is, and (b), even fewer of them would drive there for any reason. She said it
began with Santa Claus arriving in a police helicopter, which, to me, automatically makes it more interesting than any other parade. This includes the much
higher-profile Hollywood Christmas parade, which is basically two hours of
mostly future has-beens riding by on floats. Amy went to that one this year, too.
Notables included David Hasselhoff and Mickey Rooney. (My attendance to
that parade was in the form of coming out of a nearby movie theater long after
the parade was over. The gutters were filled with trash. Come all ye really fuckin'
messy.)

Naturally, the most holiday spirit she found this month was 3,000 miles away.
She flew to New York to see the big tree at Rockefeller Center, Santa Land at

Macy's, and the pretty window displays. She told me she just wanted to get away and see someplace Christmas-y (and Andrew Lloyd Webber's new show). "I keep searching for Christmas," she said, "and at the Christmas parades in L.A., it's hard to find." I guess David Hasselhoff and Mickey Rooney just don't do it for some folks.

And Amy's the only person I know who's actually seen *The Glory of Christmas*. This is a lavish stage version of the nativity—flying angels, live animals, special effects—at the world-famous Crystal Cathedral in Garden Grove, which is farther away than Montrose. Amy said the show was pretty, recalling a little boy singing a tearjerker "What Can I Give Jesus?"-type song. She also said a horse fell off the stage. "The best part, though," she told me, "was the angels on wires hanging from the crystal ceiling. As soon as they finished speaking, they were flung back into the darkness at 40 miles an hour, their flowing gowns and wings sailing overhead. It was better than a Universal Studios stunt show."

I took Amy up on her recent invitation to check out the Holiday Light Festival. In short, it's a bunch of wire sculptures ringed with lights along Crystal Springs Drive in Griffith Park. Some of them blink. It also may be as Christmas-y as it gets around here. If you don't know about this, you're not alone. I've mentioned it to people who've lived here for years and they didn't know such a thing existed. It's not even on the official Griffith Park Web site. I didn't even know about it until 2001, the first year I ever had to commute past Griffith Park. Sometimes, I'd go through it to dodge the freeway traffic. Then, all of a sudden, late one afternoon in December, I jumped onto Crystal Springs Drive, my little secret road, and it was all backed up with cars. That's how I found out about the Holiday Light Festival.

Fortunately, Amy, a veteran of the Festival, knew exactly when and how to get there. Shortly before sunset, I picked her up and we approached from the less-crowded northern route. She knew to park at the zoo parking lot and walk the route, which, because of the gridlock, turned out to be nearly as quick as driving it. We braved the 70-degree chill and headed off.

During the walk south, we hardly looked at the lights. We were so involved in the conversation about her recent man troubles (the guy was a schmuck, seriously) that we weren't paying any attention. Then near the south end of the route, she pointed off towards the tennis courts. "What's that?"

There was a low billow of smoke wafting towards us from the grass about a hundred yards away.

"Looks like dry ice," I said.

"No, that's a fire."

I saw the flames. "Hm. Maybe someone was barbecuing."

"It's there too. And there. And there."

To the left, a few flames appeared over the knoll. To the left of that, more little flames. Then more left of that. Sure enough, there was a string of tiny fires going. And some white sparks.

"Maybe it's a controlled burn," I offered.

"There's no one around."

We continued down the road to a couple of park attendants who were in charge of directing traffic and pointed it out. One of them promptly got on his walkie-talkie and ran over to investigate. Then we trotted up to the grass to get a better look at it ourselves.

It was a downed power line. An actual fire. In Griffith Park. During the Holiday Light Festival.

A moment later, we heard the siren. "Fire engine!" Amy yelled. We may have jumped up and down. We hadn't stopped to notice a single display the Department of Water and Power had so artfully mounted, but we got excited about a fire engine. And we're grown-ups.

Amy and I wondered why, when the fire department arrived, the crew just sort of stood around unconcerned except for one or two guys checking out the situation. Amy, who used to live near the park, told me that when it catches fire, it's a wall of orange at night. Between our record rainfall last winter, our dry summer and autumn, and the downed power line under a bunch of trees, all it would have taken was one ember rising into a dry leaf to give everyone more of a light festival than we'd bargained for. Next thing we knew, the fire truck drove off to the other end of the power line, presumably to begin whatever procedure firefighters do in such situations. Whatever they did, they did it right. The park didn't burn down.

On the walk back, we actually looked at the displays. We were kind of forced to when the loudspeakers playing Christmas songs drowned out our conversation. The songs were blasting because they were intended to be heard by people in their cars with their windows up. A very loud version of "Come All Ye Faithful" coming out of a speaker in the dark crossed the line from festive into disturbing.

As for the light-and-wire displays, they were largely Christmas-y stuff like Santa and reindeer, as well as elves doing cute things like making a movie. There were also displays of city icons like the Hollywood Bowl, LAX, and the Staples Center, which looked more like some kind of squat food processor. They even had Venice Beach represented by little blinking statues of beefed-up guys lifting weights.

It is in these moments that one should be finding the holiday spirit, which, I suppose, involves a Christmas-y feeling that can't be compared to anything else. I'm afraid I didn't have it. My festive red sweater and even more festive green plaid scarf only made me feel a little too warm on what was already an unusually warm afternoon. And perhaps I was just embracing my inner Christmas pig, but I couldn't help but notice how sexual the displays were. The hose that the elves were using to "spray" water over the street to plants on the other side looked like a giant phallus. Two ice-skating penguins looked like they were about to engage in anal intercourse. It didn't occur to me until later that it made no sense for penguins to wear ice skates.

Before I knew it, Amy and I were back at the parking lot. A minute later, I was negotiating a left turn at the four-way stop. Christmas was gone and we were in L.A. again. Just like that.

THESE ARE OUR
PARKING LAWS

Visitors to Los Angeles—or even longtime residents—may have noticed a curious phenomenon in our city. People will stand on sidewalks or in the gutters, for long periods of time, gazing upwards at nothing particularly interesting. They look as though they'd just asked a question of a tree and are getting a long, convoluted answer in return.

But that is not what is happening. The people are straining to understand the parking signs. They are straining because the signs can be confusing, and parking tickets have a way of materializing without warning, even to those who are careful to heed the law. Some unfortunates get too many of them too fast and become traumatized or enraged. They can't take the time off work to fight them in an administrative hearing. Failure to pay can result in substantial late fees, vehicle impoundment, attachment of outstanding fees to car registration, and even withheld tax refunds.

As a representative from the Department of Transportation wrote to me in an email, "Traffic officers provide a myriad of services to the community and are dedicated to providing parking solutions for the safe and efficient movement of people and goods in a manner which enhances and promotes the economic vitality of the city and the quality of life of its residents." A widely held consensus among residents here is a little different: Parking enforcement is a racket.

If you don't think our city's parking enforcement has a rich and interesting history, you've clearly never studied the subject. The first parking law was enacted in 1887, addressing the issue of horses—and whatever vehicles they were towing—that were clogging up downtown streets. Leave it to Los Angeles to come up with parking laws before the car was invented.

Our city's trend of keeping people confused began immediately. The law was not posted on any sign. People were expected to find out about it in the local newspaper. Even as more laws were enacted, covering more streets, the city didn't put up signs until the early 1920s. Drivers probably didn't mind because up to then the laws had hardly been enforced anyway. Even after rigid enforcement began, the laws had no teeth. In order for a ticket to stand up in court, the issuing officer was essentially charged with catching the driver in the act of getting into or out of an illegally parked car before writing the ticket. If that doesn't make you nostalgic, nothing will.

In the decades that followed, the tide turned against the car parker. The "caught in the act" part of the law was changed in 1939, when a California law was passed (and upheld in court) that granted police officers the *prima facie* assumption that any car parked illegally was done so with the car owner's knowledge, thereby freeing officers up to find only illegally parked cars and not their owners. A fee schedule was standardized, civil servants were hired to take the workload off police officers, tickets started coming with envelopes for convenient payment by mail, and all processing and collection services were outsourced to Lockheed Martin. What began in 1887 as a practice that was confined to a dozen streets and that netted about 10 scofflaws a month at one or two dollars a pop is now an efficient, leviathan monster that routinely grosses well over $100 million a year.

The unofficial capital of confusing parking laws is West Hollywood. Make no mistake, WeHo and vicinity is a great place. It is one of the regions that puts the "greater" in "greater Los Angeles." But not only is parking around there a bit of a scavenger hunt, it's not even that simple to drive down your street of choice. There is a long stretch of Melrose Avenue where it is illegal to make a left turn during rush hour. So serious are they about this law that there are not only huge signs at each intersection saying as much, but neon "no left turn" signs turn on and off during rush hour, just in case you aren't sure. It is even more challenging during the graveyard shift; in some neighborhoods, you can't make any turns at all between 10 P.M. and 6 A.M.

After you've navigated your way through the labyrinth of when and where you can and can't turn, then you have to find legal parking. Like with other parts of town, West Hollywood is so popular that residents naturally complain about not being able to park on their own streets. Fair enough. But street parking is in highest demand in the evenings, so exceptions to the parking laws are made. Generally, two-hour parking is available during the days, but none at all at night, unless you live on the block and have the proper permit—except for a weekly one- or two-hour stretch during which no one can park due to street sweeping. (I have friends who live on one of these blocks. They have a bitch of a time having people over for parties.) And these laws, days, times, and permits seem to vary slightly from block to block. I don't want to accuse parking enforcement officials of purposely being confusing, but it takes longer to decipher the signs than it does to read this paragraph.

The most confusing spot I found was just off Melrose near Robertson. This column of signs took up about eight feet of sheet metal: "No parking nighttime 7 P.M.-7 A.M. and any time Sunday, 1R permits exempt/2HR parking daytime 7 A.M.-7 P.M. Mon-Sat, 1R, 1C permits exempt." That last sign had an arrow pointing to the left. Below that was, "2HR parking, 8 A.M.-6 P.M. except Sunday and holiday." (No explanation as to which Sunday and which holiday were the exceptions.) Oh, and that sign had an arrow pointing to the right. Finally, "No parking 8 A.M. to 9 A.M. Thursday, street sweeping." The punch line? The spot below the signs had a parking meter.

My instinct when reading these signs is to ask what the point of each law is. For instance, on at least one residential block near Fairfax High School, there is no stopping allowed between 7 A.M. and 5 P.M. on school days, except for school buses. This law may have had some rationale behind it when it was enacted, but it seems pointless to have both sides of an entire block empty all day. And, in fact, I've never seen any school buses there, even when school is getting out. Another sign in the area has a P with a circle and a line through it followed by "any time/vehicles over 3/4 ton load capacity or over 24' length." (How does a parking enforcement officer determine if a car has a load capacity over 3/4 ton?) These are just a couple that seem so odd that I'd welcome an explanation in small print. But the signs are already marvels of syntactical efficiency. I suppose explanations would just make for a slower read.

As with many city departments, one hand doesn't always know whom the other hand is screwing. In front of my apartment building are signs outlawing parking every Friday between noon and 2 P.M., ostensibly for street cleaning. My landlord Ken tells me that years ago, the city's parking enforcement would come by every Friday to ticket parked cars that were flouting this law. The only problem was that the street cleaner never came at all. Over the course of months (maybe years), Ken made a series of phone calls and wrote letters to one buck-passer after another until he eventually reached a state senator's office. Only then did the Department of Sanitation finally start dispatching a goddamn street sweeping truck to our block once a week. But the Department of Transportation never missed a Friday.

The laws can also be a great source of revenue for the private sector. It is not uncommon for people to park in parking lots of businesses that are closed at night or on weekends. Seems reasonable, but the lots belong to their owners. Even if they don't need the spaces during nonbusiness hours, and don't want to hire someone to rent them out, they're entitled to keep them empty if they want. There is no shortage of independent tow truck operators who are happy to oblige them, with towing habits that can fairly be described as vigilant. One has to wonder if the property owners have more of an incentive than the aesthetic satisfaction of an empty parking lot.

Then there are the parking enforcement officers themselves, who bear the butt end of an entire city's wrath every day just for doing their jobs. While there are probably stories about incompetent and corrupt ones, I have never known of one. I've even chatted with a few of these people. I always approach them slowly before talking to them because I figure they're prepared to recoil whenever they see a stranger coming at them. And when I talk to them, they seem like personable, decent folks. I even know of one who passes my local coffeehouse and sticks her head in to warn everyone that she's about to check meters.

Personally, I think parking tickets can be infuriating. But generally, they're warranted. In fact, I'm straining to remember stories of unfair parking tickets. And if we didn't have parking laws, people would be screaming about inconceivably horrible congestion caused by parking anarchy. I didn't always think that way, so I'd park in violation of the law—and on the reliance of less-than-diligent enforcement. Of course, I'd get parking tickets regularly. But the fines kept increasing. At risk of sounding like the victim in an abusive relationship, it gave me the incentive to shape up.

But my snark never fully abated. My last ticket was about three years ago in the city of El Segundo. I was in violation of the posted sign, guilty as charged. Still, there is something about a parking ticket that causes indignation, so, just to make some clerk's life difficult, I overpaid it by five dollars. They actually sent a check back for the difference. I was amazed that any local government could be so honest and decent about such a thing.

Then I waited three months to cash it, just to fuck with their books.

Welcome to
Rancho Verde Plaza...
Wherever That Is

In a city where people traffic in bullshit so frequently that hardly anyone buys it anymore, it makes you wonder why people bother bullshitting at all. Even more mystifying is why anyone would go to the trouble to call anyone on the more trivial examples of bullshit. But the only thing rivaling the mystery behind some bullshit is just how little anyone knows about the bullshit in the first place.

I got a prescription filled recently at my local Rite Aid ("With us, it's personal"). Not because it's a sterling pharmacy or anything, but because it's close to my apartment. Everything went fine. They filled it promptly, they gouged me fairly on the markup, no complaints. But the address on the prescription label had something on it that hung me up: Rancho Verde Plaza.

You have to understand. This Rite Aid is not in a plaza. It's in a parking lot. And in one corner is a tiny medical office building with a dentist and a chiropractor. *And that's it.* There is no promenade for people to stroll at lunch. There is no row of retail storefronts for window shoppers. There is no fountain. There is nothing rancho, verde, or plaza-like about it. There isn't even any signage— except on my little prescription bottle.

Of course, I had to know what this was about. I went directly to the pharmacy. While waiting, I picked up a brochure that had an actor in a Rite Aid pharmacist's lab coat on the cover. The caption read, "Prescriptions filled. Questions answered. People helped."

A woman on the phone, presumably on hold, turned to me and asked how she could help me.

I held up my little pill bottle. "Well, here on the label, it says—"

And she turned away to complete her call. A few seconds later, she apologized and gave me her full attention. I showed her my little pill bottle. "Why is this called Rancho Verde Plaza?"

"I don't know."

Said a guy behind the counter, "I think it was a leftover from the old location."

I made follow-up visits to the pharmacy window in future weeks, just to seek other opinions. A busy woman who'd been there 10 years said it had been on the labels that whole time and she had no idea why. She also wouldn't make eye contact with me. She was clearly embarrassed by her ignorance. Another woman, also very busy, responded—twice—with "So what?" I'm still not sure if her reply fell under the "questions answered" part of Rite Aid's customer service slogan or the "people helped" part.

I wandered into the dentist's office in the other building. The receptionist had no idea what Rancho Verde Plaza was. Same reaction from the chiropractor's office.

I looked up Rancho Verde Plaza on the Internet. The only reference, apart from the automatic inclusion of it in all listings of the North Hollywood Rite Aid, was the mention of another Rancho Verde Plaza. It looked like a *real* shopping center from the pictures I saw. It was way the hell out in Rialto, a Spanish word meaning "another city in the sticks." And it had its own Rite Aid. I called it to make sure it wasn't, say, some new Rite Aid to replace the old Rite Aid that skipped town years ago like some pro sports franchise. I got a woman on the line who'd been working at that Rite Aid for 15 years. At that location. The whole time.

So I called Rite Aid. 1-800-RITEAID. After all, they have questions to answer and people to help.

The voice prompts on Rite Aid's customer service line, I've decided, represent the hierarchy in the prostitution industry. First a madam came on the phone to thank me for calling, then a breathy woman's voice came on strong by asking me if I was looking for a Rite Aid in "N Hollywood... California." When I said no, the madam came back on the line suggesting a variety of other delights, including "other services." I finally found the customer service prompt, which led me to the pimp daddy's voice, telling me to chill out while he hooked me up. Then I got connected to a eunuch who told me nothing I didn't already know. Just like with prostitution, I got what I paid for.

The next time I happened to be at Rite Aid again, I asked the cashier about the whole Rancho Verde Plaza thing. She had no idea, but she pointed to a manager stocking a shelf. I asked him.

"Yeah, that's what the property manager likes to call this lot," he said.

"Huh?"

"The man we lease the building from calls the property Rancho Verde Plaza."

"No one in the pharmacy knows this."

"No."

"The people in the dentist's office over there have no idea."

"Well, that's what the guy calls it."

"Who is he?"

"I wish I knew."

A few calls to a few county agencies led me to The Owner, who, it turns out, is the COO of a local company. I left a message with his assistant.

In the meantime, I called the City of Rialto Development Service Department. A guy who's been working there since the '70s said that *their* Rancho Verde Plaza was called that since as far back as he can remember. It was named after El Rancho Verde housing tract and golf course nearby, which dates back to the '50s, at least.

"Did you know that there's a Rite Aid here whose pharmacy labels say Rancho Verde Plaza on them?" I asked.

"No."

"I don't suppose you have any idea why that could be, do you?"

"Maybe they ordered some extra labels and got stuck with those."

"A woman at the pharmacy says it's been like that for 10 years. That's a lot of extra labels."

"A local water district once ordered 30 years of time sheets."

"Which one?"

"I don't want to say."

After several days of leaving messages with The Owner, his assistant finally gave me his cell phone number and told me that he was expecting my call. At last, I was finally going to talk to this imitator, this hoodwinker, this charlatan who'd been misleading the public for who knows how many years now.

"I own the northwest corner. Where Rite Aid is."

"Yes, exactly. I only have one question. I was wondering how it happened to be called Rancho Verde Plaza."

"Oh. I'm not aware of that. Where'd you find that?"

"That's on the prescription label."

"Rite Aid might be using old labels from another pharmacy." My image of COOs and commercial property owners paints them as too busy to give a shit about such things. That'll teach me to harbor prejudices.

"There's another Rancho Verde Plaza in Rialto that has a Rite Aid in it—"

"Oh, there you go. They're using their labels."

"Well, Rialto's, like, 50 miles away. How would they end up with their labels?"

"Did you ask the manager inside the building?"

"Yeah. He said Rancho Verde Plaza is what you call the place."

"You know what you could do is you could call up Rite Aid and ask them, because it's not Rancho Verde Plaza—unless Rite Aid did something that I'm unaware of. Maybe call and ask for their real estate division."

"Real estate division."

"Yah, and I'll talk to them at my next meeting with them. I'll ask them about that."

"Oh. That's very helpful of you. You wouldn't know when that next meeting's going to be, would you?"

"No."

I thanked him for his time. He asked me to let him know if I find out anything about his own property.

I called back Rite Aid's customer service brothel again and got the phone number for their corporate headquarters. Someone from their real estate division gave me the direct line to the Los Angeles area director of real estate. I called her up and explained all of this. After she looked at her paperwork...

"It looks like the one in North Hollywood is in Rancho Verde Plaza." My first thought was that she sounded kind of hot.

"Okay, but who named it? Because I contacted the owner of the property and he didn't name it."

"He didn't name it?"

"No.... He said, 'If you find out, let me know.'"

"There's no sign?"

"No."

And I told her the people at the dentist's office and the chiropractor's office share mutual ignorance of the fact.

She pointed out that it appears that way on the Rite Aid Web site. I told her I knew this.

She asked me if I was a historian of some sort, a classic dodge when people don't have answers. I got her back on the subject by asking her about the calculus of the pharmacy labeling system. She said the labels are completely blank and that the computer in the pharmacy prints the labels with the address on each one, thus shooting down the implausible "borrowed label" theory.

"So how did it end up registered as Rancho Verde Plaza in Rite Aid's computer?" I asked.

"I wonder if, in the past, it was named Rancho Verde Plaza."

"Well, that's possible."

"My assumption would be that it's actually the name of the center. And whether or not there's a sign on the center—in the past it had to have been called that. We don't make a habit of making up names." She laughed. She had a pretty laugh. I'm betting she's hot.

"Okay, that makes sense."

"Unfortunately, I don't have the full file on this. Maybe back in the day, it was named Rancho Verde Plaza. Maybe a broker, at one point, labeled it just as a marketing type of thing. I don't know that they're supposed to, but they can label sites, just kind of make them up like that."

"They can?"

"Like an apartment building."

"And there's nothing stopping people from just calling it that, even though it's not a legal name?"

"Yeah, it's just a name."

"And that's the best theory that we have so far."

"This is silly, but it could also be something as simple as working on a lease and somehow the wrong... you know, you're using a template and the name of the shopping center stays in from the last one you were working on."

I thanked her for her time. She said it was fine; she had needed a little break.

After all that, I never got to the bottom of things. It's either the "clerical error" theory or the "long-forgotten name" theory. Either way, people are getting away with calling this nondescript square of asphalt a plaza. A *plaza*. And no one is stopping them. Ridiculous, I say.

And if you disagree with me, feel free to tell me in person here at my apartment building, the Emerald Isle Estates. Mine is the Nights in Heaven Suite.

Meet Spencer Paltz, Part Two—and His Mother

It's high time that I write again about Spencer Paltz, which is ironic since the man has probably never had a high time in his life. He's somewhere over 50, still lives with his Mom, and could be a virgin for all I know. None of which makes him a bad person, but his limited perspective on life is constantly on display in his conversational skills.

Why, a guy could write a column about him.

The man is so harmless that, a couple of months ago, I was shocked by the following exchange. I was standing at my door when he walked by and said, "Hey, Joe, how you doing?"

"Oh, just getting over some flu-like thing," I answered.

"Yeah, you don't look so good."

That was the whole conversation. He didn't even slow down to get a good look.

I wonder if he's becoming a jerk. He used to be so... so... dorky. Take this elegant exchange from a while ago, a typical example of his inability to keep talking when you take him off his track. In the parking lot, Spencer saw me with a grocery bag in each hand.

"Hey, Joe."

"Hiiiii, Spencerrrr!" Sometimes I lapse into the habit of greeting people with a loud nasally twang whenever I'm irritated or bored. For some reason, I greet Spencer this way a lot.

"Did you know there's a song that starts off, 'Hey, Joe?'"

I paused. "You're lying."

"I think that's how it went. I think it was Jimi Hendrix. Do you know the song?"

Of course I know the goddamn song—the same way Ritas of the world are sick of being called meter maids. "Nope, never heard of it."

"It's interesting because that song goes away from the notion of tonality."

"Can you repeat that?"

"That song goes away from the notion of tonality. Most songs are tonally centric."

Then he rattled off all the chords. I don't remember them. If you'd like to learn all the chords, you might want to take a class at Valley College. Apparently, they have a great music department. To wit:

Spencer: "Valley College has a great music department. You can take some great classes there cheap. I'm studying piano."

Me: "Chicks like piano."

Spencer got conspiratorially giddy. "I know."

I don't think Spencer's had a date since the 1980s.

Me: "You're turning red."

Spencer got silent.

Me: "I'm just fucking with you."

Spencer remained silent.

Me: "I have perishables here."

Spencer: "Oh, okay. I'll talk to you later."

Not long after that, I caught Spencer coming from his mother's car, armful of groceries. His mother, Ruth, was behind him, heaving a 48-roll toilet paper package. Spencer often walks several yards ahead of her because she's about 84 years old and doesn't move very fast anymore. I also suspect that Spencer still hasn't outgrown the phase where a guy thinks it isn't cool to be seen in public with his mom.

"Hey, Joe. Did you hear that song?"

"No."

"'Hey, Joe' by Jimi Hendrix."

"Nope, still haven't heard it."

"It has no chord. No single chord. Very unusual. That's what I was trying to explain to you that day."

I looked up and saw Ruth getting closer. She walks like a wino, God bless her.

Spencer disappeared up the stairs without even saying goodbye. I was right. He is embarrassed to be seen in public with his mom. On the other hand, he was carrying perishable groceries.

"Hi, Joe, howayou?" Ruth is originally from Boston.

"Oh, fine. How are you?" There is always something with Ruth. Usually it's the weather and various medical conditions.

We talked about the cloud cover and her aching foot, then parted. She had toilet paper to put away.

While Spencer is living proof that conversational skills can be inherited, Ruth has an occasional crusty streak that Spencer doesn't have, and it makes her more interesting to listen to. Sometimes she'll get her perm in a wad about something and isn't afraid to let people know. The funny part is that her voice never rises. She doesn't speak louder or quicker. She uses the same soft, raspy tone that she uses when talking about the weather or how her latest meds are making her urinate too much. For instance, I remember one day last year, we got on the subject of President Bush.

"Did you heah what happened to him the otheh day?" she asked.

"Yes. He was somewhere in the old Soviet Union and someone threw a grenade at him."

"Yeah. Too bad it didn't go off."

Of course, she doesn't limit her contempt to world leaders. Like Spencer, her perspective on life is so narrowed that the smallest things get magnified. On the back stair landing, the broom that Ruth has hanging on a hook has fallen down twice. Ruth has made up her mind that Katie, the neighbor across the landing from her, is deliberately throwing the broom downstairs and is therefore on a par with Typhoid Mary on the humanity scale. So Ruth has started a feud with Katie. The punch line to all this is that despite Ruth's crusty streak, her inability to articulate her feelings is so crippled that it was weeks before Katie even knew that she was one-half of a feud.

I didn't realize how bad it was until I happened to be chatting with Ruth in the parking lot some weeks back and Katie walked by. Katie said a quick hello and kept walking. As soon as she passed, Ruth scowled at her. Then she did that "nose-toot" thing or whatever the hell it's called where you put your thumb on your nose and wiggle your fingers. She could have just flipped her off, but I guess that wouldn't have been dignified.

Then Ruth looked at me and said, "She's always sneaking around." I found this an interesting accusation because Katie tells me that Ruth is the one who, on more than one occasion, has tried to walk into Katie's apartment without knocking. Of course, since Ruth moves so slowly, she also moves quietly. There Katie would be, minding her own business on her couch, when suddenly her doorknob would go "click-clack click-clack click-clack." One time, her door was unlocked, allowing to Ruth walk in and complain to Katie about something that Katie may or may not have done. Then she left.

I wonder just how far the apple has fallen from the tree. Whereas Ruth thinks Katie is responsible for all the broom-tossing, Spencer, ever the pragmatist, has asked Katie to be on the lookout for local hoodlums who are tiptoeing up the back stairs to take his mother's broom off the hook. Evidently, he thinks we have a pack of thugs with obsessive-compulsive disorder who keep targeting people's cleaning supplies in our building. Katie, ever the diplomat, told Spencer she'd keep an eye out.

After all that, I'm left wondering if that one time a couple of months ago Spencer was having a bad day or if he's inheriting his mother's age-induced crustiness. A few days ago, I saw him in the parking lot. He asked me what was new, so I told him. Then I asked him what was new. He replied by looking me up and down and asking me if I'd gained weight recently.

I don't think he was having a bad day. I think he is his mother's son.

MEET CLYDE LANGTRY, PART FIVE

January 22

"I'm getting drunk."

Clyde was standing right there in the courtyard. I heard him before I could see him. The man is a ninja, I tell you.

"Huh?"

"I am. I'm gonna go get drunk." He is kidding.

"Why?"

"I'm gonna go parachuting and wait until 500 feet before pulling the rip cord."

"What's going on?"

"It's that stuff I told you about flying out to Florida." He's still irritated about having to fly to Clearwater, Florida for no reason, and all because the Church of Scientology told him to, but didn't realize they had their signals crossed until he spent the time and money to get there.

I figure this will be the last I hear of this episode. It will not be the first time I'm wrong.

January 31

Today, he knocked at my door just to say hello—and a bunch of other crap that took 15 minutes.

"What's new?"

"Ah, I'm irritated."

"About what?"

"That stuff I told you about. Flying out to Florida and back. But I talked to a guy about it." I'm beginning to think Clyde doesn't have a life.

"A guy?"

"Yeah, he's kind of an advocate who's dealt with stuff like this before. He's helping me out."

Also, after admiring that I make a living as a writer, he said, "I wanted to be a photographer. But that was back in fifth grade, the last time I was my own person."

"You're not your own person anymore?"

"I had a camera and a tripod and the whole deal, y'know?"

"Wait a minute. You're not your own person?"

"No, I haven't been my own person for a long time." He didn't explain it further. Perhaps I should find Clyde's owner and ask him for details.

After we agreed the conversation was over, he kept talking. "By the way, where do you get your shoes? I've been looking for a good pair of running shoes."

"Laszlo Tabori Sports, on Olive in Burbank."

"Bet you pay a lot for 'em."

"Oh, about ninety bucks."

"Pfft! That's outrageous. I can't imagine paying that much for a pair of Keds."

"What did you call these!?" Nothing Clyde says really bothers me, but I refuse to take that from a guy who won't buy clothes at Sears because it's too pricey.

"Keds. That's what we called 'em when we were kids."

"These are not Keds!"

"Well, what do you call them?"

"These are Adidas running shoes."

"Running's bad for your knees."

"There's no such thing as a good running shoe that's also cheap. If you think so, go find it."

He pointed to his grubby shitkickers that, several lifetimes ago, were good running shoes—maybe. "I got these in a dumpster in Tacoma, Washington. I just put 'em on and they fit." I couldn't tell if he was arguing or conceding.

"How long ago?"

"I was working on my car but I didn't have any shoes." He chuckled. Clyde humor.

"How long ago?"

"Oh, about six years ago. I only wear 'em when I'm working on my car."

Number of times he jammed his hand down the front of his pants to adjust his hernia belt during the conversation: one.

February 1

Clyde caught me again to say that he's feeling better about the whole Florida debacle and that he's decided to confront the Church's auditing department in Florida directly about this matter and that they're going to send his file back here and that he's going to try for a mutual audit of some sort where he audits someone else and vice-versa, but is still about a year's worth of classes or some such away from going back to Florida again. Keep in mind that ever since he told me a few weeks ago that he shouldn't be babbling about all this, he's been unable to shut up about it.

I do wonder, although not often, if Clyde ever thinks he should just ditch Scientology after all these years of alleged life improvement that's gotten him exactly nowhere. I figure he's so far gone in the head that the thought of truly self-actualizing by leaving the Church is just something too inconceivable for him to think, but that's no reason I can't allude to it just to see how he reacts. For instance, I may sneak into the conversation that he should rent the Marx Brothers movie *A Day at the Races* so I can get his take on the "tutsi-fruitsi" ice cream scene. This is the one where Chico, an apparent ice cream man, swindles Groucho into buying a tip on a horse. The tip is written in a code that Groucho can't decipher, so Chico convinces him to buy a book to figure it out. Groucho can't figure that book out either, so Chico sells him another book. And so on and so on until the race is over. But I suspect the metaphor would be lost on Clyde. Besides, I'm positive he doesn't rent movies. That would require both a credit card and a DVD player.

So we talked about this instead:

Clyde: "I drove across Louisiana and most of Texas with my eyes closed once."

Me: "Huh?"

Clyde: "Yeah, I didn't even realize I could do it until I tried. I just started driving and around that stretch, I checked the clock on the Scientology meter and then later I checked it again and sure enough, I'd fallen asleep."

Me: *"You actually drove a car while you were asleep?"*

Clyde: "Yep. You see, the brain remembers everything even if you don't have a conscious memory of it. But the meter recorded all of it. And I wasn't sure how many times I'd fallen asleep, but I thought it was 12 times and I asked the administrator and she said, 'Yep, 12 times.'"

He asked me how the writing was going and I told him it was going just fine. Naturally, he responded with unsolicited advice, suggesting I buy a three-book series by L. Ron Hubbard about management, at about $125 per book. "And see if you can find a dictionary guide too, because he uses words in there that most people don't understand."

Maybe he *has* seen *A Day at the Races*.

February 6

Clyde knocked.

"Hi, just thought I'd say hello and let you know I'm still alive."

"Thanks, Clyde. I was lying in bed last night thinking, 'I haven't seen Clyde in a few days. He might be dead. Maybe I should go over there and check. Nah.' And I rolled over and went to sleep."

"'Cause there were fire engines here last night."

"There were?"

"Yeah, they picked up Ruth." (She came home a few days later and appears to be fine.)

"They did?"

"Yeah, that's what the guy told me. She didn't look too good when I saw her yesterday. She looked like she needed a kick."

"You wanted to kick Ruth?"

"You know, a kick, a..." He made a thrusting motion with his finger, like a fencer would with a sword. "A compliment. Something to lift her up." But he didn't compliment her and now she's in the hospital. Nice going, Clyde.

"Oh, that kind of kick. I was gonna say—why would you kick an old lady?"

"You know, every time I see you, there's this word I want to use about you but I can never remember it. It's a real common word."

"Asshole?"

"No."

"Prick?"

"Nope."

"Dickhead? Jerkwad?"

"No, it means, like, a 'what the fuck' attitude."

"Well, if you think of it, write it down and let me know."

"I can't believe I can't think of it. Say the secret word and win five hundred dollars.... Ah, the world's gonna end in several years." He got this faraway look on his face and stepped back and looked up off to the side at something, so I looked off to the side too. All I noticed was that my hummingbird feeder wasn't out.

"It is?"

"Yeah, Bush is destroying it."

"He is?"

"Yeah, he's just evil. You know how I can tell?"

"How?"

"Because I'm extremely good at reading people. I can tell what people are thinking just by looking at their faces. As a spirit, I have the ability to do that. People wear their intentions on their faces."

I wonder if he could tell by the look on my face that I was thinking about how he's told me about that skill of his several times now.

Later that afternoon, Clyde knocked again. It's moments like this that make me wish I had a full-time job at some office far away.

"Cynical. The word is cynical. That's what you remind me of sometimes."

Goddamn neighbors these days. Can't count on any of 'em.

He also explained to me that he talked to someone in Scientology about that whole Florida mix-up from a few weeks ago. He finally figured out what happened. What happened was this: There was a mix-up.

"I just didn't want you to think badly about Scientology," he said.

Hmm. After all that, I'm not sure what to think of Scientology now. I guess I'll need Clyde to tell me more about it in the days to come. I can only hope he won't be shy about it.

THIS IS HOW WE RECYCLE

One day back in the '90s, while working for a former employer, I went to a printer's shop to run an errand. In a little cardboard display stand on his desk were a bunch of brochures about recycling in Los Angeles. I picked one up and put it in my shirt pocket.

The printer laughed. "Those have been there for three years and you're the first person who's ever taken one."

Los Angeles may be the place where new age ideas are born, but we're hardly at the forefront of the recycling movement. We were far from enacting the first curbside recycling program. That honor goes to University City, Missouri, in 1974. We didn't get around to it for another 15 years, when the state assembly passed a bill requiring jurisdictions throughout California to divert some of their trash from landfills or face financial penalties. The idea was to make people aware of the state's growing garbage stream and shrinking landfill capacity. Gee, if the state assembly said so, then it must have been true.

Hence, in Los Angeles, curbside recycling became a function of the Bureau of Sanitation. All homeowners were given small yellow bins, which were just big enough to hold a foot-tall stack of newspapers. They quickly proved inadequate, and were replaced with 90-gallon bins. The blue one is for paper, plastic, and aluminum—and lots of other stuff, I would find out. The green one is for yard waste. (It is worth mentioning that the bins in the city of Beverly Hills are large to the point of freakish. Either everyone there just likes large things, or rich people generate more crap.)

The story is different for apartments. Apartment owners hire private trash collection services for the emptying of dumpsters. These companies have no incentive to subsidize separate collection for recyclable materials. For those of us who live in apartments, recycling is not usually a simple task.

Somewhere along the way, I decided I didn't like the idea of throwing away recyclable materials. Without the benefit of being an expert on the subject, reducing our garbage flow and increasing our landfill capacity just seem like good ideas to me. Or maybe I'm one of those people, as Penn & Teller surmised in their TV show *Bullshit!*, who recycles because it feels good. Except that it doesn't feel good to me. I've gone from being pleased that I'm helping the environment to being neurotic about not throwing away recyclable materials. Every scrap of paper ends up in my bag full of scrap papers and junk mail. I rinse out my spaghetti sauce jars, let them dry, and put them in bags in my kitchen, where I keep my beer bottles, wine bottles, plastic soda bottles, rinsed-out soup cans, and collapsed cereal boxes. I stack my newspapers in a corner until there are enough of them to fill a grocery bag. The result is a bunch of bags of crap filling up my apartment because it is a pain in the ass to recycle them.

I schlep them to my car and put them in my trunk—and backseat—where they might stay for days because an opportunity to recycle them doesn't present itself. I could dump them in a blue recycling bin that I see on the street, but this becomes problematic. First of all, these bins are not out on the street all the time, just the one day a week that the recycling trucks come by. Even if I do see them on the street, there is the issue of parking. With everyone putting their trash, yard waste, and recycling bins out at the same time, a lot of curb space is taken up. Unless I'm on a street that isn't near any apartments or businesses, there may not be a parking space, which would force me to stop in the middle of the street and risk blocking traffic. Blocking traffic is the worst thing any human being can do to his fellow man in Los Angeles. It is worse than homicide.

Even if I can let go of my ethos long enough to block traffic, I don't want to get caught filling someone else's bins with my crap. I'm always afraid that they might see me and get mad. They may need all 90 gallons of space every week. Plus, I hear it's illegal to tamper with other people's bins, even if you are trying to reduce the garbage stream in your local jurisdiction.

Fortunately, there is a Whole Foods Market conveniently located near me. For those of you not familiar with Whole Foods Market, it is a store that sells hormone-free milk, free-range chicken, shade-grown coffee, and other healthy, environmentally conscious things that require hyphens. A typical store has an entire aisle devoted to homeopathic, ayurvedic, and herbal supplements, with experts on hand to help you figure out just how much bee pollen you need or which kind of flaxseed oil is right for you. They could even tell you what the hell "ayurvedic" means.

The store near me is so progressive about the environment that it has a giant recycling bin in the corner of its parking lot—that it provides and empties at its own cost, I found out recently. This is where I take my recyclables. On occasion. Parking at this Whole Foods outlet is so difficult that sometimes I just drive around a few extra days with bags of recyclable crap in my car.

The last time I went, I fought to get into the driveway, squeezed between two SUVs to get into a parking spot, and handed off my bags of stuff to the nice scavenger lady who frequents the bin. There is no shortage of people in Los Angeles who go around collecting cans and cardboard. Then I moseyed over to the smaller bins to dump my mixed paper, whereupon a volunteer with a clipboard came at me. She wanted to hit me up for something on behalf of the Democratic Party. Money, signatures, courage not to fuck up another election—I don't know what. I was in no mood to listen. Recycling bags of crap really shouldn't be this difficult.

Once, I was doing a thorough cleanout of my crap. I mean a big-time, go-through-the-closets kind of overhaul, part of which included dumping a lot of paper: magazines, old mail, catalogs, and so on. I didn't want to fill up the bin at Whole Foods with all this paper, so I found a place in the industrial part of Van Nuys that actually pays people three and a half cents per pound for recycled paper. I figured if I was going to this much trouble, I should scoop up few bucks, anyway.

I drove into the place, whereupon a man directed me to drive onto a scale that looked as if it would collapse and eat me and my car. Then he pointed to a giant pyramid of phone directories and told me to dump my paper there. I drove over to the pile, got out, and started heaving. It was sunny and windy. Papers I'd written in college started swirling around me, into other piles of paper. Some swirled into no piles, but just lay on the ground where paper-pushing trucks drive around.

I got my car weighed again after I was done, and was told that my car was now 310 pounds lighter. Then I had to turn in my receipt in the office for my cash payment. At three and a half cents per pound, all that labor resulted in $10.85. And I was nice and sweaty before work.

Cans and bottles are a more lucrative trade, mainly because $10.85 worth of them weigh a hell of a lot less than the same amount of paper. Ergo, the Ralphs grocery chain has put recycling machines in their parking lots. Anyone can wander up with their bags of cans and bottles, feed them into a machine, and get a receipt that can be redeemed for cash in the store. This is a great idea except for one thing: It is a colossal inconvenience.

The machines themselves are slow; users have to feed bottles in one at a time. Furthermore, they are only "open" during daytime hours, and only while an attendant is on duty, which kind of undermines the whole idea of having self-service machines. And there is always a line. My girlfriend, Nicole, thinks it's a swell idea to save our cans and bottles and then make a trip to the local Ralphs and stand in line with the other nice folks and occasional meth addicts, then get her hands dirty feeding the bottles and cans in one by one, then walk into the store for her money. I've gone with her twice, and both times it took over half an hour and didn't net her more than $10.85. I'll do a lot for Nicole, but I've asked her never to take me to these goddamn vending machines again. I'd be just as happy taking them to Whole Foods so the nice scavenger lady can take them and go recycle them herself.

I wanted to find out more about the city's recycling program, namely how I can recycle bags of crap more easily. Can I dump stuff in blue bins that don't belong to me? They had no such information on the site. What I found out, though, blew my little mind. Our city recycles an awful lot of crap, over 240,000 tons of it each year: wrapping paper, arts and craft paper, telephone books, note cards, blueprints, file folders, Post-it notes, catalogs, window envelopes, shoe-boxes, detergent boxes, the cardboard thingies inside rolls of toilet paper and paper towels, corrugated boxes, pie tins, aluminum foil, paint cans, aerosol cans, wire hangers, bi-metal cans (Can metal cans be bi?), margarine tubs, yogurt containers, plastic planters, dishwashing liquid bottles, and dry cleaner bags. And that's only about half the list.

Just to make me more neurotic, there are lots of things one can't recycle: soiled papers, bags with oils and food waste, broken glass, plastic trays from frozen dinners, plastic six-pack rings, plastic hangers, plastic toys, electrical cords, cloth, styrofoam, appliances, mini blinds, kitchen utensils, lawn furniture, and wood. And that's only about half the list.

And there is another list of things for which the city provides special pick-up services and drop-off locations: extra yard trimmings, bulky items, Christmas trees, dead animals, used tires, concrete, asphalt, bricks, gypsum, wallboard, plate glass, scrap metal, and hazardous materials. And crap. Horse crap. In fact, they give you a special bin just for horse crap, and the city will empty it for 10 bucks a month. To put this in perspective, a single ticket for a front-row seat at a Los Angeles Kings game costs $424.50.

I also found out that restaurants can donate extra food, and participate in a program to recycle grease and cooking oil. And fat. Fat can be recycled! It can be used to make soap products and animal feed. It's in your business telephone directory under "Rendering," FYI.

But I could find no link for a page for people who live in apartments and don't want to negotiate the parking lot at Whole Foods Market. I called the Bureau of Sanitation to find out exactly what the law is surrounding the blue bins on the street. I spoke to a very nice woman whom we'll call "she" because I wasn't listening when she gave me her name.

"From what I understand, once someone puts their blue bin on the street, the contents of the bin, at that moment, belong to the city, correct?"

"That's correct."

"So what is the penalty for someone coming by and opening the container and taking the aluminum cans out?"

"We don't have anyone to go around and enforce that regulation."

"So there's really nothing stopping someone from doing that."

"That's right."

"Okay, well, what about *putting things in* the blue bins? To take a random example, can a guy who lives in an apartment take his newspapers and walk down the street to a house and drop his papers in someone else's blue bin out on the street?"

"Yes, that's okay."

"It is?"

"Yes."

Oh. Well, that settles that then. But no word on how to dump them from a car to a bin without blocking traffic.

Just for the hell of it, I decided to hunt down that printer and ask him if those recycling brochures ever gained in popularity. He's gone out of business. Come to think of it, I don't think I ever read the brochure. I hope I recycled it.

Meet People with
Extra Cars

For whatever reason, people in L.A. collect cars the way people in the Pacific Northwest collect umbrellas, I'd imagine. As with umbrellas in rainy climates, people here feel that extra cars are just good to have handy, even though a person can only use one at a time, they're too large to carry around in the trunk, they break down quickly due to disuse, they can cost more than they're worth, finding a parking spot for them can be a hassle, and neighbors complain that they're eyesores. But make no mistake: They're good to have handy.

An audit of my neighbors alone cuts across a cross-section of the extra-car society. One neighbor, Paul, got an extra car several months ago. I think he got it from one of his parents who is now too infirmed to drive. But he kept his old car parked on the street for a while. Finally, after getting a parking ticket, Paul gave the car to someone who needed it. He probably figured that if he kept the car and paid the ticket, he'd suffer a net loss on an eventual sale.

My neighbor Katie bought a new car several months ago, a brand new Subaru station wagon that's so big you could play racquetball in it. She felt she needed it for the reliability that comes with a new car. But she won't sell her little hatchback, which presumably gets good mileage, looks to be in okay shape, and might fetch a good price. So she moves it around just often enough to avoid parking tickets and keep the battery from dying. Last week, the Department of Transportation put a little green notice on her car, warning her that it would be towed after 72 hours of continued nonoperation. So she raced out on a weekday morning before work to get it washed, then she parked it up the street. This is a woman who works about 60 hours a week as it is, and presumably could do without such extra chores.

But when I asked her why she'd go to so much trouble instead of selling it, she had a disarmingly logical answer. "It's paid for and only worth three hundred dollars," she said. "I pay 10 extra dollars per month to insure it over the price of insuring my new car, so figured I might as well hold onto it to use for certain purposes. I'll be using it to commute this huge 50-mile-a-day commute, but I was waiting for it to cool off a bit because it doesn't have air conditioning." Such is the importance of the extra car in Los Angeles.

Mac and Brandy are a two-person car opera. They have an SUV, and they had a Mercedes coupe that was stolen recently, and then found completely stripped. They're awaiting judgment from a claims adjuster. Mac has a van that he rents out to studios as part of his work as a teamster. He parks it on the street because he parks the SUV in their one available spot in back. He also puts the van on the street because when he first got it he parked it in back, but it took up so much room that Spencer's four-foot-ten-inch mom chewed him out for encroaching on her parking spot.

He also has a motorcycle, which he puts in a parking space with another motorcycle. The other motorcycle belongs to Jezbo, who either lives here part-time or visits a helluva lot. I'm still not sure which. Jezbo has a large, white, jumbo pickup truck because his large, white, jumbo van "hit a hunnerd thousand miles and started havin' problems." Like Mac, he also has a large van he rents out to studios, which he leaves parked on the street when it's not in use.

Despite simplifying (he and his psychotic former live-in girlfriend had, at one time, five cars between them), Jezbo is still hung up on economizing the space where one can put extra cars. He recently said that he considered painting lines in the street between the driveways out in front of our building. "You kin fit five carzh out there if ya' pack 'em in right," he explained. In the same speech, he also complained to me that the two cars along the side of the building are taking up too much room. "You kin fit three carzh over there," he said. He was practically simpering.

His simpering isn't without merit. Not only do the two cars on the side have a fair amount of elbowroom, but they're both dead. Clyde's dead Corolla is one of them. Actually, his wife, Priscilla, used to drive it. But Clyde is too busy being unemployed ever to get around to fixing it. When I asked Clyde yesterday what his plan was for that car, he admitted that he had to get it fixed. (He told me a bunch of crap about cat reincarnation and flying saucers too.) After all, it only needs carburetor repair and a new battery. "Plus, Priscilla really needs it," he said. "She's teaching at different schools, she gets tutoring work at different places. She's gotta have a car." This is the same Priscilla who's not only been taking public transportation to her various jobs ever since I can remember, but she likes it.

The aforementioned Milt Dorfman, who sometimes says hi, has an old, white nondescript thing that he drives every morning to go eat a fattening breakfast. His second car is a Datsun. The model is a 210, which, I'd estimate, is the car's value in Mexican pesos. It's an economy-sized station wagon, making it both fuel-efficient and just big enough to comfortably seat five midgets. It looks avocado green, meaning it was probably forest green when he bought it a quarter of a century ago. The vinyl seats are shredded; the exposed foam underneath is now dark yellow. Far be it from me to call it a piece of crap, but yesterday it actually had flies on it.

Milt drives it around the block once in a blue moon just to keep it on life support, although it's been so long since I've seen it move that I'd suspect it has expired. He says he'd sell it if someone would buy it. He seems to have over-looked the step of posting an advertisement somewhere.

It didn't occur to me until I wrote this that I'm doing more than mere sniping. Extrapolating a statistic from my apartment complex unearths a potentially staggering reality. Of the 21 cars parked on this property, three have more or less broken down. That's 14.3% which, when applied to the number of cars in the entire city, multiplied by the amount of square footage the average car occupies, means that the broken-down cars in the Los Angeles metropolitan area occupy, by my calculations, roughly $11 billion worth of real estate. All statistics about Los Angeles can be converted to the cost of real estate. All of them.

If we sold all the extra cars, all those people would have extra disposable income, stimulating the economy, and freeing up space for construction of new homes, thus increasing the supply—and lowering the price—of housing. Do you know what that could mean for L.A.?

An influx of people—and their cars.

MEET OUR JOGGERS

With all the entertaining and thrilling ways a person can exercise these days, people who do things as vanilla as running have got to be crazy. I don't want to rant about marathoners and the questionable logic of spending months training for the chance to wreck yourself running 26 goddamn miles all at once—on asphalt, no less. There are many people in Los Angeles and around the world who don't find that strange at all. But there are runners in Los Angeles who happen to be strange. I'm only putting a spotlight on them because I happen to live here.

Let's start with my buddy Reynaldo, who is less of a case than he used to be. There was a time when, after running, he'd go straight to the gym to do leg presses. That clever combination made him so sore that he wouldn't be able to run for three or four days. Meanwhile, he ate fast food all the time. And he couldn't figure out why he wasn't losing any weight.

Reynaldo runs with a knee brace, but he's afraid to put it on in front of our running coach, Laszlo, because Laszlo yells at him for it. So when he starts running, he carries it with him until he gets to the other end of the track, then hides behind the bleachers to put it on. And the other day he told me that his knee actually doesn't hurt anymore. But it used to, so he wears the brace just to be safe.

He's also admitted to enjoying singing along with chick songs. Soft-rock ballads from the '70s, mainly. I've heard him playing them real loud in his car when he pulls up. He's so unabashed about it that he recently bragged that he bought a collection of '90s chick songs from an offer he saw on a TV commercial. He calls them "pussy" songs, but won't take God's name in vain because he was raised Catholic.

It is worth noting that Reynaldo is a nice guy, and as nice guys go, he is a pain in my ass. He keeps reminding me that this year's official Burbank calendar has a picture of me in it. The July photo is a picture of the track where we run, and the picture includes a bunch of the runners from our running group. Everyone else in it looks cool and relaxed. I'm the only one in the picture who's soaked with sweat and appears to be in total agony. I think it's a terrible photo of me, but Reynaldo, pain in my ass that he is, wants me to fuckin' autograph it.

For some reason, the teenagers who run with us never last. They have trouble understanding what Laszlo wants from them. Admittedly, Laszlo has a thick accent, but that doesn't excuse these kids' behavior. Two kids in particular come to mind. A few years ago, this skinny teenager named Victor was with us for a few months. He always wore this anguished expression on his face. I couldn't tell if he had bad indigestion or if he just witnessed a homicide, but every day was clearly a bad day in Victor's world.

He also had this weird habit of moving farther and farther away from us during calisthenics. After every stretching exercise, he would move about five feet to the side. Then five feet more, then five feet more. Then Laszlo would notice and yell at him for being 20 feet away from the rest of us. Laszlo gets mad if you tilt your head down too much during running. Victor's obsessive-compulsive shit didn't stand a chance.

But it ended one day when Victor came up to Laszlo and said he needed to talk to him about his workout. He said it as if Laszlo was doing something wrong. Laszlo didn't wait around long enough to listen to Victor's learned opinion. Victor was gone before any of us knew what happened.

The classic example of a kid who wouldn't—or couldn't—do what Laszlo told him was Davey. About 13 or so, Davey was a polite enough young man, but he had the attention span of a gnat. He'd either forget or not understand the assignments Laszlo gave him, so he'd just follow some other runner and do what that person did. But he wouldn't let on that he was doing it. So he'd run behind them about 20 or 30 yards. I know this because I caught him doing it to me once while I was running some intervals. He started running with me, so I ran harder. During the walking parts, I walked fast and eventually got a ways ahead of him, so he raced to catch up. So I slowed down to let him pass me. Then he slowed down because he got too far ahead of me. So I slowed down more. As we were walking back to Laszlo for our next assignment, he kept looking back at me to see if I was getting closer. I wasn't, so he slowed down more. Finally, I just stopped walking entirely. I can tolerate a lot, but that drove me bananas.

He used to run on the curb, that little cement strip that separates the grass from the track. I've sprained my ankle on the damn thing at least twice, but Davey would run on it on purpose. One foot on, one foot off. Then both feet off. Then back to one on and one off. On off on off on off on off. Off off off off off

off off off. Sometimes I used to get in his way on purpose just to see how he'd handle it. He'd run around me, then go back to running on the curb. He'd even do it when Laszlo timed him in a lap and ordered him to run hard. He'd run a little harder maybe, but still run on the curb. I kept waiting for him to sprain his ankle on it. He never did. (Lately I've been seeing Davey and his little brother at the track on Saturdays. Damned if his little brother doesn't do the same thing with the curb.)

And he wore this little smile the whole time he ran, even when he was getting yelled at. I don't mean to pick on children, but imagine smiling while you're running. I mean honestly.

Laszlo threw Davey out of his group a while back, probably for general aggravation, then let him back in for some reason. That ended several months ago when Laszlo asked him why he didn't show up for the previous session. Davey blurted back in his cheery, harmless way, "I have better things to do." Laszlo told him to go do them and threw him out again. Davey is the only person in Laszlo's group I've ever seen get permanently barred twice.

But there's one runner in the group who's the last guy I would have guessed to have a strange side. Let's call him Charles. A longtime runner, he's about 60 and can outrun me at any distance. When I first met him, I didn't meet him. It's not that he was shy or rude, but there are so many people who try Laszlo's group once or twice and never show up again that Charles had gotten in the habit of not doing much more than saying hello to them. That's how Charles viewed me. But one day, long after I'd proven that I'd become a regular, we somehow got on a subject that cracked Charles open like a walnut.

Dolls.

Charles is far from a girly-man. In fact, he's a former Marine. So when his wife was on a plane one day with R. Lee Ermey, the Marine-turned-actor, she called Charles from Dallas during the layover and told him about it. By the time she landed at Los Angeles International Airport, Charles was there with his R. Lee Ermey doll for the actor to autograph. Ermey obliged.

Charles also has a randy sense of humor, as evidenced by the following story, which I'll recall as best I can. This one time at his work, a health inspector was coming in for a tour. So Charles prepared for it by dipping a tampon in ketchup and tossing it on the floor around a corner in the warehouse. During the tour, the inspector and a gaggle of managers and other employees came by and saw it. The inspector demanded to know how it got there. Charles picked up, licked it, and said, "I don't know, but it hasn't been here long because it's pretty fresh."

But the dolls appear to be the greatest inspiration for his humor. "One time," he said to me with his slightly raspy, slightly garbled enunciation, "I took this Rosie O'Donnell doll and carefully opened the box and took it out. Then I took the arm off. Then I got this GI Joe doll with a .45 automatic in his hand. I took that arm off, melted it over an open flame so I could bend it at the elbow and the wrist, and popped it onto the Rosie O'Donnell doll so that the .45 was pointed right at her head. Then I put it back in the box and sealed it up like it had never been opened." Remember, this man is a former Marine.

I was at his house once for a backyard barbecue. He invited me in to check out his modest collection of dolls. Sure enough, he had a pristine, sealed box with a Rosie O'Donnell doll inside. She was pointing a tiny automatic handgun at her head.

It was on the same shelf as his Oreo Barbie.

For those of you who weren't subscribing to *Racist Toys Monthly* at the time, Mattel put out what it called an Oreo Barbie doll in 1997. Nabisco sponsored it in an effort to cross-promote its Oreo cookies. The first one was a Caucasian Barbie, and it sold so well that they put out an African-American one. Unfortunately for Mattel and Nabisco, it wasn't until these lovely dolls were on store shelves that they found out that the term "Oreo" is also a racial slur. The African-American Oreo Barbie was quickly pulled from stores. But Charles got one.

I don't want to call Charles a bigot, and he certainly doesn't act like one, but on "doll day" at the track, I got this side of his subversive sense of humor:

Charles: "What do you call a black bumblebee with a machine gun?"

Me: "What?"

Charles: "An African killer bee."

He had that doll on display at his house too.

Meet the Actress
God Sent

The other day at my favorite coffeehouse, my office away from my office, I was minding my own business chatting with Russ, fellow writer.

Russ: "How's your column?"

Me: "Oh, fine. Typical of a Wednesday, I have another one due Friday morning and have nothing prepared."

This was true. It's not that I'm out of ideas. I'm just always looking for something better, always keeping myself receptive to whatever comes my way. And stuff always does. God, in addition to His other talents, supplies tons of material.

Shortly thereafter, a friendly, attractive woman, late 30s, I'd guess, sauntered in. She saw the book I had on the table: *How to Write a Book Proposal*. She asked me what my book proposal was about and I told her, followed by, "Do you think that's an interesting topic for a book?"

She smiled broadly. "Yes. Here, give me your hand."

I thought she was going to introduce herself. Instead she held my hand in both of hers. We'd known each other all of 30 seconds and she hadn't told me her name yet.

"Close your eyes," she said.

I turned to Russ. "Watch. This is where she steals my stuff."

Russ: "You don't have anything worth stealing."

The woman, Ellen, said gently, "This is quiet time."

I put my head down. A moment later, she said, "Do you feel that?"

"Feel what? All I feel is your hands."

She pulled her hands away. "I just transferred energy. This is what I do with artistic people." She may have said "autistic people." I couldn't quite tell, but before I could ask, she went on. "I helped you put your idea out there to be received. You asked me, 'Do you think…?' By doing that, you kept your idea in, you held it in, you didn't let it out there for the world to receive it. Instead say, 'The world wants my idea. The world wants my book.' By saying it that way, you give power to your idea."

"Nicole Kidman wants me. Nicole Kidman wants me."

"By putting it out there, you've given flight to your desire. Now, her or someone very much like her, with her qualities, will come into your life."

"Someone *like* her?" I turned to Russ. "Wow, she's hedging already."

Ellen continued. "My biological twin is out there, and we're supposed to be together, but we haven't met yet. But he's very famous, and my acting coach was his acting coach 15 years earlier and he said that I was his female equivalent in every way."

Russ: "Is this a long-lost twin, separated at birth kind of thing?"

"No, just someone I'm destined to be with." They had the same acting coach 15 years apart, they've never met, and this famous person has no idea who she is. But they're destined to be together.

"Can you say who this famous person is?" I asked.

"Someone who knows Nicole Kidman really, really well."

"Who?"

"Think about it. What really famous person knows Nicole Kidman really well?"

"Oh. Him."

"Everything I'm doing in life is getting me closer to him. I have a friend who knows him and my friend is taking me to a black-tie fundraiser in a month where he's going to be."

"Well, good luck. But how are you going to get what's-her-name out of the way?" By "what's-her-name," I of course mean the famous person's famous fiancée who destined herself to be with him just before their respective movies came out this summer.

"Oh, we're not going to become romantically involved. We're just going to talk… and maybe become friends… or something."

Just then, another guy, Jim, walked in and started hitting on her because he didn't know any better. This gave me a chance to casually pull out my notebook and scribble down as much of this as I could possibly remember.

I wrote furiously, including parts of Ellen and Jim's conversation:

Ellen: "I'm an actress and a life coach."

Ellen: "Christ would never want his church divided."

Ellen: "I'm studying Buddhist philosophy with my voice coach."

Ellen: "My fiancé left me two weeks ago. He's 42 and had a mid-life crisis and stole my car, but it's okay because I've realized that he was only with me because of the success that I'm going to achieve, and, it just so happens, I just signed a major contract."

Jim: "A major contract? What kind of major contract?"

Ellen: "It doesn't matter what kind. That's between me and...." She gestured upwards. "But I'm blessed because it's opened me up to all these new and wonderful people."

A moment later:

Ellen: "...but I should keep my voice down because this gentleman [Russ] is working on his novel, and he's working on—what are you writing?"

I didn't want her to know that I was scribbling down everything she was saying, so I tried to disarm her with something so outlandish that she wouldn't possibly believe me. "Oh, I'm not writing. I'm just scribbling down everything you're saying."

"Really? I want to see."

She abandoned Jim and invited herself down at my table. I showed her what I'd written. It was the only known instance in my life where my chicken-scratch printing worked to my advantage. After a moment, she gave up reading it and asked, "I want to see what you're going to do with it."

"What I'm going to do with it?"

"Yes, what are you going to do with this? I want to see what this will become."

"Here, let me show you."

I turned my notebook to the next blank page.

"That's it?" Keep in mind she's maintained the same even, cheerful, harmless tone since she walked in the room.

"I don't know. I guess. Why, do you think I should publish this or something?"

"See, you said, 'Do you think...?' again. You're not giving energy to your idea." Shortly she was droning on about God and meaning, with lots of words and pauses. I can't possibly remember it all, but it went for at least 30 seconds, something like this: "God brought me here for a reason.... It's like a sculpture, a... block of marble... through which... a way that I can... express my... gifts... and the marble is chipped away and... a sculpture emerges that... puts forth my expression.... God puts a light, an energy, in all of us.... It moves through us.... I'm experiencing something with God right now."

She stopped talking.

"Maybe we should tell the manager."

"What?"

"Maybe we should tell the manager."

"What manager?"

"The manager of this place. I mean, maybe we should let them know that God's doing stuff to the customers."

She smiled. "Noooo."

A little later she said, "You're going to write your book, and when you're done, you'll have time to write another book. And I have a story to tell, but I'm waiting for a writer. But it's got to be the right writer."

"What kind of story?"

"I can't really say until I talk to my attorney."

"Oh, legal, privacy issues you have to deal with?"

"No."

After revealing only that her story was personal and deep and "will affect all of America," she gave me her phone number and email address. I guess her only criterion for the "right" writer was that he must have a pulse.

"So when it's time for you to write my story, you call me."

"Okay."

"I was meant to come here today. God sent me here for a reason."

Yeah, you could say that.

Meet Walter Tennant: The Friendly Neighborhood Bullshitter

Several months ago

Russ: "Why don't you write about Walter?"

Why would I do that, I thought? He's just another regular.

Wrong again.

I must have missed something about Walter when I first encountered him at my local coffeehouse. He was another seemingly nice, harmless old codge—one of many—who frequented the place. He reminded me of the voice-over guy from the old Smucker's Jam commercials, but without as much avuncular warmth. The first time I remember seeing him, he prattled away into his cell phone about some lawsuit. He did go on for about 40 minutes, but still, that kind of self-absorption is nothing new in Los Angeles.

But the evidence slowly began to accumulate. In the months that followed, there were off-hand run-ins I'd have with him. One day, as he and his beverage were heading for another room, we got on the subject of Las Vegas. "I can go to Vegas, sit down at a blackjack table with a hundred dollars, and in... three hours, I can turn that hundred dollars into... twenty thousand dollars." He had to think about those numbers for a beat before he said them. On-the-spot horseshit is tricky business.

"How?" I asked.

"I can't tell you that." He smiled his friendly piano-keys smile and walked away.

I also remember him mentioning that his father either built or owned the Aladdin Hotel & Casino in Las Vegas.

Walter also made sure to say into his cell phone periodically—loudly enough for everyone in the room to hear him—that he owned lots of property, including houses and warehouses. Not only did the whole property ownership thing seem suspicious, I can't even be sure there was anyone on the other end of his cell phone.

At any point along the way, I could have asked him why someone this remarkable spends so much time sitting around a coffeehouse, but I think that would have just shut him up.

It was also not uncommon to find him transcribing notes from one little notepad into another little notepad, so I asked him about it once. He explained to me that he knew a lot of people and wrote down every phone number in this little notepad, and therefore he had to transfer them to a new notepad every month. I don't think there was any other information before the "therefore" part. He just liked rewriting phone numbers into a notepad.

One day, he pulled a subtle but major blunder in his bullshit routine. He got up and wandered away without his cane. Maybe his hip was getting better—after all, he did jog six miles a day—but it's the sort of thing that stirs doubt. (And yet, when I found out that Dean Martin didn't really drink gin during his alkie crooner routines, I was more fascinated than accusatory. Go figure.)

Then there were the stories that others had about him. Another regular, for instance, told me that Walter told him that he could kill a man 500 different ways with his cane. Someone else testified that Walter claimed to have, in fact, killed six people. And Walter dumped so many lies onto one guy that when I asked him to recount them all, he said he didn't have enough time in his schedule to do so—and he's unemployed.

The best tale I heard was this one, related to me by Russ. The government had sent Walter down to South America, perhaps to kill someone. (Maybe he was going to use his cane, maybe he wasn't. Walter didn't say.) He wandered into the jungle to ask some local tribespeople where he could find this guy. Eventually, he reached a clearing where he chatted up a tribal chieftain. In the middle of their conversation, they looked up and saw a bull that promptly decided to charge them. While the tribal chieftain was wetting his skirt, Walter simply looked at the bull and raised one hand. The bull stopped and dropped to its knees. That was when Walter truly gained the chieftain's confidence—along with Russ' confidence that Walter was truly full of crap.

The thing that made me a believer in this unbelievable guy happened a couple of months ago. On a crowded Saturday, he was at the table next to me, telling a couple of people God knows what. I had completely tuned out, reading or writing whatever I was working on. When I stopped for a moment, I tuned in long enough to hear Walter say this:

"So I grabbed the gun out of the cop's hand and threw it into the volcano and said, 'If you do that again, I'm gonna kick your ass.'"

I didn't catch the rest of the story, but somehow I doubt context would have helped.

Four days ago

At the coffeehouse, I walked in on a couple of locals, Sid and Edith, gabbing about how someone had saved Siegfried's life. Or maybe it was Roy's life. And it may or may not have had something to do with a tiger attack.

"The worst was when he said he gave mouth-to-mouth to [Robert Blake's former wife] Bonnie Bakely," said Sid. "This was after her head was half blown off."

"Are you talking about Walter?" I asked?

"Who else?" said Edith. "He also said he got to push the button for the space shuttle."

"You mean to launch it?"

"He said his nephew worked for NASA," said Sid.

"Has anyone seen him lately?"

"He moved to Las Vegas."

"I've heard that. But is it true?"

"That's what he said."

"Well, Walter says a lot of things. Is it true?"

"As far as we know."

Sid also said that if you're going to make stuff up, you'd better have a good memory so you can keep track of it all. But it seems that Walter has been going around telling everyone that he's moved to Las Vegas. Everyone. Son of a bitch. At last, Walter wasn't bullshitting about something, and he's not around to confirm it.

Several months ago

Russ: "Why not write about Walter?"

Nah. Who'd believe it?

MEET OUR
LANGUAGE MANGLERS

Ever since the pilgrims gave England the finger and fled to this continent, we've been wailing away on the English language as if it were a sparring partner. That proud tradition is on display in Los Angeles too. Sometimes we just slur and sometimes we mispronounce things entirely. But on occasion, what comes out of our mouths is so cryptic that it can't be defined.

Last week, I went out to run an errand, and returned to find a homeless guy with shopping cart, standing next to my driveway. I didn't think twice about it. Homeless people are entitled to our sidewalks, and if they want to stop and smell the flowers, I see no reason to stop them.

That changed an hour later, when said person erupted in shouting that vaguely resembled English. At first, I thought it might have been one of the neighbors practicing *a capella* rap in Sanskrit. Then I decided that didn't make sense.

Then I heard my neighbor open his back door. I did likewise and the two of us were treated to the sight of aforementioned homeless man about 50 feet away, stomping around our driveway on the other side of the gate. He looked like Charles Manson minus the charm. I'd repeat what his ranting was about, but it was incomprehensible. But he was clearly mad at someone who—to my eyes, anyway—wasn't there.

My neighbor and I decided it was time to call the police, seeing as how the homeless guy was getting rather exercised. While my neighbor went in to get his phone, I stood there and looked at the homeless guy, all at once amazed at what I saw, but ashamed that I was quickly getting bored. Like everyone else, I've grown accustomed to looking for the entertainment value in everything.

My neighbor got through to 911 and described what we were watching. At that moment, the homeless guy spotted us and decided that real people were better to yell at, so he directed his complaints our way. Now he was mixing it up with curse words, English that everyone understands. Included in that was an invitation for my neighbor's girlfriend to come over and service him.

Then he did something I didn't expect. He opened his dirty, tattered blue jeans and proceeded to urinate in our direction. Not that I've consciously measured such things, but it was the longest uninterrupted whiz I've ever seen (or heard). It kept going and going and going, like the last *Lord of the Rings* movie. He made a sizable puddle, which I suppose might have done us some agricultural or animal control service, but I'm not sure what.

Like all men who are done, he wagged and tapped, but turned it into a full-on taunt, again exhorting my neighbor to tell his girlfriend to come over and do things to our visitor's junk while it was openly available. My neighbor, still on with 911, described this too. I told him to add that the police better come fast, because this guy was becoming pretty angry. I actually got a tad concerned for my safety. If one of the other residents had pulled up and clicked their remote control gate opener, this guy may well have stormed down the driveway at us.

The homeless guy disappeared just in time not to be seen by the police, who rolled up to take a report. When we mentioned that the guy had urinated at us, the officer told us that the stakes had been raised.

"That makes him a sex offender."

"It does?"

"Yes. If you can identify him in court."

"This will end up in court?"

"Probably. If he's looking at a conviction for that, then he'll probably try to fight it. But if you can identify him in court—the guy, not his, you know—then he has to register as a sex offender."

"Register where? He doesn't have an address."

"He has to check in with the department every 30 days."

So he took a complaint from both my neighbor and me, in which we attested that the guy had exposed himself. We were also told that they were going to go look for the guy and if they found him, one of us would be called to verify the guy's identity. As I write this, neither of us has been called. The guy could be urinating and screaming at people anywhere.

The whole thing reminded me of something that happened about five years ago, but I remember it like it was only four years ago. I was driving home from running (yes, we drive places to go exercise here; we even piss and moan if we don't get a good parking spot) when I saw a car accident right in front of me. The guy ahead of me, driving an old economy car in the fast lane, swayed way over the double yellow and sideswiped a jeep that was in the left-turn lane, pointed the opposite direction. And he kept going.

I called 911 on my cell phone and followed the guy. By the time I'd gone half a mile, the guy who got hit, along with one other car, had sped past me. The three of us trapped the guy in the left-turn lane. All of us jumped out of our cars, all of us on our cell phones to 911.

The hit-and-run driver got out. He was a little Latino man, maybe 40 or so, feebly waving his arms around and pointing off in the distance, like he was late for poker night and he was bringing the cards. He slurred at us in what sounded like Spanish. Or maybe it was Klingon. He was so drunk that the actual language didn't matter, but it definitely sounded like whining. Every language is only understood by a certain percentage of people, but whining is universal.

After more than two minutes of this, we were all still on the phones to 911. No one was picking up. Finally, a police car happened by. We waved them over, they directed us to a nearby parking lot, and called for more officers. I hung out and waited to give a statement. The drunk driver was handcuffed and ordered to stand at the back of a patrol car. While an officer wrote down my answers, the drunk guy kept turning around bleating something totally unintelligible and trying to walk away. The officer had to keep telling him to stand still. It would have been funny if it weren't so pathetic.

In a moment, I was done. I went over to wish the hit-and-run victim good luck, whereupon I found out that the drunk guy had no driver's license, and, presumably, no insurance either.

I never found out what happened to the drunk driver. I guess he didn't fight it in court.

It says something about Los Angeles that I can only think of a grand total of two examples of such blatant destruction of language. But I consider it a good sign that it seems to happen so infrequently. Maybe my city's image as a land of slurrers and botchers will turn around. It also speaks well of public safety. In my admittedly narrow study, 100 percent of all incidents of language destruction coincide with felonies.

Meet Clyde Langtry, Part Six

April 27

I raced up the walkway after working on-site for a client. Clyde was on his stoop.

"You okay, Joe?"

"Yeah, just busy, why?"

"Haven't seen you in a while."

This was the first time Clyde has ever shown anything more than baboon-like curiosity about me. His voice betrayed something resembling concern, like the kind he might show towards his best friend. Then again, for all I know, I might be his best friend.

April 28

It was night. I don't mean evening. I mean after 9:00 sometime. It was dark and quiet and someone knocked at my door.

"Hi, Clyde."

"You wanna go for a walk, buddy?"

"Uh, why?"

"So you can hear stories you've never heard before. Maybe learn something."

"Uh, no thanks."

"How's the writing going?"

"Oh, fine."

"You know, Hubbard was a great writer." That's L. Ron of Scientology fame. Mr. Hubbard if you're nasty. "He used to type out his stories on a manual type-writer at 90 words a minute and with no typos. That guy was amazing."

L. Ron Hubbard started an entire religion—possibly as a joke or on a dare, depending on whatever rumor one's heard—and Clyde can't get over what a great steno he was.

May 7

A hummingbird has made a nest on a slender branch of a bush along our walkway in front of Clyde and Priscilla's apartment. Just below eye level. Today, during a rare moment when the mother hummingbird was not only off the nest but not hovering nearby, I took the opportunity to grab my camera and get a few shots of the newborn hummingbirds in the nest. The mother hummingbird didn't swoop down and tweet menacingly at me. Instead, the father humming-bird came out of his apartment and tweeted at me.

"You're disturbing him. C'mon, man. That's enough." Clyde the ornithologist. A minute after he complained about me taking pictures of the baby humming-birds, he asked if he could see them.

"I don't think man will ever create a machine as good as a hummingbird," said Clyde.

"I think the same could be said of all animals, couldn't it?"

"I mean, they migrate thousands of miles and every year, the same humming-bird comes by out back and looks at me in the window as if to say, 'I'm here.'" Kind of how Clyde does with his neighbors, minus the migration part.

I told him he was insane in my usual way: "Hmm, interesting."

"This isn't the first time they've built a nest here. One year, a hummingbird built a nest in the branch right above our front door. Of course, they do this because they know I'm an ally."

It couldn't have anything to do with the fact that Clyde and Priscilla have more foliage in front of their apartment than anyone else here, could it?

A moment later, Clyde said, "I'm not myself."

"You're not?"

"No. I haven't been myself since January. There's this objectivity course I can take here, but you have to do it with a partner. I do you, you do me." I don't want to imagine Clyde Langtry doing it with anyone.

"What do you do, exactly?"

"Well, I tell you, 'Go to that wall.' And you go to the wall. I tell you, 'Touch the wall.' And you touch the wall."

"What's it called? An objectivity course?"

"Well, there's lots of 'em. The ones about you are called subjective courses, because they're about you. This is an objective course, because it's about every-thing outside of you. The idea is to get you out of your head. And I need that right now. I think too much. That's really the only thing that's wrong with me."

"Hmm. Interesting."

"I gotta do what my supervisor did. This guy is amazing. He's at a really high level in Scientology. He practiced bouncing two tennis balls off a wall, crossways at the same time, and catching them with the opposite hands. I gotta practice something like that."

If he's interested in doing something objective, he might consider practicing something the rest of us call a "job."

May 8

I ran into Mr. Near-Perfect in the parking lot tonight.

"How you doing, Clyde?"

He was slouching with his arms folded. "Oh… okay."

I laughed. He was nearly pouting. "What's wrong? Are you still… not your own person or whatever it is?"

"No. Not yet. I gotta stop thinking so much. Thinking is the enemy."

Add thinking to his list of enemies—which includes the police, the government, doctors, dentists, psychologists, university professors, processed food, processed pet food, regular exercise, buying retail, ironing.…

May 9

In the parking lot.

"How's your little car working?"

"Great," I said. "Sixty-eight thousand miles and the only thing wrong is that the battery died once. But that could happen to anyone."

"I just got a whole bunch of stuff done on mine. I got a new alternator, a new battery, a new catalytic converter, a new regulator.…" He rattled off things that I'm not sure exist in cars. He may have said "toaster" for all I can remember.

"Did you do it yourself?"

"No, I had to get a guy to do it. But I knew what parts needed to be replaced. I can sense these things." He can't tell when he's annoying the shit out of his neighbors, but he can sense when a car part is broken.

"Hmm. Interesting."

"I also got a clear muffler put in. That's a muffler you can see through. Now the car runs really quiet. Have you heard it?"

"I haven't noticed." That was a lie. The truth is that his car still makes the same noise it always has, a labored roar as if it had been repaired by a guy with a marginal understanding of auto mechanics.

May 10

Today, I discovered a little note taped to the branch below the hummingbird nest. It read, "Hummingbirds should fly 27–29 May."

A little while later, Clyde saw me and said, "I taped a note over there saying when the baby hummingbirds should fly. I went on the Internet, did some research about their gestation period."

Gestation refers to the period *before* an animal *comes out of the womb*, not *after* it has *hatched*. Anyone wanna bet that the hummingbirds won't fly May 27–29?

This Is How Our
TV News Programs
Cover Our Weather

Monday morning, I happened to turn on the TV to a local news update during *Good Morning America*. One quick story told us of a big rig accident on Interstate 5. It happened at about 2:00 A.M. and traffic was severely backed up. They showed footage of a big rig fully engulfed. Then they went on to the next story. I was left wondering what happened to the driver of the rig.

Admittedly, it was just a brief newsbreak, designed mainly to allow the *Good Morning America* crew to go out and smoke, I'd guess. They probably would have rushed to the next story anyway, but because of the nature of the next story, the driver's status never had a chance.

You see, the next story was about the rain.

People joke that summer lasts nine months in Los Angeles. This is not true. It's actually about *eight* months. The rest of the time, it's a blur of spring and autumn. The last time we had winter was in 1989, in February. I think it was a Wednesday.

In the face of all that relentlessly mediocre weather, the first rainstorm of the season is interesting stuff. When it happened to us Monday, it was so remarkable that people literally stopped what they were doing to run outside and look at it. I know this because I was one of those people, and had conversations with my neighbors when they did likewise.

And in case we don't know it's a big deal, all the local TV news programs are here to remind us. Rain, like scandals and awards shows, warrants what all the stations seem to call "live team coverage." This means instead of dispatching one reporter to cover, say, a kidnapping in Bell Gardens, one to cover a holdup in Carson, and one to cover the discovery of a body in a dumpster in Chatsworth, they go out to Bell Gardens, Carson, and Chatsworth to talk about the rain.

They were at it again Monday. The happy happy joy joy morning show on channel five ("You will not believe what happened on *Desperate Housewives* last night!") provided team coverage for live reports of what the rain was doing to various communities throughout the southland. How's the flooded trailer park in Santa Clarita? How are the cliff-dwellers in Laguna Niguel surviving this go-round? It's not that these things aren't newsworthy, but the coverage is broad to the point of absurd. My personal favorite was the chatty clown who went all the way out to Palmdale to do little more than narrate cars driving through a flooded intersection. Although he included neither the particulars of his data-gathering techniques nor a margin of error, he concluded that "many" cars were going "too fast."

This exact same type of reporting happens in the summer, when L.A. weather is so predictable that even *The Old Farmer's Almanac* couldn't get it wrong. On the hottest of those days, the hydra of team coverage rears its blow-dried heads to go into the field to tell us what we can already tell by stepping outside our front doors. These experienced, credentialed professionals usually insert taped on-the-spot interviews from people who give incisive quotes like, "It's hot," and "I'm drinking water." If they're lucky, they'll get a real scoop, like from a roofer or a pothole-filler, who gives even more incisive quotes like, "It's really hot," and "I'm drinking lots of water." (One day this summer, a reporter from channel two struck gold while trolling for quotes in Pasadena. He ran into Gene Gene the Dancing Machine—and promptly chatted him up about how hot it was outside.)

This kind of cutting-edge journalism is nothing new here. These schmuck-on-the-street interviews have been going on since as far back as I can remember. My favorite of these intrepid reporters is a guy named Conan Nolan of channel four, the NBC affiliate here. He's since graduated to real news, but back in the day, he endured all elements. Whenever strong Santa Ana winds came in, the station would send this poor bastard all the way out to the Inland Empire, a vast wasteland about 50 miles east of Los Angeles that lies beneath the Cajon Pass. This pass is where the winds from the high desert funnel straight down and make the big rig drivers pull over. The station would show clips of truckers saying things like, "It's too windy to drive," then they'd cut back to a live shot of Nolan standing in front of pulled-over big rigs, shouting into his microphone, trying not to fall over. I can only assume a guy with Nolan's otherwise impressive credentials was paying his dues all those years, because every time the winds came, Nolan was always the guy they sent out there for a report, and it was *always* the same report. The only things that changed were the truckers he found and the color of his tie.

As for the weather forecasters, they're always inside giving detailed explanations as to why rain, wind, or extreme heat is interrupting our otherwise predictable weather. I can't tell if it's because they're not qualified to stand outdoors asking strangers what they think of the weather or if it's because reporters aren't qualified to stand indoors and recite reports from the American Meteorological Society. And for reasons I can't figure out, all of our weatherpeople fall into two categories: attractive women wearing revealing skirts, or men who look like my junior high vice principal.

After the *Good Morning America* smoke break, I flipped to channel five's program, where they gave more extensive coverage of the big rig accident on Interstate 5. The live team coverage included a reporter on the scene telling us mainly that it happened at 2:00 a.m. and that traffic was severely backed up. That was about it. No word on the driver. Not that my opinion of local news journalism could get any lower (*Daily News* headline on Tuesday: "KABOOM!" with an above-the-fold picture of lightning strikes), but was channel five in that much of a hurry to get to the puddles in Palmdale that they couldn't tell us what happened to the guy?

Just then, an in-studio anchor asked matter-of-factly, "What happened to the driver?"

He was dead.

Everything about It Is (Usually Not) Appealing

Meet People in Show Business

Show business is so pervasive in this town that it seems like everyone has had a job in it at one time or another. About half the people in my apartment building currently work in it. Even yours truly has held some industry jobs. And you may be surprised to learn that insanity runs rampant in show business. Before I share a few tales in that vein, just know that stories like the ones below are everywhere. These are just the ones that happen to be mine. And these are only some of them.

Years ago during a stint as a production assistant on a big-budget feature, there was this driver named Fred, a squat, agreeable fellow who talked like he had marbles in his mouth. He was the one who, in this rock quarry where the company was doing nighttime shooting, told me that you could hypnotize rabbits by whistling at them. So I happened to be riding with him in a stake bed truck around 12:30 one night in this giant rock quarry. Nothing but dirt, brush, little hills, and curvy roads for the mile between the parking lot and the set. Total darkness except for the headlights. We came around a turn, and there were about a dozen jackrabbits in the light brush. Fred gunned the gas and whistled out the window while trying to navigate a windy road at an unsafe speed. He was so marble-mouthed that he could barely whistle to begin with, and it was completely drowned out by the roar of the engine. The rabbits were not hypnotized. They just ran for their lives. I might have too if the whole thing hadn't been so ridiculously funny.

That was the very first entertainment industry job I ever had.

Soon thereafter, I ran errands for the wealthy owner of a production company, a guy we'll call Jordan. I don't want to generalize about all rich people, but this one was a bit of a case. One day, I had to get some papers signed and a check deposited at a bank, so I idly glanced at them while waiting in line. Turns out Jordan was spending $22,500 to buy a military uniform worn by a grunt who later went on to become an American entertainment icon. And for that money, he only got half-ownership. Then he'd turn around and grouse about the cost of things. For instance, he once sent me to a baseball card store to buy a limited-edition card for his son. The card was $139. So Jordan wrote out a check for that exact amount because he felt the sales tax on top of the retail price was an insult.

On the one hand, Jordan could be really generous with the money. He gave me what remains the biggest Christmas bonus I've ever received. On the other hand, this is the same boss who dragged his feet when I asked for a raise after four months of sterling work. I got my raise a month later: $25 a week. And I was making poverty-level wages to begin with.

Sometimes the procedure was crazier than the people. One afternoon, I got a call from a production coordinator of a network sitcom. He'd gotten my résumé off a pile and wanted to know if I had a car, car insurance, a clean driving record, and any interest in delivering scripts to actors' houses at night. I told him I did.

"Great," he said. "Can you come in tonight around 6:30?"

"For what? An interview?"

"No. You're hired."

I showed up, filled out paperwork, met the principals, learned how to operate this huge copier, and was given address labels of where to deliver the scripts. Then everyone left. So there I was, on a major studio lot, at night, all alone in the production offices of a successful show, with the home addresses of the cast in my hand, access to God-knows what else at my fingertips, and none of these people had any idea who I was. Seriously, didn't they know there were nuts out there trying to break into show business? I could have been anybody.

In that same vein, I once got a phone call/job offer from a production coordinator on a cable show. He wanted to know if I would monitor the double-parking of cars in the tandem parking lot of this little studio in Hollywood. Just hold people's car keys at the front desk if they block another car in, move cars to let other cars out, that sort of thing. I told him that I didn't know how to drive a stick shift. His response? "That's not a problem." Not a problem to him, maybe. His car was an automatic transmission. But some of the stick shifts made scary noises when I drove them. Did I get fired? Nope. They were happy I stayed for the remaining two months of the production. The guy before me had lasted only one day.

Movie producers can be an especially wacky lot. In fairness, they have a lot of pressure on them. However, I've never understood how some of them can maintain control of huge productions but get bent out of shape over the smallest things. For instance, one high-powered producer I worked with complained to me one afternoon that he was having Hanukah dinner with some people that night and, oy, he didn't know what food item he was going to bring. I reassured him that if he could produce mega-budget movies starring Tom Hanks, he could probably find a side dish at a kosher deli on short notice.

But a few years back, I temped for a world-class whackjob of a producer, a wizened, middle-aged guy we'll call Kevin. Equally whacked out was his first assistant, Jamie, a walking stress fracture of a woman who had spent years cultivating a symbiotic insanity with Kevin. (Big-name producers always have two assistants: the first to help with business; the second to answer the phone, schedule lunch, and quietly look for a new job.) Jamie seemed to think the producer was helpless. One day, for example, everyone told me all day that a prescription at the local drugstore had to be ready for Kevin by six o'clock sharp so his housekeeper could pick it up for him. At around 5:30, Kevin called from the road. His meeting ended early. He asked me which drugstore was holding his prescription so he could go get it himself. Seemed reasonable to tell a man where his drugs were, so told him and hung up.

Jamie heard the tail end of this call and asked me who it was, so I told her. She nearly panicked. "No, no, no. You have to call him back, tell him just to go home. Tell him his housekeeper will pick it up."

"Um, okay. But why?"

"He'll walk into the drugstore, see the long line of people, and freak out."

The nuttiest episode was saved for last. One night while driving home, Kevin got sick in his car and had to vomit. He neither pulled over nor put down the window, so he simply turned his head a little to the right and puked all over his gearshift, as well as the carpeted sidewall leading down towards the gas pedal. Three days later, he decided it was starting to smell, and Jamie decided it was my responsibility to take $40 from petty cash and get it cleaned up as quickly as possible. I raced to the nearest car wash and gave the whole $40 to the manager. To expedite matters, I had to explain to two guys who spoke no English that they had to move the gearshift from P all the way down to 1 and back to locate and scrape up any residual barf that had slid around under there.

The last time I ever saw Kevin was at the end of that day. He bade me farewell by getting into his clean car with damp floor mats and saying, "See you again sometime?"

"Sure you'll see me again," I told him. "I'll be around in this business. I'm too crazy to leave this business."

I haven't had a job in the entertainment industry since.

MEET OUR ACTRESSES,
PART ONE

This week, a sane, talented actress threw her hands up and moved back home to marry her high school sweetheart. I don't know who it was, but I know it happened. It happens all the time, and I consider it one of the great tragedies of this city. It's compounded by the fact that few people notice or care, particularly in the entertainment industry. Just once I'd like to see in *Daily Variety* a headline something like, "Jane Doe Nixes H'Wood for Beantown Bean-Counter."

Meanwhile, a crazy one moved here and has no intention of leaving. She'll spend years spreading insanity, bad cheer, and her legs. Then she'll reproduce.

You've probably heard plenty about actresses. They're bitches. They're pill-poppers. They're materialistic. They're superficial. They're masochistic. They're slutty. They're dumb as bread. And so on. All I can say to such charges is, you left out, "They're nuts."

But don't take my word for it.

"Thirty percent."

I had asked Russ what percentage of actresses, in his estimation, were *not* nuts. I was surprised he thought it was even that high.

"Then there are the ones that don't have time for you," he added.

"So you combine the self-important ones with the 70 percent that are nuts and you're left with a really small percentage of actresses. Like what, 10 or 20 percent?"

"Around there."

I mentioned to my friend Max that I was pondering a column about crazy actresses. He groaned. "I could go on all night."

Said my friend Juli, L.A. native and non-actress, "Don't forget self-centered. I don't think there's any good actress that's not self-centered." Her answer neglected to account for the excuse of the non-good actresses.

I asked my friend Amy if she thought actresses are nuts. She answered, "It's a well-known fact." Amy, incidentally, is an actress.

A divorced screenwriter I know told me that he considered dating an A-list actress (he didn't say who) until a friend said, "You realize that she's just as crazy as your ex-wife but with lots more money, right?"

The meanest woman I ever worked with in the entertainment industry was, I found out months later, an ex-actress. I don't consider that a coincidence. I'm at that age where friends of mine have gotten divorced. In all the cases, the wives are actresses. I don't consider that a coincidence, either.

You just don't hear that kind of talk about any other profession. Then again, actresses labor under stresses that other professions don't have. They come out here from some town where they were voted Most Talented by their graduating class, only to be surrounded by others who earned the same honors from their high schools. They're practically hit over the head with the message that thin is in, so the ones that aren't blessed with high metabolism are obligated to adopt a long-term practice of malnutrition as part of their career strategy. They show up to auditions and sit in rooms with other actresses competing for the same job, all of whom are just as thin and made-up as they are, then wonder why they don't feel a stronger sense of individuality. The 95 percent of them who can't make a living at acting are forced to not make a living waiting tables in the meantime. And since the industry places such a premium on youth—a standard to which it does not hold men nearly as stringently—they can practically hear their dreams sputtering like a Fiat every month they don't land a job. (In an industry where the money flow can stop as arbitrarily as it can begin, this dread also applies to the 5 percent who *can* make a living at it.) And we wonder why they're such stress fractures exhibiting all the attendant symptoms.

What intensifies the perception that all actresses in this town are nuts is the attrition factor. One thing that induces people to give up and move back to Missouri or Illinois or wherever they came from is that they have a loving family waiting for them after they've had enough of the entertainment industry. The actresses that are more inclined to stay are the ones that don't have a loving family waiting for them back home, which is, in part, what made them so unstable in the first place.

In general, actresses are considered so difficult that men actually have a rule about dating them: Don't. When you say "no-actress rule" in this town, everyone knows what you're talking about, so wide and deep runs the reputation of the actress. Rules for teachers, nurses, cops, doctors, librarians—if such rules even exist—aren't applied remotely as often. I don't even know anyone with a no-singer rule.

However, God, having a keen sense of humor, has also made actresses among the most beautiful women in the world. Take the following exchanges.

Me (to my now-married friend Matt): "Did you ever have a no-actress rule?"

Matt: "I probably did at one point, but broke that rule many times."

Me: "Why?"

Matt: "In retrospect, it was probably for hormonal reasons."

Me (to another friend): "Did you have a no-actress rule before you got married?"

Another friend: "Even after I got married, I didn't have one."

I'd like to add that the above observations are merely generalizations, and that actresses generally get along with everyone else just fine. Some of my best friends are actresses—and it's likely going to stay that way. For whatever reason, actresses have never been very interested in me. Furthermore, I'm not without integrity. I have a no-actress rule of my own, and I gave up trying to violate it when I found out Joan Allen doesn't live here.

With some actresses, the whole insanity thing is no joke. Consider the following tale. It's the kind of thing that makes you feel just helpless.

Years ago, this actress—a person I know casually—allegedly checked herself into a room on the top floor of a high-rise hotel with the full intention of jumping. Ultimately, she didn't jump. Instead, she did what so many actresses do, what seems to come naturally for them. She wrote her insanity into a one-woman stage show.

Which got her into a comedy festival.

Which got her an agent.

Who got her a network TV development deal.

Meet Roberta Porter: You Can't Spell "Screenwriter" without "Screwier"

It all began last year when I answered an ad soliciting new members for a screenwriting group. With nothing more than an email, I was admitted. No interview, no résumé, no writing samples, nothing. I was in.

Screenwriting groups in L.A. are formed by screenwriters for the purpose of giving notes—some verbal, some written—on each other's work so we can all get better. You need to get better because you want either to sell a good script or to get hired to rewrite someone else's script. Sure, chances are it'll get made into a bad movie, but that's not the writer's job. A chore that important is usually reserved for studio executives.

The point person for this group I joined, the one who welcomed me in by email without so much as a secret handshake, was Roberta Porter. The most I can say about Roberta is that she was so fiercely devoted to doing the right thing that she literally lost sleep over it. She was slender, probably in her late 40s, wore a leather biker jacket and faded tennis shoes. She kept her long straight hair in a ponytail. She also had this hurried walk that looked like it had once been ladylike before the stress demons kidnapped her. I couldn't tell if she walked that way because she was late for something or because she was upset about something. This could be because she usually arrived to the meetings late and upset. After showing up late to one meeting, she volunteered that, on the way there, she'd had to pull over to the side of the road and cry because she'd been so overburdened lately. Minutes later, when we needed someone to type up a new contact sheet with everyone's phone numbers, Roberta insisted on doing it, citing her ability to type 120 words a minute. Stuff like that explained why her hair was white. Not gray. White. All of it.

Her typing may have been unmatched, but her writing needed help. The first script of hers I read was over 160 pages, which is unconscionable. (It's common knowledge that anything over 110–120 pages gets round-filed unless you're some A-list writer who can break rules like script length.) The second one was a chaotic story featuring a female lead character brimming with anxiety and who was angry at almost everyone around her. Can't possibly imagine what she drew on to create such a world.

I think she submitted such drafts because as long as she didn't put too much time and effort into her writing, the result would be so assailable that the humbling experience of constructive criticism wouldn't hurt her. Getting honest feedback on your script takes courage, less so when your script's biggest opponent is you. And it was the one thing she did graciously, except for the thing about the pencils. She would take out a sharp pencil, scribble notes as people delivered them, then put the pencil down and take out another sharp one a few minutes later. "I like them really sharp," she'd say.

The funny part, except for the fact that we'd be in a room with an overstressed woman who had a dozen sharp objects at her disposal, is that she didn't need any of us to tell her that her last opus was riddled with flaws. She said so herself. In an email she sent out before distributing the "angry female" script, she apologized for it by stating she wrote it in about a week and that it was "10 notches worse than merely sucking." If she said such things in pitch meetings, it might explain her lofty success after years of screenwriting.

Even funnier: She spent six years teaching screenwriting. I'm surprised she lasted so long. Her notes were trenchant, but she surrounded them with so much crap that they were almost not worth getting. Before she gave a note, she qualified it by warning us that it may be stupid, redundant, off the mark, too small to be worth mentioning, or all of the above. She had this habit of raising the pitch of her voice and lingering on the last syllable of a clause, sometimes raising her voice to a screech when she was suppressing a laugh. And she did it really fast, like she wanted to get her long speech out before the men in white coats showed up to trim her fingernails.

She once prefaced a script note with this: "As many of you know, I have a relationship with a beautiful El Salvadorian man." I don't remember anything after that.

Roberta's neuroses were on shiniest display whenever someone slighted her. The smallest disrespect sent her into such a frenzy of hatred that she was unable to confront the person, give or receive an apology, or do anything other than bitch about it behind the offender's back and invest eternal excoriation in them. The first I saw of this was with a woman who was in the group but too busy to make the commitment of showing up regularly and reading the scripts. While the rest of us were in calm agreement that this woman had to go, Roberta had grown to hate her guts. I could never figure out why.

In the weeks that followed, Roberta had two more run-ins with other members as they were out the door. Her biggest war came with a new member, Tricia. Tricia's behavior was bad form from the start. She missed her first two meetings and made little effort to give notes on the scripts she wasn't there to discuss in person. After she received Roberta's “10 notches worse than merely sucking” script, Tricia left a message on Roberta's answering machine telling her that it wasn't that bad, but that it was so rough that she wasn't sure what notes she could possibly give. Roberta explained all this to me in an email because I was now the coordinator. I was now the coordinator because the previous coordinator had left and no one else wanted the job.

The next day, Roberta emailed again, telling me that she made a cassette tape of Tricia's phone messages for me, and printed a note on her thoughts, but decided I'd get angry if she sent it to me. Then she said she decided to send it anyway. The next day, Roberta sent another email, telling me the cassette was in the mail along with a note explaining her take on Tricia. The next day, I got the cassette in the mail, along with a note explaining her take on Tricia. Some guys get mix tapes with love songs on them. I got one with half a chick spat.

Tricia left the group after attending one meeting. She sent out a farewell in which, among other things, she ripped Roberta a new one for being mean. Roberta did the same in her rebuttal email, except she didn't leave the group. And that was really all of it, except that before the next meeting, a sixtysomething biker dude in the group shook his head and muttered to me, “Chicks.”

The other to-do she'd had with another member around the same time was with a guy we'll call Curt. For reasons I can't remember—but I'm sure they were insignificant—Roberta had called, emailed, and possibly snail-mailed Curt repeatedly one week, to the point where he had become slightly annoyed. So at the end of the next meeting, Curt calmly came up to Roberta and informed her that all that reaching out had been a bit much. Roberta replied by disappearing into the ladies' room and bawling.

Minutes later, after we'd folded up the tables and chairs, one other member and I were idly chatting in the meeting room when Roberta came out of the bathroom. She told us that she'd come undone because Curt had just yelled at her. The truth is, Curt had merely spoken to her, and rather quietly and discreetly. I know this because I'd happened to be near him when he did it. But to Roberta, it was yelling, and she had fallen apart because of it.

I figured the last thing a woman in her condition needed was to be told she was wrong, so I pretended this was the first I was hearing of this matter and calmly told her that I was sorry to hear it. She started crying again and told me and the other person that she was sorry for crying. I told her again that it was okay. She prattled away about a lot of things, namely about how mean Curt was and some other ancillary revisionist history. I told her it was okay.

Then she hugged me.

I'm all for compassion for the needy, but I'm also all for boundaries. The two-second invasion of personal space—that I can live with. But at that moment, it occurred to me that the only thing worse than Roberta hating someone is Roberta liking someone. This poor, fragile, confused, catty, annoying, manic woman decided I was a friend—or at least someone she could hug. What loyalties did she presume came with this? Was I going to have to dodge invitations to hang out? Were there going to be other huggings?

A few months later, I exercised a potentially suicidal choice. I decided to quit the group. I'd simply had enough, a not uncommon sentiment after staying with a screenwriting group for any length of time. Of course, my biggest concern was how Roberta would react. Multiple phone calls? Showing up at my apartment? "I won't be ignored, Joe," I could hear her saying, as rabbit stew boiled over on my O'Keefe & Merritt.

I wasn't really afraid for my safety. Just afraid. I'm sure the question "How are we going to break the news to Roberta?" was a common one among her family members. Now it was my turn. Even though leaving was no crime, it was still bad news. No telling what she would do. We weren't having an affair or anything. We never even talked to each other outside of the group. But still, me leaving was exactly the kind of thing that, like all other events in life, Roberta wouldn't handle well.

I figured the best way to keep her replies short and sweet was to issue a short and sweet resignation—by email. The first member to reply to my farewell didn't quell my anxiety any: "I hope you sent Roberta some medication before you sent this!"

I had written specifically in my farewell that it wasn't because of anything anyone had done. Roberta replied by email that afternoon to ask if my departure was caused by something she had done.

Twenty minutes later, she sent another email, this time to the whole group, talking about how to go about picking a new coordinator and going over all the various little duties and issues. And she asked me to reconsider. Twice.

Eleven minutes later, I received another email from her. She wanted to know if it was because I switched script analysis dates with her. She asked me if I was feeling down on my work. She also said my departure was "really threatening" to her. Now, what does that mean? Was *I* threatening her?

I won't be ignored, Joe. The woman wasn't homicidal. Just persistent.

I wrote back reiterating my original resignation email, but shorter, assuring her that she'd done nothing wrong. It was brief, clear, and best of all, not vague.

The next day, she sent out an email to the group, nominating a new coordinator—and begging me to reconsider. What does her beautiful El Salvadorian boyfriend do with all this?

The woman was officially annoying. I didn't respond.

The next day, she sent another email. This was her most impassioned and personal email yet. It was brief, clear, and not vague. She praised my writing ability.

It was her last email—her last contact entirely. No boiled rabbit. No psychotic episode. Just one writer urging another not to quit writing.

Thanks, Roberta. Consider yourself not ignored.

MEET PEOPLE WHO'VE INTERACTED WITH FAMOUS PEOPLE

Celebrity is rampant in this town. This month alone, I saw Walter Koenig, the guy who played Chekov on *Star Trek*, coming out of my post office. I saw Leonard Maltin at my Trader Joe's—where, last week, I also saw William H. Macy and Felicity Huffman getting out of their car. At my coffeehouse, Morgan Fairchild made one of her regular visits, to the regular excitement of approximately no one. Also at the same coffeehouse, I saw some guy claiming to be a music producer hit on a pretty blonde who herself was claiming to have been the star of *Bring It On Again*, the straight-to-video sequel to *Bring It On*. I don't know what the star of *Bring It On Again* looks like, so no telling if it was really her. Then again, who'd lie about such a thing?

Of course, just by mentioning the above names, I risk being accused of the regional crime of name-dropping. Name-droppers are people who try to prove to everyone how cool they are by their brushes with fame. In truth, these people can get annoying. You ask them what's new, and invariably, it involves a celebrity. I have this casual acquaintance, a musician, who always mentions some known music personality among his latest gigs or recording sessions, never anything personal like he has a new girlfriend or he took a vacation to Peru or anything like that. One time—this goes back some years—when I asked him what was new, he said his band was going to appear on *The Tonight Show* in a month. It didn't happen. Next thing I know, he was fired from his band. (He was the backup percussionist.)

The line between merely mentioning celebrity sightings and trying to appear exceedingly cool due to such mentioning can be a fine one. On the one hand, if someone asks you what's new, you'd be a fool—a fool, I tell you—not to mention that you had the chance to gawk at Winona Ryder's ass in a movie theater lobby to see if she wore underwear or not. (I couldn't tell.) Since stories like that would be considerably lamer without saying the famous person's name, your only other option would be not to tell them at all. But then you'd have no one to share your excitement with. If you practice this form of self-censorship too much, you find yourself stifling your excitement entirely. Before you know it, you're seeing Adam Arkin squeezing produce at the market and not thinking twice about it.

However, a charge of name-dropping is as much a function of the accuser as much as it is of the accused. I've noticed that not just anyone accuses other people of name-dropping. The same small group of people always levels the accusation. Let's just call them what they are: name-dropper finger-pointers. These are people who get instantly or unnaturally irritated just by the dropping of a name, regardless of the context. My theory is that they're just jealous that the woman who played Ted Baxter's wife on *The Mary Tyler Moore Show* didn't ask *them* to put a letter in the nearby mailbox because she couldn't reach it from her car. (Happened to me. Happened to me. Swear to God.)

Then there are insiders, people who have so many of these stories and sightings that they look at garden-variety name-droppers as merely annoying. Some just ignore name-droppers, but some are insecure enough to one-up a name-drop, either with a bigger name-drop or a request to stop gossiping about a friend of theirs. A writer friend of mine witnessed this up close and painfully once. She was talking to an agent when Norm McDonald's name came up. "Did you see him on Leno last night?" she asked him. "The guy was out of it!"

The agent responded, "He's my golfing buddy."

Getting back to the name-dropper finger-pointers, they do have a point: Famous people are just like the rest of us, so why get all animated when you see or hear about them doing mundane things? Good question, yet we're still fascinated when we hear stories reiterating this. To give just one random example of boring celebrity normalcy, I recently heard on good authority that an A-list movie star was permanently banned from a local spa because he kept asking the masseurs to massage his rectum. Now, I ask you, what's so interesting about that?

At this point you're probably wondering who the movie star is. And if there were any way of telling you without getting sued, I'd do it. Why? Because we're fascinated with famous people. This is why name-droppers drop names, why name-dropper finger-pointers are jealous that they don't hear such stories, and why insiders volunteer either that it's old news or that _____'s rectum is looser than the Cahuenga Pass.

And these are just my stories. Everyone in town has their own. And as interesting as the stories are, it ultimately doesn't make much difference if you have a brush with celebrity or not. Would my friend Max be a lesser friend if he hadn't played darts with Eric Idle one night at a pub? Would my friend Sally have a void in her life if Tobey Maguire hadn't flirted with her at the Oscars a few years ago? Is my friend Jennifer a better person because George Clooney once bought her a drink at the Formosa Café?

No, no, and no. Now, if you'll excuse me, I have to go back to my coffeehouse to see if the star of *Bring It On Again* shows up so I can hit on her. With any luck at all, she'll go with me Saturday night to a club to see an actor/musician friend of mine play. And who wouldn't want to go? My friend, it just so happens, is the guy who says "Toasty!" at the end of the talking-baby Quizno's commercials.

MEET KYLE GOLDEN:
THE INCREDIBLY SPEEDY FILMMAKER

Kyle Golden and I were introduced by a mutual friend who's never been forgiven for it. All I remember about Kyle was that he was a manic moviemaker and that we got along. Somewhere along the way, he found out I was a writer. Then he told me he was going to make a movie and asked me to collaborate with him on the screenplay. For free. My philosophy was always to work your way up in the industry with your most powerful contacts. At the time, Kyle, an assistant to a suit at Sony, *was* my most powerful contact.

His movie idea was about the tensions that boil over when a bunch of old friends get together for a party. He also wanted the story to involve Ecstasy, a drug Kyle enjoyed so much that he mistook it for a food group. He urged me to try Ecstasy during the writing of the movie to help me gain a better understanding of the subject matter. I declined. I doubt it would have helped. I think he just wanted to see me on drugs. He also told me that Ecstasy gives people the uncontrollable urge to hug and touch other people. Since Kyle is among the straightest males I've ever known, I wondered just who he was expecting me to hug and touch upon taking the drug.

His idea was a hard one to wrap an entire movie around. It was even harder as we wrote it: All his male characters sounded like him, all his female characters sounded like his girlfriend, and none of them had much of anything to do. It was also difficult because I had something resembling a life, as well as that pesky condition called "needing sleep," while Kyle seemed to have neither. Kyle called or paged me daily, sometimes repeatedly, asking about the outline, what time I was coming over to help that night, and so on. After cobbling together plot points and conflict and some of the other stuff that screenwriting books tell you to include, our outline was finished.

Kyle woke up at 5:00 a.m. the next morning and began writing the script. He took a break around 2:00 p.m. to go for a bike ride, then came home and wrote until he fell asleep at 3:00 a.m. He was done. I don't mean done for the day. I mean he was done with an entire first draft. A hundred and forty-six pages. In one day. Now, few first drafts of screenplays are any good. Screenwriters have a bunch of nicknames for their first drafts, including the "vomit" draft, as in you need to vomit up a script and then build from there. But 146 pages in one day is a near-inconceivable amount of vomit. As if you can't tell by now, Kyle's way of writing was essentially practical, if not caveman: Put words on paper. While we worked on the outline, the thing he asked me most often was simply what happened next. He didn't seem to have much concern for intricacies of character or plot twists. He just wanted to get it done. He ate the same way. One night, he had green beans for dinner. His entire preparation consisted of opening the can.

This stripped-down approach existed elsewhere in Kyle's life. It's been a long time, and maybe he's grown more complex, but back when I would see him at our mutual friend's parties (and when he was single, I would hope), he had this way of hitting on women that could most charitably be described as efficient. A friend of mine told me that Kyle was chatting up her sister for a spell, during which time she told him she was married. Kyle walked away. It may have even been in the middle of the sentence where she mentioned that she was married. As with moviemaking and food preparation, time is the enemy in Kyle's world.

It was decided that I should rewrite his first draft. So there I was, working on the script alone, while Kyle had nothing to do. I told him that between my full-time job and my need for sleep, I would need at least three weeks to finish a rewrite. To a guy who can write an entire draft in one day needing nothing more than a bike ride, my request must have seemed ludicrous. Still, he acquiesced, and three weeks later, I delivered a rewrite. I didn't have time to go over the whole script, but at least I was on time.

Kyle read it and reacted by telling me that he felt that I didn't really give it my best. I explained to him that back on Earth, writers are given a month or two or more to do rewrites. And we're talking about people who don't have day jobs. He decided that, despite me not giving the rewrite my best effort, it was time to shoot his movie. Not because the script was ready, but because he was in a hurry.

He was impatient about casting his movie too. He called me one day to complain about how only 11 headshots had come in after he'd placed an ad in *Backstage West*. He called me on a Thursday. The paper comes out on Thursdays. This means that the only people who had sent headshots, I explained, were those who had mailed them on Wednesday, which means they saw the ad online, and I suspected that only a handful of people who subscribe to *Backstage West* do so electronically. Most likely, I continued, when everyone else gets print copies of the paper on Thursday, they'll send out their headshots that day, or Friday, or Saturday. By Monday, Kyle had approximately 500,000 headshots all over his living room. I just remember thinking that I never would have tried to become an actor if I'd known the competition was this fierce for a nonunion, nonpaying role in a movie written by a guy whose greatest creative influences were Ecstasy and pathological haste.

Since the bulk of the movie took place in an apartment, Kyle needed to find a suitable location. He chose his girlfriend's apartment, a cozy place with a loft. His girlfriend, however, wasn't crazy about so many actors spending all those late nights in her apartment. It seemed she wasn't crazy about Kyle, either. She drew up a lengthy contract with numerous clauses guaranteeing the safety of her apartment and compensation for letting him use it. One clause even read, "Director promises to be nice." Ridiculous as that sounds, it's actually a hell of an idea. The only reason that the rest of show business hasn't caught on is that if every contract in showbiz had a "nice" clause written into it, the breach of contract lawsuits would start before the signatures were dry.

With a lot of his own money, he shot the whole movie in about a month and a half—on weekends—then edited the whole thing on his PC in his bedroom. It was about five minutes after he finished editing his movie that a movie called *The Anniversary Party* came out. *The Anniversary Party* was about a bunch of friends who get together for a party and drop Ecstasy. Kyle shrewdly counteracted this threatening competition by throwing a chair through a window. Then he wrote a new beginning and a new ending to his film, raced out and shot them, and tacked them onto his cut. He didn't want to take any chances that people would confuse the two movies. *The Anniversary Party* had Jennifer Jason Leigh and Gwyneth Paltrow and Kevin Kline. Our movie had a guy who was on *General Hospital*.

The new cut came to nearly four hours, which, under ordinary circumstances, would require a script longer than *Titanic*. Lacking a giant boat and a clichéd love story, Kyle eventually chopped his film down to a more traditional length, which I eventually saw at a screening at a condominium of one of the actresses. One of the people at the screening was a guy sitting in the kitchen, peering at the television through a wrought iron wine rack. Hardly anyone talked to him all night except Kyle because no one knew he was. That was me.

The film never sold. Kyle tried to make his money back with a three-pronged fiscal plan. He got a new job, made another movie, and bought a house, although it may not have been in that order.

When I emailed Kyle to tell him that I was writing about him, he said what director-producers say in this town every day: "I love it." He only asked that I plug his company and tell everyone that he's seeking investors for his latest feature. Unfortunately, to avoid any risk of litigation over all the nice, flattering things I've written about him, a lawyer advised that I change his name and not mention his company. Poor Kyle. I hope he doesn't throw a chair through a window.

Meet People in Show Business, Part Two: Writers

How long can a person be not working on their screenwriting before no one considers them trying to break in as a screenwriter anymore?

There is no rule, but since I haven't done any screenwriting in a while—and don't exactly have a long list of credits anyway—it appears that my "career" in show business is over. In honor of it, allow me to share some true adventures of writers and scripts.

I worked on a sitcom pilot that featured a brain-dead, narcissistic star/creator/ producer, whom we'll call Gabbie because she knew how to talk. One day, she gave me $20 and told me to go buy her some cigarettes. But not a carton. Just one pack because she was going to quit. Anyone under the stress of trying to get a pilot off the ground isn't going to quit smoking. So us production assistants took turns going out to buy one goddamn pack of cigarettes at a time for her. Soon, the production coordinator, who *was* a bright woman, used petty cash to buy a carton and kept it in her desk. Every time Gabbie wanted a pack, we told her we'd get it on the next run, then pull a pack out of the coordinator's drawer. And by show's end, she hadn't quit smoking.

This is the same comic genius who insisted that she could only write with candles lit. Her sitcom was such a turd that the pilot never aired. Maybe she should have tried writing with jokes.

I had to pick up her kid from high school one day and drive him home. Naturally, as he navigated us from his high school to his mother's townhome, he got lost. Apple doesn't fall far from the tree.

The other executive producer, a friend of Gabbie's, once sent his assistant on an errand to pick up "a box." The circumstances surrounding the errand were so suspicious that curiosity got the better of her and she opened the box before delivering it. It was full of pot. She submitted her two weeks' notice shortly thereafter.

Wacky as these show runners were, they can't take all the blame for the failure of their show. The truth is that it's not easy to make a good sitcom pilot. Since no episodes of the original script have been shot yet, no one knows what the show is supposed to look like. Therefore, pretty much everything about it is subject to change as various creative and noncreative people at the production company, the studio, and the network take turns destroying it beyond all recognition. This thoughtful process is called development and can cost millions of dollars by the time a script gets a shooting date. Since there's often weeks between a commitment and a shooting date, what were good jokes eventually sound unfunny and stale because everyone's heard them over and over again, so they're mistaken for duds and rewritten with bad jokes, sometimes during long, long nights. Then after it's shot and edited, the network doesn't order any more episodes because no one thinks it's funny.

People who have actually worked in development—as a writer or otherwise—can describe worse things, but the most unbelievable development story I heard was when I worked briefly on a UPN sitcom called *Grown-Ups*. It was originally sold as a one-hour comedy-drama about a Jewish guy in New York. By the time it went through development, it had become a half-hour comedy about a black guy in Chicago.

And a friend of mine has been dragged around for two years on a TV show idea that has been restructured into every length and format imaginable. Keep in mind, it has never been made. The suits at the network just keep beating the script to death. They had yet another meeting a few weeks ago to discuss changes they'd like to make. They neglected to invite my friend to the meeting. She is, of course, the writer.

Several years ago, right after I got hired to work as a production assistant on a network sitcom, I dug deep for the guts to try the direct approach to breaking in as a writer. On my second night there, one of the producers asked me to walk her to her car. This was my first conversation with her. I asked her how I could go about writing an episode of the show someday (it does happen). She danced around it and essentially gave me a noncommittal answer. It was about what I expected, but at least I'd planted the seed for a later chance to ask her again and, dare to dream, get my episode.

She never asked me to walk her to her car again.

When I was delivering scripts for a network sitcom, I pulled up to a townhouse complex in Brentwood late at night. The big gate at the driveway opened automatically (er, um, what's the point of having a gate at all, then?), so I drove in. Jumped out, dropped the script at the actor's door, and split.

When I drove back to the gate from the inside, it didn't open. So I drove around to the other side. That gate didn't open either. I went back to the first gate. To the second gate. To the first gate. Nothing. There was no security guard. There was no call box or keypad for a person to punch keys angrily. There was no one around. It was 2:00 in the goddamn morning. Then it was 2:01. Then it was 2:02. I started thinking bad thoughts. Then I considered screaming.

Finally, a young couple wandered in through the pedestrian gate. The guy felt my pain, but the girl was suspicious. She was reluctant to let a stranger out of her complex, since she didn't know who I was or how I got in there. I considered screaming again.

Fortunately, I calmed down just enough to rant about how I just wanted to get the fuck out of this fucking place and go to fucking Van Nuys and drop off more goddamn scripts at the houses of other actors who were never going to be famous so I could go home to my ratshit guest house and if she didn't open the fucking gate I was going to start honking and wake everybody up.

The guy said something like, "Brother's gotta go home."

It was two against one. Or maybe she just wanted to get inside with her guy friend and drink the hooch she just bought at the liquor store across the street. She relented, explaining that she could only open the gate from the phone in her apartment. After about a minute and a half, I thought about screaming. At last, the gate swung open and I got the hell out of there.

Could have been worse. I heard a story recently about another fellow night script delivery guy who parked outside a gated complex but didn't set his parking brake. His car rolled and smashed into the gate so hard that it wouldn't open and no one could get their cars out for hours.

I developed such a sterling reputation as a guy who could photocopy scripts, put them in envelopes, and dump them on doorsteps that I was retained to do the same for a pilot on the same lot that spring. As we've learned about pilots, rewriting can be a bit haphazard. The last night of rewrites on this show was so chaotic that I wasn't able to start photocopying until about 3:00 A.M., and didn't get out of there until about 5:00 A.M. My first job was to drop off a box of scripts to the stage. I drove across the lot with arrangements to wait for a security guard to show up and unlock the stage door. Unwilling to wait, and in a hurry to get the scripts to the actors' homes *before* they left to go to the studio that day, I tried the door. It was unlocked.

This studio was like that. I used to park on the street and wander through the pedestrian gate on a side street. The guard never asked who I was. At the main gate, whether you were driving on or walking on, you had to be on a list. But at this side gate, all you needed was to walk through. And when I was temping there once, I used to eat my lunches in one of the screening rooms and use the phone for personal calls. No one ever came in. Ever.

Walking around, having lunch alone, no one bothering me. It was like not being in show business at all.

Meet Our Actresses,
Part Two

Last fall, I made a mistake. I wrote a column describing actresses as crazy. The mistake I made was not including actors. Let it be said here that:

+ just as some men won't date actresses, some women won't date actors
+ actors have a reputation, not entirely undeserved, for egomania, narcissism, immaturity, and raging insecurity
+ no actress ever made *Battlefield Earth*

I can attest to those statements personally. I used to be an actor. During that time, few women wanted to date me and I didn't make *Battlefield Earth*. Also, I had a larger ego, was less mature, was led around by my fears, and, on occasion, was accused of narcissism. As I got more therapy, I got less egomaniacal, more secure and mature, and fewer accusations of narcissism. I also lost the urge to act. That can't be a coincidence. I'm convinced that losing the urge to act is directly related to sanity.

Last fall, I made a mistake. I dated an actress.

I'd sworn off actresses until I met this one who was just lovely. And funny, and smart, and sweet, and multi-talented. Not long after we met, she read a few of my columns, including the one about crazy actresses. She assured me that she wasn't like them, as her burning desire to be an actress was on the wane.

She also admitted to a chronic fear of relationships, which she fed and cared for by practicing communication skills that could best be described as constipated. I endured such emotional gymnastics trying to figure out and please this woman that, after a month and a half, I was getting headaches and diarrhea, which, all things considered, is nicer than getting the clap.

Among her other talents, she was a singer/songwriter. A few weeks after we started dating, she had a gig at a bar. I wanted to go and told her so, but told her I would understand if she didn't want me to go. We hadn't known each other that long, maybe she was too self-conscious to have me there yet, I wasn't sure. I'm still not sure. We talked about it for what seemed like 10 minutes and I don't remember a word of it. She didn't say one way or the other whether or not she wanted me there. She didn't tell me why it was so complicated for her. She couldn't even admit that it was complicated.

It was this sort of crippling inability to say what she wanted—or inexplicable urge not to—that sent me into fits of confusion and frustration. All this fun culminated in a fitful two-day span around New Year's, when she complemented her poor communication skills with a previously unseen layer of game playing: telling me one thing then acting like she'd told me something else, passive-aggression without telling me what I'd done wrong, fun stuff like that. She also called to cancel a dinner I'd made for her because she was reluctant to drive to my place in the Valley. She'd recently driven all the way to Texas for Christmas but didn't want to drive over Laurel Canyon because it was raining.

All her disinterest in me had an effect: It made me disinterested in her. When I told her that, she was shocked. Rather than own up to my accusations or acknowledge hurting my feelings, she got defensive. So I broke my no-meanness rule, raised my voice, and told her straight out that she was by far the worst communicator I've ever known. She didn't know how to respond to it.

At least not right away. Once it seemed clear to her that I'd had enough and probably wasn't coming back for more, she pulled manipulation out of her arsenal, pouring the praise and the contrition on thick. First came an email about two hours after I told her goodbye, then a voicemail message three days later. By then, my headaches and diarrhea had been gone for two days. That's how I knew not to respond to her.

Wherever she is, she's probably still lovely, funny, smart, sweet, and multi-talented. I hope she's found a therapist who challenges her to do more than wear green to attract wealth into her life.

Last fall, I made a mistake. In the aforementioned column describing actresses as crazy, I accidentally picked at a scab of one actress in particular.

All I did, or so I thought, was relate her story: She developed emotional problems and nearly committed suicide, but instead channeled her energy into writing about her problems into a one-woman stage show that eventually got her a TV development deal. I even left her name out of it to protect her identity. To her, however, the anecdote was not only factually flawed but took a shot at her, both of which she wrote in a rebuttal letter published by the online editors of the column and neither of which were my intention. She also signed her real name. So much for protecting her identity.

A few weeks ago, I went to *The Los Angeles Times* Festival of Books at UCLA. It's a great chance to browse the wares of vendors, hear authors speak at panels, and shake hands with publishers who rejected your book proposal earlier in the year. I'm hoping to be an author, believe it or not, and would relish the chance to speak at panels like the ones held at UCLA every year. In a recurring daydream, I can see myself speaking at the book festival at UCLA someday, author of the book version of this column, dazzling the crowd with my quick wit. Sometimes, the daydream is interrupted by this actress stepping up to the audience mic and asking me in front of an entire auditorium how the hell I could have justified the awful things I wrote about her. I'm not very good at daydreaming.

I was heading through the throngs to get face time with one last publisher when a woman coming the other direction said, "Helloooo, Joe."

It was her. *The Actress.*

She was with a friend and introduced me to him as the guy who wrote that column about her last year, filling him in with the particulars. I couldn't tell what her attitude was. She didn't seem mad about it, but I wasn't so sure. She actually tried to play it off as if the column and her reply had all been in good fun. I wasn't so sure about that either.

Her main beef about the column, she told me, was that she felt it had made light of a serious problem and that I was intimating that she was being an opportunist by using her own then-serious emotional issues for material gain. I hardly knew her well enough to make that accusation, and, after repeated readings of the anecdote as originally published, I can't read that into it. Nor can anyone else whose opinions I've solicited. Still, I told her I was sorry she took it that way.

In her rebuttal letter, she wrote that most of my facts in the article were erroneous. So I asked her what facts I got wrong. She said it was so long ago that she couldn't remember.

In the last two weeks, I've sent her two emails asking her to explain what I got wrong so I could clear things up. I didn't get a reply.

After our conversation, after repeatedly checking my facts, and after scanning her rebuttal letter all those months ago, I could only find one thing I got wrong: I called her an actress. She'd intimated in her letter and told me in person at the book festival that she had no desire to do theatre anymore. This loss of desire, as I've attested above, is a sure sign of sanity.

Just for the hell of it, I did an Internet search for her. The first thing I found was her professional Web site.

She does voice-over work.

Maybe I Should Move

Meet Clyde Langtry,
Part Seven

May 16

Tonight, I came back from the laundry room and found Clyde standing by my door.

"How's my door, Clyde? Still up there?"

"Haven't seen you in a while, thought I'd check in." We see each other all the goddamn time.

I spent the day—not the whole day—thinking about my incredibly rude neighbor, Mac; the inconsiderate assholes next door who keep throwing their cigarette butts in our driveway; and a jerk who stiffed me on a freelance job. For all the dumb things Clyde says, he takes a little of all that pain away.

"Yeah, I got a long-term day job on-site."

"I know. How's that going?"

"Oh, fine. Nice people, low stress."

Clyde turned this into a conversation about Scientology. (Clyde turns everything into conversations about Scientology.) "Hubbard said it on this last tape I listened to: We're all turning into robots. I forgot exactly how he said it. Something like…. Well, we're turning into robots. That's what he was saying."

Then Clyde talked about past lives. I tried to pin him down on how exactly Mr. Hubbard was able to prove all this. "I'll give you the short answer," he said. Then proceeded to prattle away for several minutes about other Scientology things that seemed unrelated. He ended it with, "It's logical. There isn't much logic to it." I couldn't agree more.

He also reminded me how good he is at reading people's faces. "For instance, I can tell by your face that you're puzzled by all this." The fact that I'd told him a few minutes earlier how puzzling I found all this was what might have clued him in a little.

"So, if you're so good at reading people, why don't you try playing poker?"

"You know, I have a friend who does that."

"Why don't *you* try it?"

"Eh, I don't know. I should. I guess I don't have the discipline."

Never mind the bankroll.

May 19

Today was the day I noticed that the hummingbird nest was gone, as were the two baby hummingbirds inside. So was Clyde's note that said that they'd fly around May 27–29.

"What happened to the hummingbirds?"

"Serendipity got 'em." Serendipity is one of Clyde's cats.

"How? This branch is too thin to support a cat."

"She jumped up and got 'em. Serendipity can jump. Our last Abyssinian could jump about seven feet straight up." I looked up cat breeds on the Internet. Domestic cats can't jump that high, especially a lard-ass like Serendipity. And it looks nothing like an Abyssinian.

"Oh. Well, that's too bad."

"I shoulda' known it would happen. She knew they were out here. I should have put up some netting up on posts around here with lots of space between the strings so she couldn't climb on it." For a guy who's neither Jewish nor Catholic, Clyde sure traffics in a lot of guilt.

Incidentally, there wasn't a trace of either bird left. The prevailing theory is that Serendipity ate them. Who can blame him? It was probably the first time he'd ever tasted meat.

May 23

As I headed through the darkness to the laundry room, Clyde greeted me. I couldn't imagine what he was doing wandering around out there. I didn't ask because I figured he'd tell me anyway.

"Hey, Clyde. Wanna watch me throw my clothes in the dryer?"

"No. Have you seen Misty?" Misty is one of Clyde's cats.

"No."

"There she is. I'm trying to get her in for the night."

I threw my clothes in the dryer. A moment later, Clyde was still chasing his cat around.

"You know, they're cats," I said. "They'll come in on their own, won't they?"

"Yeah, I know but I worry about her. She's roaming around, under the building, out in the parking lot. This is new behavior for her. She just started doing this a few weeks ago. Who knows what they're thinking." Proof again that pets are like their owners.

A moment later, Clyde knocked at my door. His cat was in his arms. "You didn't see Tom Friedman on *Charlie Rose* last night, did you?"

"No."

"Oh, it was great. You know who Tom Friedman is, right?"

"No."

"He's a reporter for *The New York Times*. He's really a brilliant guy."

Misty meowed at Clyde, the unhappy meow of a cat that's uncomfortable.

"I'll take you in in a minute," said Clyde. "I only saw the last part of it. I wish I'd just recorded what little I could. I was hoping they'd rerun it on channel 58 or something today, but they didn't. Anyway, he was talking about oil and the Middle East and our future. He was pretty optimistic about things. He says China is screwing up and India is screwing up."

Meow!

"I'll take you in in a minute." The cat swiped its claws at Clyde's free hand. "Do you know what Nicola Tesla did with electricity?"

"No."

"Oh, he was amazing. He figured out how to use the Earth's natural electricity field…" Over the next several minutes, the cat got squirmy. I can't say I don't know the feeling. So Clyde put her down, whereupon she promptly wandered away. The whole time, while Clyde yammered away about how Nicola Tesla approached L. Ron Hubbard with this invention that would harness all the electricity needed to power everything on Earth, he kept looking back at his cat disappearing into the dark. It was the sort of thing that really messed up a good story. That and the fact that the story was probably complete bullshit.

June 14

Clyde likes to brag about his affinity with his cats. But it is worth noting that when their cat, Marmalade, was a kitten, he had a kitten's friendly instincts. You could come up to him and pet him. But Clyde and Priscilla disabused him of that sweet nature. Now whenever someone comes near him, he just runs like hell.

Yet Priscilla is the one who calls them in at night. Well, it seems that Marmalade hasn't been responding to Priscilla's calls. So, like Misty, Marmalade hasn't been coming in at night. Poor Clyde was out tonight looking around for him. Serendipity, the other cat that runs like hell when anyone comes near him, was following Clyde around, meowing as if to help Clyde call Marmalade in. At least that was Clyde's interpretation. Serendipity may have been trying to call Clyde in.

Hm. First Misty, now Marmalade suddenly doesn't want to come in. Kind of makes you wonder what Serendipity is thinking. My guess is something along the lines of, "I told you I could outlast you two."

Also, we got to talking about my recent trip to Italy. Clyde said, "Italians are a nationality that I really identify with."

"Why's that?"

"Oh, you know. Art. Auto racing."

June 15

"Did you find Marmalade, Clyde?"

"No, but Ken [the landlord] said he saw him this morning."

Tonight, Clyde and Priscilla were out looking for him again. Not long after they gave up and went inside, I went out and Marmalade was rolling around on the walkway all by himself. He looked like he was having the time of his life. Can cats laugh?

June 18

Mystery unraveled.

Clyde explained Marmalade's entire disappearance. "Yeah, he was about a thousand feet away."

"How do you know?"

"I have a friend, Jim, who can sense where animals go. He tracked Marmalade to a neighborhood about a thousand feet from here. And I know why Marmalade left too."

"Why?"

"He wanted to be a protector. Not like a watch dog, but just, you know, hanging out around the front here."

"Weren't you letting him?"

"Well, yeah, but not exactly."

"The cat told you this?"

"No, Jim told me."

"How does he know all this?"

"He has a thing with animals."

"Excuse me?"

"He can track animals and their thoughts. That's how he found Marmalade."

"Wait. Did he go and get your cat and bring him here?"

"No, he lives two towns over."

"Then how did he know?"

"Marmalade is a free spirit, just like his earlier being. This is the reincarnation of the last one we had."

It's not much of an answer, but honestly, if Clyde could have said, "Jim doesn't know, he's full of crap, and I'm a moron for believing him," don't you think he would have said it by now?

June 22

Since the summer heat is upon us again, Clyde has taken to sitting around with his door open.

"Hi, Joe."

Clyde jumped off his couch to come out and greet me. I'm almost convinced that I'm his best friend.

Imagine what a person would look like if he never exercised and avoided most food because he thought most food was poison. Now imagine that person around age 60 wearing only Bermuda shorts. That's what I had a conversation with today after work.

"I didn't see you in there. That's why I didn't answer. That's why I don't answer you when you say hi to me from your bedroom window. I don't want to look like I'm having a conversation with the plants."

"Maybe it's a ghost trying to talk to you."

This prompted him to tell me about his one and only encounter with a ghost, which I found remarkable. Not the story. That wasn't much. The remarkable part was that a guy who claims to have past lives has only one ghost story.

Just to make sure I got my facts straight, I asked him to explain again why Marmalade ran away.

"Well, Jim said that Marmalade wasn't feeling appreciated for being a protector. So we've tried to make him a member of the family."

Just when I thought Jim was a crackpot, Clyde said this: "Jim got in touch with the first Marmalade after he died. 'Tell him to come back as a person,' I said. Jim said, 'No, he wants to come back as a cat again. Just get another body and he'll join you.'"

For all the crazy things Clyde has told me over the years, he has never ever snuck glimpses at me to make sure I believed the twaddle he was passing for truth. He didn't do it today, either. If he's playing a joke on me, it's damned elaborate.

Meet Our Morose Russian Woman

The acreage on which my apartment building rests has not, to my knowledge, expanded. Nor have we added units. But in the five years I've lived here, the population of our building has increased about 20 percent. This is a tiny example of the steady population increase of Los Angeles despite the qualities that generally make my fair city unlivable, such as heavy traffic, crumbling infrastructure, the high cost of unlivability—and encroachment of new arrivals.

A couple of months ago, I glanced out the window and saw a woman with a baby in a stroller in my apartment courtyard. The woman looked about 50, had her hair pulled straight back, and wore a long topcoat. She was shaped like a giant shampoo bottle. At first, I didn't think twice about it. Residents have visitors sometimes, and sometimes those visitors go outside. But this woman wasn't waiting for anyone. She didn't look at her watch and then up at someone's door as if to say, "Let's get going already." Finally, after her toddler had made many little squealing noises at one of the cats, the woman steered around and moseyed off. She was just wandering around in our courtyard.

I didn't think about it after that. While we have this history of the occasional interloper, we never get regular interlopers. But this woman kept coming back. Several times. The more I saw her, the more I wanted her to go away. Like our other visitors, this woman and her toddler were not hurting anyone, but I don't care for strangers roaming around my apartment courtyard. It could lead to, well, more strangers.

Naturally, Clyde beat me to it. They had a brief exchange as she was leaving one day about three weeks ago. When I asked Clyde about it, he said, "I said hi and all she said was 'Russian.' I guess she's Russian." Let no man ever question Clyde Langtry's powers of deduction.

Even more notable, however, was that it didn't deter the woman. One afternoon two weeks ago, I spied her sitting on the steps across from my place. Her little girl was bopping around Clyde's porch looking for cats. I was about ready to go out there and stare at her conspicuously or something, but I stopped when I saw the look on her face. She seemed tired and sad. She dropped her forehead on her hand as if some awful reality weighed her down. I further sensed this when her little girl bounded over to get her attention, but the woman ignored her. She seemed too wrapped up in her own forlornness even to humor the girl. Then she put the girl in the stroller and left. I stared inconspicuously.

A few moments later, I got in my car to go meet friends for dinner. I passed her and watched her in my rearview mirror as she disappeared behind Pizza Hut. And she never came out the other side. At first, I wondered how the slowest woman in the world could have possibly given me the slip. Then I turned around and drove through the Pizza Hut parking lot.

The little gate, the kind that separates dumpsters everywhere from ne'er-do-wells who want to monkey with other people's garbage, was ajar. The woman and her stroller were standing inside the gate. She was looking around, exhibiting a self-consciousness she certainly doesn't betray in our courtyard.

As I rolled past her, she looked at me. She was definitely looking at me because her head turned to follow me. She couldn't have possibly been looking at my four-door Toyota. Chicks never check out the car. Never. She was looking at me to see me looking at her. She'd been caught standing beside a dumpster—which, in L.A., is not only no crime, but shouldn't merit anyone taking nearly this much notice.

A few days later, after she made another morning stopover, I got in my car and followed her around the corner. I pulled over and watched her disappear behind a cinder block wall in a parking lot. What was she doing in there? I had to know. So I turned on my engine and rolled forward until I saw her, sort of hiding between a building and a parked car...

...smoking a cigarette. Was this why she hid near the dumpster the other day? To sneak a cigarette?

Eventually, she loped through the Rite Aid parking lot to the far end, the area where no one parks. She found what looked like a small piece of cardstock paper in an abandoned shopping cart. She handed it to her baby, then took a detour through the alley. That's where I saw her, sitting on an abandoned couch, holding her head in her hand again as if life was too much for her. Then again, if my only source of entertainment was walking around Valley Village, I suppose I'd grow despondent too.

Finally, she forced herself to stand and left the alley and headed up the side street. I'd been following her for 40 minutes and she'd gone two blocks.

February 16

Today, around 5:00 in the afternoon, I head through the courtyard to the street. I get halfway... and there she is coming right at me.

I stop and deliver a very neutral "hi."

She smiles back. "Hi." And doesn't stop walking.

Her toddler freezes at the sight of me and decides I'm friendly, so she smiles at me. The woman tells her something in Russian, something along the lines of stop dawdling and come along. This whole time, I'm giving the woman my best what-the-hell-are-you-doing-here glare and she's ignoring it.

The two blow right past me and go look for Clyde's cats.

In the past week, I've been keeping an eye out for her, determined to put an end to these visits. I figure a stern tone of voice and a frown should be plenty. I've decided it would be silly to go to the trouble of hunting down some translator to find out how to say in Russian, "You know, lady, it's really inappropriate for you to be using our courtyard as a public park."

Meanwhile, I've been interrogating every neighbor I can find. I ask Paul, the genteel middle-aged neighbor, if he's ever seen her.

"Oh, yeah, I figure she's just a foreigner and doesn't know the rules of our society, so I say hello to her and let her roam around."

Perhaps I have a stick up my ass, but I think I'm entitled to a courtyard free of morose Russian broads.

February 21

She hasn't shown in a while. She's probably dying to see this place again. She does morning visits and late afternoon visits. I'll be here today during both of those periods. So I keep my window wide open so when I hear her squealing toddler coming, I can race out there to stop her.

Throughout the day, I leave my listening post to go for walks outside and check to see if she's coming—or if she's passed. I peer around the front edge of the courtyard so as not to scare her off; she *does* have to enter in order for me to tell her to leave. Until then, she's just another person on the sidewalk.

She never shows.

February 22

This morning, I wait again. I take a break, peer around the corner down the street... and she's coming.

I run back to my apartment. Should I be looking out the window? No. I can't see the sidewalk. I stand on my porch. And look. And wait. And a minute later, I see her coming down the sidewalk...

...and she keeps going.

Maybe another neighbor barked at her in the universal language of territorialism. Maybe she was late for a date with a lawn jockey in the next neighborhood. Maybe, like everyone here in the entertainment capital, we got too boring for her.

No matter, she is merely part of the ebb and flow of newcomers. She may have drifted away, but the tide will keep rising. There will be more people to overpopulate this building. There will be more strangers to wander the courtyard. Sometimes I think there will be so many people packed in so close here that even I will fall out of love with my highly imperfect hometown and move someplace quiet and less crowded.

Then, other times, I think I should just be thankful that I'm already living in a place that so many people want to move to, and that I don't spend my spare time sitting around in public with my head in my hands.

THESE ARE OUR CASINOS

In *The Day of the Locust*, an apocalyptic novella about Los Angeles, Nathanael West wrote a line that's always stayed with me: "Few things are sadder than the truly monstrous." He wrote this in 1939, before there were any casinos in Los Angeles. If he were here today, he might gloat.

The first time I had ever visited a local casino was about eight years ago. I was a tiny bit curious, since we only had—and still only have—a few of these around greater Los Angeles. But the main reason was because I had to pee. I was driving back from Orange County and decided zip into the Commerce Casino, only because it was right off the freeway. Plus, I figured it had nicer bathrooms than any gas station.

I don't remember much about the place. I don't even remember going to the bathroom. For something so unique to Los Angeles, it was amazingly unremarkable. All I remember about it was thinking that I'd probably never have a reason to go back.

Until two weeks ago.

I've been to plenty of casinos in Las Vegas, the city that can make anything fun, and some of those casinos can be depressing places. I had a feeling the potential for depression was much greater at the casinos in Los Angeles. I had a feeling that that potential could be even greater if one visited them during the holidays. So, on December 30 and 31, I went out at night just to see what our casinos—all eight of them—were like during the most wonderful time of the year.

My initial prediction was that if you lived in Los Angeles and really liked playing cards, these casinos would probably be your best options. I was wrong.

You'd be better off driving four hours to Las Vegas. If Vegas is the devil's playground, then the casinos in Los Angeles are the dog that the devil kicks after a bad day at work.

December 30

Hawaiian Gardens, I'm told, is a pit of a city and doesn't resemble Hawaii or gardens at all, but it was my first visit and the only thing I could see in the dark was the giant sign for the Hawaiian Gardens Casino. All the casinos had giant signs, which would have given their neighborhoods a Vegas feel except for the fact that there were no other similarly large signs anywhere near them.

The Hawaiian Gardens Casino is under a giant, hardtop tent. At 9 P.M., the parking lot was packed. It took me five minutes to find a parking spot, and about as long to hike all the way to the big top. Once inside, I was paralyzed by the sight. It was nearly wall-to-wall card tables. The gamblers appeared to have minimal interest in social interaction and even less in the aesthetics of their environment. And every seat was taken.

As soon as I walked in, some card player's elbow knocked a Styrofoam cup off a poker table right in front of me. The impact of the crash tore a hole in the bottom of the cup and water streamed out like dog pee. The card player didn't pick it up. He didn't even look.

I turned to the security guard standing by the door. "Does that happen often?"

He gave me a long look and a slow nod.

State gaming law prevents the casinos from being truly in the casino business. They are not allowed to profit from gambling losses, so they do not have games like slots, keno, or most of the other casino games where a player plays against the house. To be more accurate about it, they're in the cards, chips, chairs, tables, walls, and electricity rental business. They make their money by charging gamblers to use the facilities (so to speak). Private companies act as banks by hiring people who are grossly underpaid to sit at blackjack tables to give chips to and take chips from people who, according to a grossly underpaid buddy of mine who works as a banker at Hawaiian Gardens, are ungrateful, ill-mannered, and generally miserable.

I thought I'd look for my friend the banker and say hello. Sure enough, he was sitting not far away. It took me a while to get his attention because of the brace of people surrounding the tables. Plus, he was slumped to one side, holding his head up like he'd been waiting too long at an urgent care facility. When I finally got his attention, his face lit up as if my arrival was the best thing that had happened to him all night. It probably was. He doesn't speak highly of the job.

"I just thought I'd come down here and see what it was like."

"Go for it," he said. The sarcasm would hit me later.

This was not a fun place. No one looked like they were enjoying themselves. Not even people who were winning. My banker friend told me that some of them play for days at a time. Some of them looked scary. Every room looked largely the same. There was nothing for the non-gambler to look at except distant televisions showing sports highlights. The heavy security presence made the place feel more dangerous than safe.

I would soon learn that all our casinos are essentially like this.

I've never heard anyone speak highly of Compton, and the Crystal Park Casino will do nothing to help that. In the dark, I got off the 91 freeway only to end up on something resembling a bobsled run. The only way to get off that was to make a right onto a labyrinthine route to the self-parking lot. On the walkway to the casino, the palm trees bore paper signs warning patrons that the property was monitored by surveillance. I should hope so. I don't think it would have been hard for someone to pop out from behind one of those trees, demand my wallet, and flee in a getaway car.

The owners of this place have big expectations for it—or had them at one time. Inside the west side of the building was a large, dark room that was being used for exactly nothing. Further on was the hotel lobby, where the desk crew had no one to help. On a Saturday night. I went into the restaurant and was completely ignored. The tables were empty. A server walked by and I asked if they were open. She said yes—barely. And kept walking without looking back.

The active part of the casino was fair-sized and buzzing with gamblers. A poker tournament was going on in a nearby room. And unlike the Hawaiian Gardens Casino, this one had plenty of walking space. Although at one point, I nearly bumped into a guy crossing my path. I stopped to let him pass, and he thanked me by ripping a two-part fart right in front of me. And kept walking without looking back.

On my way back to the car, I noticed that the Blue Line train ran just beyond the back of the parking lot. I drove to that end to see if there was pedestrian access to the platform. There was. Can't entirely fault a place that encourages use of public transportation.

Gardena is the area capital of casinos. It has two, both conveniently located as close to the 110 freeway as possible without being outside city limits. First I hit the Normandie Casino, which likes to boast that it's the oldest casino in Los Angeles. This isn't exactly a brag, because it also happens to look like the oldest one too. However, with age comes character, and if it's one quality these places are begging for, it's character. Normandie's character lent an air of something vaguely resembling friendliness to the place. Vaguely.

After about 15 minutes of all that vague friendliness, I left. Then I saw motor homes in the parking lot. On another side of the building was another parking lot, also with a few motor homes. I had to know. I went back in and found a security guard, who explained to me that as long as the owners of the motor homes gambled a certain number of hours at the casino, they could park in the lot indefinitely for free as long as they moved to the other parking lot every few days. He also said the casino had a name for these people: VIPs.

Larry Flynt had already conquered the commercial potential of one vice, so a few years ago he staked a claim on another by opening the Hustler Casino not far from the Normandie. It's new and sleek with blues and purples and manicured grounds. Give Flynt style points for eschewing the glorified warehouse look of most of the other casinos in town. Now if only he could do something about attracting riff-raff. In the 20 minutes I was there, one guy was escorted out for being a sore loser and slinging his remaining chips across the room. (He yelled, "Fuck Larry Flynt and fuck his wheelchair" on the way out.) Another guy was calmly escorted from a blackjack table to a back room for questioning after security guards decided he matched the photo on a computer printout. If Larry Flynt's people wanted him out of there, I figure he was either a known casino cheat or a member of the Moral Majority.

Adding to the unsavory element, someone told me that this casino in particular is a popular place for criminals to end car chases because they think they can elude police by getting lost in the crowd inside. (Everyone in L.A. knows that when you're fleeing the cops, you drive to LAX because even police helicopters aren't allowed to hover near commercial airports. The only people who don't seem to know this are the criminals.)

After two hours of this, the casinos became a blur. I had given up looking for anything special about them. They were all depressing and uninviting and in unpleasant neighborhoods far from home and I had run out of ways to stop being curious about them. They had become merely the crowded one, the scary one, the old one, and the new one. By the time I got to Hollywood Park—which, naturally, is in Inglewood—all I could focus on were its most monstrous qualities, namely the word "CASINO" in gargantuan letters on the grandstand roof. My guess is that it was to advertise to people flying into LAX that there was something besides strip bars near the airport. Inside, there was a column of escalators leading to floor after floor of multi-purpose rooms. And they had horse races there. Other than that, there were lots of people playing cards.

December 31

I wasn't invited to any New Year's Eve parties this year. It happens. Off I went.

The Bicycle Club is in Bell Gardens, yet another one of our cities that sounds more festive than it really is. This casino is neither the largest nor the smallest. It is not the grungiest or the nicest. It is not the northernmost, southernmost, westernmost, or easternmost. All that nondescript, however, makes it the most comfortable—or the least uncomfortable. And, like with Hustler Casino, the architects of this place were shrewd enough to create a room that was technically outdoors so people could smoke in it but with a louvered roof so they could play cards and not get rained on.

Club Caribe in Cudahy is an anomaly as far as L.A. area casinos go. It is aberrantly small. The good news is that parking is incredibly easy. The bad news is that even on New Year's Eve, there were probably more exciting places in Cudahy. Let history record that on New Year's Eve, 2006, at about 9:30 at night, Club Caribe was a morgue. The place has a grand total of 12 tables—far smaller than any other casino in L.A.—and only three of them were in use. No one was using the pool table that took up about half the coffee shop, which itself had only a few patrons. There was one bartender, talking to one customer. The security guard looked like he was sleeping with his eyes open. I had a brief chat with a very nice woman who worked the change booth. The vending machine sold cigarettes and Reese's peanut butter cups. I left after about four minutes because I ran out of things to observe.

Which led me back to the Commerce Casino, where it all began with a pee eight years ago. It did not resemble what little memory I had of the place. It must have undergone an expansion. It was rather ostentatious. And loud. And like Club Caribe and the Bicycle Club, appeared to betray no indication that it was New Year's Eve and that midnight was only two hours away. All of which made me wonder if holidays or current events or anything else existed inside these places.

I went home to await midnight alone, where I didn't try to trick myself that I was having fun in an un-fun place, where I didn't try to ignore that it was New Year's Eve, and where things were neither sad nor monstrous.

This Is What Bigotry
Is Like Here

When I was in fifth grade, I went to an elementary school about half a mile away from my house. It was a nice integrated school, and the Los Angeles Unified School District saw to it that it was integrated by bringing dozens upon dozens of black students in on buses every day.

I also had a neighbor named Mary. She was a friendly woman with a husband and a grown son, and she would come out with her two little dogs every day. She also had a mild southern drawl that she only exaggerated when she asked me how I was doing. "How are you?" always came out, "Hah you?"

One day, she asked me about my school and if they had busing going on there.

"Yeah, they bus lots of other kids in."

"The niggers," she replied. There wasn't a bit of vitriol in her voice. She betrayed no more disgust than if she were describing a neighboring house in need of a paint job.

I don't remember what I said. I did wonder why she felt that way about kids she'd never met. I got along with them just fine. In fact, the only thing I knew about them was that they probably had to wake up a lot earlier than I did every day, probably got home from school later than I did every day, and I never heard any of them complain about it. Not once.

I also remember at that moment in front of Mary the nice neighbor trying not to act surprised. After all, I'd known this woman for over a year and never suspected that she was prejudiced. More than that, though, I remember fearing that if I said anything that indicated I disagreed with her contention, she might come down on me for being too friendly toward other races or disrespectful toward elders or God knows what. And I have no idea what compelled me to be that way. It had just been ingrained in me somehow—maybe the same way she'd been taught to hate black people.

In the amount of my life that I've lived in L.A.—that is to say, all of it—awkward moments like the one above do pop up. I'm thankful that they don't pop up often, which I take as a sign either that I don't keep company with bigots or that there isn't much bigotry here. Hopefully both. I can hardly control how much bigotry there is here, but I can control the company I keep.

I had occasion this year to make friends with a woman from Israel. Let's call her Miki. One night not a couple of months ago, Miki and I were out at a restaurant, whereupon I asked her about the whole Israel-Lebanon mishegoss, whereupon her dander got a bit elevated. She responded—and I quote verbatim here—"The only good Arab is a dead Arab. I don't care if the whole restaurant hears me."

Well, the whole restaurant was loud, so no one in there heard her. But I heard her.

I've heard that old expression about people sliding down in their chairs in embarrassment, but I always thought it was just an expression. For the first time in my life, I slid down in my chair. The fact that she'd already bitched to the waitress about her dinner—three times—just contributed to my discomfort.

I'm not Israeli, so I don't know what it's like to live in a little country surrounded by 700 million Arabs, more than a few of whom want to push all of Israel into the sea. But I've known many Jewish people. I've even known some Israelis. I'd never heard any of them advocate genocide upon Arabs.

Miki told me we should hang out some more. Maybe she likes me because I don't call her on being a fussbudget—or, it turns out, a racist. I haven't spoken to her since then. Her demanding streak in restaurants already makes me uncomfortable. But her open season on an entire race is too much for me to sit with.

We wouldn't be a large American city if we didn't have any racism, and Los Angeles has had its share. Like all cities, we try to ignore such scars on our past, but even the winners, if there are any in such a conversation, can't rewrite history quickly enough.

In the mid-to-late 1800s, Los Angeles was at its violent peak. At one time, it had more murders per capita than Tombstone. Chinese people here at that time were just trying to make a living when, in 1871, 19 of them were killed in what may have been our city's first race riot. However, egalitarians that the white rioters were, the riot happened on a street the locals called "Nigger Alley."

Eventually, we went from a group of outlaws who shot each other in the front to sophisticates who stabbed each other in the back. (I don't consider it an accident that this coincided with the arrival of show business.) Despite the fact that overt violence was no longer in vogue, the Ku Klux Klan flourished. Chapters popped up all over the southland, but they failed to do anything splashier than have rallies, cross-burnings, and the occasional murder. Naturally, the most high-profile Klan-related event that ever happened here occurred in show business. *The Birth of a Nation* premiered in Los Angeles in 1915, complete with actors dressed in sheets at the premiere festivities.

Since then, every generation got at least one major riot. In 1943, the zoot suit riots. In 1965, the Watts riots. My generation's riot came in 1992, after the jury in the Rodney King trial acquitted four white police officers of beating the hell out of a black man, first one night in real life, then night after night on television for a year. And I had my own run-in with African-Americans during those riots.

The night the mayor issued a curfew, I raced out from my home in the Valley just before dark to return a video. I parked my car, got out, and walked toward the video store. Two black people were walking toward me. What were they going to do to me, I wondered. Had they been watching the riots erupt on TV like I'd just been doing? Were they going to start their own riots in the Valley? Should I get back in my car? I figured the best thing to do was act like nothing was going on, so I just kept walking towards them.

They came at me... and walked past me as if nothing was going on that night. That was the only time I was ever afraid of black people. And all because of something else that was going on 20 miles away.

Los Angeles has a large Latino population as well, but the racial tension toward this community seems much different. I'm not saying that bigotry doesn't exist, but it seems less rampant toward Latinos than it does African-Americans.

Oddly enough, what I have heard is that Latinos are prejudiced against other Latinos. A Mexican-American I used to work with told me that if you're from Central America and you're passing through Mexico to the United States, you better pass fast. There is nothing Mexicans hate more, he said, than illegal Latinos. (I remember hearing once, but have been unable to confirm, that even on the soccer fields here on weekends, Latinos segregate themselves by country of origin.)

Black Angelenos, by contrast, continue to endure their share of bigotry. Whites-only beaches and swimming pools existed well into the first half of the 20th century here. During my father's day, so the saying went, it was illegal to be black in Glendale at night. I still hear likewise about Beverly Hills. There is still the occasional report of a cross-burning or some other un-neighborly incident aimed at a black family or a black community. And a friend of mine told me that she once ended up driving her friend's pimped-out VW Bug through Malibu and was pulled over by police, not for the way she was driving, but for what she was driving. So nervous were they about this very un-Malibu car that they walked up to it with their guns drawn. She told me that when the officers saw that she was white, they were astonished.

There are also the periodic incidents of police shootings of unarmed black people. The story seems to unfold on the news the same way every time: An unarmed black person is shot by one or more police officers, usually white officers. Black people in the community are understandably outraged. Community leaders hold press conferences and demand justice. The officers involved may be placed on indefinite leaves of absence or suspension while an investigation ensues. And then the news stops covering it. We never hear if the officers lose their jobs, if the city has to pay a civil settlement to the victim's family, if a law is passed or amended to help deter such shootings in the future. We never hear anything about it again, from which I can only conclude that nothing's done about it. Then one day it happens again. And we wonder why black people riot every 27 years in this city.

You may wonder what a straight male WASP knows about racism. The answer is not much. The above is only what I've heard and seen. I haven't gone around asking minorities what kind of racist incidents they've been involved in or heard about. I won't even ask the soccer players if they segregate themselves. It's not because of any preconceived notion I have about how people of other races feel about such inquiries. I don't have any fear that they will think I'm a jerk or an idiot for asking. What I have is a fear that they *might* think I'm a jerk or an idiot for asking. Even though opening up a dialogue is the best way to combat racism, I'd rather not if the dialogue ends with even one black person or Latino going around telling everyone what a dumb cracker I am.

Still, I think about bigots I've encountered over the years. The New York actor who told me that he wouldn't rent an apartment from Armenians. A contingent of Persians in Encino who were consistently mean to a white woman I know, or so she told me. My old southern neighbor Mary. Miki, the Israeli woman. They back up what my friend Ken said to me once about the most rotten people in Los Angeles: They all seem to come from someplace else.

Meet Mac Stenerup:
Biker with a Heart of
Cuervo Gold

Lest you think all my neighbors are namby-pamby, bothersome head cases, allow me to introduce Mac Stenerup, a type-A, bothersome head case. When he's not working as a driver for the movie studios, or riding the world's loudest motorcycle with his wanna-be Hell's Angels biker gang, or polishing the world's loudest motorcycle for hours at a time, or putting away beers by the pool.... Wait, I think those are the only four things he does.

I don't want to call Mac an asshole, only because he's never actually done anything to me. That and "asshole" is so clichéd. Because of this diplomacy, however, I'm able to have conversations with him about such things as how much he hates the neighbors or how much he likes the latest vehicle he bought. He's eager to oblige because these are the only two topics he's capable of discussing.

But what's curious about his neighbor rants is that they're always based on apparent truths that aren't common knowledge. One day, for instance, out of the clear blue, he went off on me about Spencer. "What a bum," he said. "Won't even drive his mother to the hospital." Don't know if "bum" is the fairest description, but the rest of it is true. How Mac knew about this, though, is beyond me. It's not like Mac and Spencer hang out. Imagine Don Johnson hanging out with Stan Laurel.

I ran into Mac checking his private mailbox at the nearby post office about a month ago. There are at least three people in our complex who have private boxes there and I find this curious, so I asked Mac why he has one.

"Oh, you got people sniffing around the mailboxes where we live. You got Paul sniffing around. And fucking Clyde. You know what that fucker did? He went around to all the notices—you remember those rent increases that Ken put on everyone's door a couple of months ago?"

"Yeah."

"Clyde went around and looked at all of 'em to see what everyone was paying. The fuck does he care. He's paying the cheapest rent of anyone. His wife's been living there, what, 30 years?"

I can understand Mac's indignation, but he strangely left out the part about how he came down the stairs drunk and angry one night and kicked his own mailbox door off. The fact that the locking mailboxes in our complex are so old that most of the doors permanently hang open in the unlocked position is hardly an excuse.

Mac went on. "I told him that if I caught him doing it again I'd punch him in the nose. What a bum. Guy hasn't worked an honest day in his life. I hate people like that. And he makes his wife take the bus because he doesn't fix her car. All he has to do is put a starter in it, but he won't do it because he's so fuckin' cheap."

Whew. This guy could start a column.

His disrespect for the neighbors extends to deeds as well as words. He has a parrot, which in itself is no crime, but he's averse to the idea of covering it at night to shut it up. I know this because one of the neighbors, whom we'll call The Confidante, has asked him to do this and he has always declined—angrily. He also has two dogs. One dog is such a sad, blind old pile of hair that once, upon crashing into my shoes, it simply walked over them like some ornery geezer who's grown tired of showing the world any respect. The other dog is a Chihuahua, a noisy, contemptuous rat straight from Satan's anus. Can't imagine where these dogs could have possibly picked up their demeanor.

As lunatic as the neighbors can be, I have the same neighbors Mac does and I don't despise them the way he does. So it isn't the neighbors. It's him. This vitriol is on display in his very walk. Every time I see Mac walk anywhere, he looks like he has to go give someone the finger. Whenever I say hi to him, I half expect him to say, "Not now, kiddo, I have to go give someone the finger." Recently, however, he had knee surgery, so he's been walking with a cane and what can best be described as an angry limp—like he has to go give his doctor the finger.

Then again, loath as I am to admit it, there are moments of solidarity with Mac. One night, I came home to find that some rude assmunch parked his car in front of our driveway, prompting me to call a tow truck immediately because no one else would have (and because rude assmunches piss me off). Mac happened to come out moments later and stood there on the sidewalk with me until the tow truck came and hauled the car away, a good half an hour, at least. If you hate what Mac hates, he'll commiserate—and on this night, anyway, stand by your side.

Of course, this is just me. I suppose I'd hate him if I lived as close to him as, oh, let's say another neighbor who tells me of his late-night drunken rampages, including a very special episode of Chez Stenerup in which he demanded that his live-in girlfriend, Brandy, tell him where she put his gun. This was followed by the sounds of him tearing his apartment up, presumably to look for it.

Mac went through a spell not long ago during which he took to carrying a baseball bat with him when making trips to the parking lot in back. I happened to see Brandy during one such trip, and when I asked her about it, she just smiled, shook her head, and said, "Don't ask." I guess he couldn't find his gun.

Yesterday, I saw Ken the landlord and thought I'd pick his brain to find out what's new with Mac since I'd neither seen him beached with his stereo by the pool nor heard his chopper fart down the driveway in a while.

"Got his car stolen," Ken said.

"When?"

"Monday night."

"Which one?"

"The coupe."

"Where was it? In back?"

"Not Monday night. It's usually in back, but that night they parked it on the street."

"How come I haven't heard his Harley lately?" I was hoping for a similar answer, I suppose.

"He got a new one. It's much quieter."

Then Ken told me that Mac's motorcycle gang either suspended him or threw him out, apparently for conduct unbecoming a weekend warrior mid-life crisis alcoholic. Biker gangs have codes of ethics. Who knew?

And I don't know where I'd heard it, or even if I'd heard it. Maybe it was something that registered subconsciously when I'd last talked to him. Maybe it was because he hasn't been around lately.

"Did he quit drinking?" I asked?

"For now," Ken said.

"You mean, he's tried this before?"

"Yeah, but never for this long."

A couple of months ago, I had a quick chat with neighbor Paul, the same Paul whom Mac accused of "sniffing around." Paul's a fiftysomething, part-time scenery painter for the studios. He tends to the plants in the courtyard. He puts out jugs of tea to brew in the sun. He's actually one of the more normal people around here, which is remarkable considering that he's the one with a steel plate in his head.

"I tried saying hello to Mac today," Paul said. "He just kept walking with his head down and didn't say anything."

"Yeah, he's an interesting character."

"True. But if it weren't for interesting characters, we'd have nothing to write about."

You don't say.

Meet Jezbo Vickers:
Professional Dumb-Ass

What do you get when you take Johnny Cash, replace that deep, Arkansas baritone with a nasally North Carolina twang, replace all artistic talent with the ability to be a human crash test dummy, replace the tour bus with a gaudy, white-trash van, and keep the alcohol abuse and craggy, middle-aged face?

One of my neighbors.

In the two years since Jezbo Vickers arrived, I have been unable to determine a single thing about him that can't be found in the "don't" section of a user's manual for a human life. Let us start with his drinking problem, for which I'd have more sympathy if he were actually making an effort to beat it. Tecate beer isn't just a drink to Jezbo. It's a way of life. It's a diet, it's a hobby, it's a personality quirk, it's a talking point. On occasion, he'll head out to his van with a beer and leave the can on the sidewalk before driving off, so it's also a signature—and, it would seem, potential evidence in court.

Jezbo owns too much stuff—nay, crap—and he doesn't know what to do with it. His crap must be seasonal because he's always moving it in and out of his apartment, to and from his parking spot, in and out of cars, going to and coming from who knows where. He's fond of going up and down stairs with arms full of his crap, invariably dropping something down the stairs. He manages to drop something only when he reaches the top of the stairs so as to maximize the amount of noise he can make with a single object, thus annoying his nearest neighbors as efficiently as possible. I know this because his stairs are on the other side of my living room wall. I can tell a dropped can of beer from a dropped can of silicon spray, a suitcase from an ice chest, exactly how many wire coat hangers just by the noises they make when Drinko McThumblefuck lets 'em go.

One particularly crappy item is his Indian statue, an atrocity so pitifully devoid of art or craft that it might not even be useable as firewood. Once, when it was the statue's turn to be moved out of Jezbo's apartment, it ended up only as far as the base of Jezbo's stairs—that is, right in front of my apartment.

The next morning, when I saw this fright, I caught Jezbo hunchbacking through the courtyard for a quick getaway and asked him if he planned on moving this thing.

"Yeah, I—I—I jes' need somebody to hep me."

I turned and went into my apartment. It disappeared later that day. He must have found someone else to help him. Or he dragged it out back and shot it.

Naturally, a man of Jezbo's temperance and obvious physical dexterity makes him ideally suited for his career as a stunt man. He'll disappear for weeks at a time to work on a movie, then show up for a while, then disappear again. Ken the landlord says that he was watching one of those "stunts gone wrong" kind of shows recently and in one segment, they showed some artful video of a guy bashing his face in by jumping a motorcycle over a big rig or something, followed by an interview with the poor bastard who did it. It was Jezbo. "He doesn't do stunts," Ken said. "Stunts require skill. What Jezbo does doesn't require any skill other than the courage to do something stupid."

Jezbo had a dog when he first moved in, a beautiful white German shepherd named Chuy. Chuy, put simply, was psycho. One day, he got hot and bothered by the sight of a cat outside, so he jumped through Jezbo's window screen—on the second floor—to chase it. The dog took a 10-foot header onto the cement, apparently on purpose, taking this whole "you can learn a lot about people by their pets" thing to a degree I never would have imagined.

Chuy hated me and everyone else on sight. Typical of an oblivious dog owner, Jezbo used to let it run around the courtyard without a leash. Once, when Chuy growled at me for the second or third time, Jezbo swatted it on the nose and explained apologetically, "I don't know why he's like that. Normally, he only dud that to black people."

The dog only growls at black people??

After the 10-foot header incident, Ken the landlord gave Jezbo an ultimatum: either Chuy goes, or they both go. So Jezbo and the dog got in Jezbo's van and disappeared. A few weeks later, Jezbo came back without the dog. I've always been afraid to ask.

Jezbo promptly replaced one dog with another. This one's name was Jolene, a used dishrag of a woman who had the manners of Jezbo's previous roommate but not its good looks. She was pushy, loud, forced a disingenuous friendliness on some of us who clearly didn't want it, and cursed behind the backs of neighbors who dared to call her on her behavior. She clearly wore the pants in

her relationship with Jezbo, as evidenced by the fights they used to have where she did all the yelling. But she was somewhat discreet in her psychosis. It was long after she was gone that I found out that Jezbo had to get a court order against her, apparently at the urging of Ken the landlord, who told him either she goes, or they both go. Even Jezbo knows the value of a good apartment in Los Angeles. People would rather get rid of their dog and their girlfriend than move.

Still, he appears unable to hold down enough employment to pay for his lavish lifestyle, which consists mainly of an inexpensive one-bedroom apartment, lots of golf and Tecate, and frequent trips back to North Carolina. So he shares his place with Garth, who I believe is Jezbo's ex-brother-in-law. Like Jezbo, Garth is exceedingly fond of Tecate, but Garth can hold down a job, doesn't have an excess of crap, and all the tenants seem to like him. What I can't figure out is why Garth needs Jezbo as a roommate.

Yesterday, as I was finishing this, I thought I'd been too hard on Jezbo. Chances are that he's doing the best he can. He'd long since sold the two extra cars he came here with, he hadn't done a major furniture shuffle in a while. Maybe he was settling into a regular work regimen on location somewhere. I was hoping to strike up a conversation with him, just to see what I could divine about the new Jezbo. When I saw him racing through the courtyard with his jumbo bag of golf clubs, I followed and spied him and a woman shuffling his crap into his truck.

The woman was Jolene.

Ken confirmed that Jezbo has been seeing her for a while now. "Didn't you tell him to get a court order against her?" I asked.

"Yeah," Ken said. "Leave it to Jezbo to nullify his own court order."

Even the non-philosophers in our apartment complex have wondered how on earth Ken ended up renting to this clown. The answer: He was referred to us by Mac Stenerup, the same tenant whom Ken once dragged into court for repeated failure to pay his rent (among other transgressions). When I asked Ken why he'd take a recommendation from Mac, Ken said of Jezbo, "He was only supposed to be here a few months."

It certainly seems like two years, but come to think of it, maybe it only *has* been a few months.

Welcome to Vernon, Only without the "Welcome" Part

In light of the recent elections and the particularly profound effect this round will have on our democracy, I'm reminded of a place where the democratic process has all the effect of a bum pissing in the ocean. The place is not some far-off dictatorship. It is a small city called Vernon. And it is literally next to downtown Los Angeles.

Like all major metropolises, Los Angeles has its share of industry. And just as they do in other large cities, we manage to shove it off to one side, look away, collect the business taxes, and hope the pollution it creates doesn't kill us. The majority of our industrial areas are south and east of L.A., in places with sexy names like Commerce, Industry, and Irwindale. Those cities, however, are incorporated. This means that in exchange for letting all those ugly, dirty buildings blanket their cities, they reap huge tax gains for *their* residents and infrastructure, while all of us get to breathe—and look at—their businesses' polluted air.

Then there is Vernon. Like those other cities, Vernon is a mecca for industry, filled with over 40,000 people—by day. Those 40,000-plus are employees. At night, the population dips a little bit.

To 91. Not ninety-one hundred. Ninety-one.

The lack of population, combined with the fact that some immediately surrounding areas appear to have the basic trappings of civilization, has resulted in a near-total evaporation of anything remotely resembling common culture. But

I didn't want to judge it without seeing it. So yesterday morning, I got up early to beat traffic down to Vernon to find out what no fuss was about.

Driving around Vernon is like hanging out with a guy who's always cranky and always has B.O. The entire city is abrasive on the eyes. Most buildings are models of architectural inanity, boasting irresistible combinations of gray and black, on streets with long stretches of sidewalks conspicuously absent of pedestrians. The place feels dark even in the daytime. It makes the neighboring City of Commerce seem inviting. I didn't think that was possible.

People who drive in Vernon have an aggressive streak that I found annoying at first. Then I realized that if you have to drive through Vernon, there's probably no reason to prolong the trip. City planners are on the same page. They helpfully discourage lookie-loos by dotting many of the major thoroughfares with "no stopping" signs.

What little culture it enjoys is a small assortment of chain restaurants and mom-and-pop stores—and at least one strip club. A place called Ben's General Store boasts that it is the home of the 28-inch pizza. A sign on another store marquee read, "Cristin your plants are ready please call." The intended small-town feel of such a personal message in such an impersonal place was a nice try, but hardly helped offset the sense of gloom that pervades the city. The easy availability of naked women and comically large Italian food didn't help either.

Word is, there are 26 housing units in Vernon. In two hours of driving around, I could only find about 17 of them. A few times, I'd chance upon a set of apartment buildings down this street or that street, but I knew I didn't have to look at the map to realize that those residences weren't in Vernon. What began as a much more populous city (the rules of city charterage require a minimum of 500 residents) has been gerrymandered down to a much more manageable few.

The question isn't why 91 people would live in a city that is so devoid of most things that make cities feel like cities. The question is why it is so impossible for outsiders to move in.

This brings us back to the election thing. Seeing as how Vernon is an incorporated city, members of the city council—the mayor, the mayor pro tem, and the three councilmen—are subject to a city vote every four years. If the number of candidates equals the number of seats available, the election is legally cancelled, thus saving the city the monumental ballot-printing costs for all those voters. Since most of the residents are city employees living in city-owned housing, potential challengers are either bribed or cowed into forgetting they ever heard the term "All politics is local."

In January, three men challenged the status quo. They moved into a cinderblock building, declared themselves residents, and filed papers to run for the city council election in April. The reason they moved into a nonresidence is likely a function of city housing construction rates, which just happen to mirror Vernon's population growth: zero.

This is undoubtedly the way city fathers like it. The fewer residents Vernon has, you see, the lower the chance of any of them having the temerity to run for city council, a fact the council learned the hard way in 1980, when the retiring police chief dared to try. He was promptly evicted from his city-owned house and disqualified from running for office since he no longer met the residency requirement. He countered by moving into the house of the president of the chamber of commerce, and the duo both ran for city council. In the end, the city administrator circumvented democracy when six votes—all of which happened to be cast for the challengers—were tossed out. The incumbents won by three votes.

This time, the council pussyfooted around with passive-aggressive tactics like turning off the power and charging the trio with converting a building without a permit. No luck. Then they turned to the old standby of eviction, thereby claiming the trio were no longer city residents, canceling not only their candidacies but their right to vote in the city, just for insurance. When a judge ordered the council to reinstate the three men as candidates in time for the election, Vernon's acting city clerk—the son of the city administrator who threw out six ballots 26 years earlier—outdid Katherine Harris: He refused to count the ballots.

Legal wrangling included legislation that would have transferred election supervision from the city to the county. It died in committee. Finally, last month, a Los Angeles Superior Court judge denied Vernon's claim of voter fraud. The Vernon city clerk opened the ballot box to find that the incumbents had won in a landslide. For real.

Which goes back to the question of why anyone would try to run for office in Vernon. The trio of challengers claimed that they simply wanted to take part in the political process. It wouldn't be such an implausible story if there weren't reason to believe that they were backed by the deposed treasurer of nearby South Gate, who may have been attempting some kind of coup—before his jail sentence for corruption as treasurer of South Gate, I mean.

As with everything else in life, all arrows point to the money. Once a city pays for everything it needs, it is a fair question to ask what it is supposed to do with the overage. Vernon's overage, according to an article published earlier this year in *City Beat*, runs at around $100 million. While Vernon spends plenty on its infrastructure, there appears to be plenty to spare. The mayor and his family are alleged to live in a two-story mansion in Hancock Park, although it can't be said for certain that Vernon paid for the house. A clearer observation can be made about the former city administrator, however. At one time, he drew a salary of $600,000 a year—believed to be the highest of any politician in the state.

The good news, unless you're on the Vernon City Council, is that the Los Angeles District Attorney's office is doing an ongoing investigation of corruption among Vernon city officials. The office doesn't have enough dirt to pass out indictments yet, but it may just be a matter of time. Until then, Vernon remains the home of the super-quick business license, the 1.1-million-dollars-per-resident tax base, and the make-believe democracy. And as far as Vernon's leaders are concerned, the rest of us can go piss in the ocean if we don't like it.

Author's footnote: Five days after this article was first published online, the Los Angeles District Attorney's office filed corruption charges against the mayor, his wife, his son, and the former city administrator.

THIS IS HOW WE DEAL WITH EARTHQUAKES

Wednesday morning, an earthquake measuring 3.4 on the Richter scale hit us. It was centered under the San Gabriel Mountains, near a little hamlet called Monrovia. There were no reports of damage or injuries, as the saying goes. And since it was only 3.4, chances are pretty good that no one even felt it. There was one thing about it, however, that resonated with the relatively few of us who heard the news.

It happened at 4:30 A.M.

People who've lived here long enough can tell you what 4:30 A.M. means in earthquake parlance. That's what time it was when the Northridge earthquake hit. (Okay, technically, it was 4:31 A.M.) Such a reaction is one of the signs of being a true Angeleno. Yes, you may know how to text message someone while driving, and you may begin practicing aloofness and isolation while complaining about how hard it is to make friends here, but you haven't been indoctrinated until you've lived through an earthquake big enough to get national news coverage. For many of us, our earthquake cherry was popped by the Northridge earthquake on January 17, 1994.

When it hit, most of us were sound asleep, but we have never forgotten what it was like and what happened to our property: We shook like hell and our homes became big fuckin' messes. That's what it was like. With the exception of the small percentage of buildings that partially collapsed and the small percentage of people who got injured, there weren't many variations on these stories.

Same with the stories about how people woke up 10 minutes before it happened or how their kitty cat was running in circles and humping the venetian blinds the night before. I got tired of hearing these stories after about three days. My favorite story was from a family friend in the west Valley, a woman who lived only about 10 miles from the epicenter. When we spoke to her not long after phone service was restored, she told us that she "thought she felt something" that morning, and noticed that a few knickknacks had fallen over. That was a great story. Not because it was exciting, but because it was unique.

Worse than the clichéd stories were the bullshit ones. I honestly believe that some people mistook the Northridge earthquake for the Tet Offensive. If they weren't showing off a cut on their finger or some other crippling injury, they bragged about how close they were to the collapsed this or the burned-out that. At the time, I worked with a guy who liked to tell people how close he lived to the epicenter. On a few occasions, I'd hear him on the phone, saying to some poor schmuck, "We were four blocks from the epicenter." The man lived three miles from the epicenter, for God's sake.

Then there were the overreactions. The suddenness and awesome force of these things have the power to scare so much crap out of people that some residents got in their cars and drove the hell away. A good number of others used the opportunity to stock up on earthquake supplies and Velcro all their belongings to the floor. This activity was at its highest right after the quake hit, that is, right after years of built-up pressure between tectonic plates had just been released. In other words, people took extreme measures of caution and preparedness at a time when the chances of a major quake hitting were at their absolute lowest.

The Northridge earthquake taught us all a few terms. "Red-tagged" was what we called houses and apartment buildings that were so damaged that the city refused to let residents back in. Everyone knew someone who lived in a building that got red-tagged. For a while after the earthquake, there was a disease called "valley fever." The shaking of the ground kicked up heretofore un-kicked dust that included a fungus that, when inhaled, could cause symptoms resembling the flu and lead to meningitis and even death. The disease had existed before, but no one had ever heard of it. And no one can explain why wind gusts before or since never seem to kick up the valley fever fungus. The 1994 earthquake also bore a phrase that has mysteriously become an overused term not just in earthquake conversation, but in testimonies about other natural disasters too: flying television. Whether it's an earthquake here or a twister in Indiana or a tornado in Florida, everybody gets hit by flying televisions. To this day, nothing else flies during natural disasters. Not remote controls, not books, not cans of tomato paste. Just televisions.

This being showbiz, even the earthquakes get makeovers. The epicenter of the Northridge earthquake was just west of Reseda Boulevard, between Saticoy Street and Roscoe Boulevard. This, of course, would put the epicenter in Reseda. But someone decided that "the Reseda earthquake" didn't have the same ring, and the fake name stuck. The spin doctoring didn't surprise me. What surprised me was that it wasn't the first time we'd done this. I recently found out that the Sylmar earthquake of 1971 had its epicenter about eight miles to the north-northeast, near Sand Canyon, an outlying rural burg in another valley entirely. But "the Sand Canyon earthquake" doesn't sound so menacing. It sounds more like a children's story.

Earthquakes are the only things left in Los Angeles that are both incredibly obvious and zero percent bullshit. But that didn't stop one local news outlet from deciding that we needed even more evidence after the fact. Not long after the Northridge earthquake, the news brainiacs at the NBC affiliate here came up with something revolutionary in earthquake coverage. It's called the "Seismo-cam." It consists of a video camera pointed at a seismograph. Whenever an earthquake hits, they're eager to show videotape of the seismograph needle jerking back and forth. It's even more exciting on their Web site. Any time you want, you can click on their Seismo-cam window, where you will be treated to a regularly updated Web stream of a straight line.

Since the terror of the event keeps fading in reflection, we've developed a cavalier attitude towards the inevitable next "big one." In fact, some of us are all but praying for it as soon as possible. We know from 1994 that when a big one hits, a small but substantial percentage of the city clinically freaks out and leaves permanently, and another percentage of would-be transplants is instantly dissuaded from moving here. This reduced demand for housing far outweighs the drop in supply caused by red-tagging, thus driving housing prices down. Show me someone who thinks this is a sign of misplaced priorities, and I'll show you someone who isn't faced with the reality of paying $1,545 a month for a decent one-bedroom apartment.

We're periodically reminded about the importance of earthquake preparedness. Like all messages we hear on a regular basis, we kind of ignore them. I'd guess the average Los Angeles resident has enough water stored to last him two days. However, no matter how unsure we are about the severity of the next big one, Hurricane Katrina made us quite certain about our government's inability to give a shit about us. That was a motivator for some of us to load up on a helluva lot of food and water. Like with any person with an excess of food and water, the urge to be generous takes over. I've had a few friends invite me to walk or ride a bike over to their houses (downed power lines will have closed all the streets) for food and water when the next big one hits. But they don't make it sound like a chance to huddle together to save each other's lives and boost morale when our city becomes an apocalyptic scrap heap. They make it sound like a chance to catch up.

Thus completes the circle of the earthquake deflowered. The importance of being alive inevitably shines a spotlight on the importance of having a life. Like with all the other days, Wednesday so filled us with our other priorities that there was little place for trifles like news items about a minor earthquake in the mountains behind a remote suburb.

Besides, we don't need any more reminders that the big one is coming.

Meet Clyde Langtry, Part Eight

Clyde Langtry is never short of an answer for anything. The lunacy, the hilarity, the irony, they're all bonuses. I just take notes. But there is more to a man than his lunacy, hilarity, and irony.

July 20

Today, I worked all day, then went running. And it's been hot lately, so by 7:30 in the evening, I was tired and sweaty as hell. Then I heard something I've never heard before.

"Hey, Joe!"

It was Clyde. He sounded like an angry drunk.

"Yeah?"

"C'mere!"

I walked up to his apartment door. As usual, it was open.

"Come in," he said.

I stepped over the threshold.

"You can come all the way in. I don't have a gun."

I stepped in a little more.

"Sit down."

"Clyde, I've had a 12-hour day. I just went running. I'm hot and tired and sweaty. I'm not going to sit down."

"Okay, okay. I'll try to keep it short. It's hard to explain to someone who's not a Scientologist. But basically I've had an epiphany. I talked to a guy today and it's like I'm a new person." I was tempted to tell him that this is kind of what they do in, um, therapy, which Scientologists find evil, but I didn't want to yank on his rug while he was dancing on it. "I've never been happier in my life. Everything makes me happy. I went out and bought a fan. That made me happy. I rearranged the shelves. That made me happy."

"Oh. That's great. Congratulations."

"I can never tell if you're being serious."

"You told me you were happy, I'm congratulating you."

Already, the lining of his new Happy Coat is beginning to fray. Like with everything else Clyde believes, he gets uncomfortable if his audience isn't completely sold.

August 2

Ken the landlord and I were standing in the courtyard. He was complaining about something, which Clyde mistook as an invitation to come out and join us. Actually, any time Clyde sees anyone in the courtyard for any reason, he takes it as an invitation to talk.

Clyde ambled out munching on a bowl of berries. "There's nothing like fresh strawberries. And these are organic."

Ken responded with his usual deadpan dispassion. "Organic doesn't mean what it used to."

Then Clyde did something he's never done before. The happiest man in the world lost it. He threw his now-empty bowl and spoon into the bushes, but gently.

"Dammit, Ken! Why the hell do you have to go and say stuff like that? You don't know what you're talking about."

It's worth noting that Clyde was actually right about something. If Ken's diet is any indication, Ken's knowledge of organic foods couldn't fill a thimble. It's also worth noting that Clyde took Ken's grossly uneducated opinion so personally.

Ken was so sorry about it that he let out a little laugh and walked away.

"I can't stand that guy," Clyde said. "He doesn't know what he's talking about and he tries to bring me down."

This was the closest to going postal I've ever seen Clyde Langtry go. I wasn't sure what he was going to do next.

Then he did it.

And it freaked me out, but gently.

He became calm.

"So, how you doing?" he said, as if nothing had happened.

"I'm fine."

"The job going okay?"

"Yeah. Tell me, how is it that a few seconds ago you were so angry, and now you're so calm?"

"I'll tell ya' how. You ever see babies, how they're crying one minute and happy the next?"

"Yeah."

"That's how. I live in the moment, just like babies do. If they're upset, they cry, then they move onto the next emotion."

August 16

As I got home from the office today, Clyde summoned me. He must not have had the kind of father who needed a scotch first thing after work or else he'd hit mommy.

"Come on in. I wanna show you something." Never before has Clyde made such an offer.

He took me into his bathroom to show me that he's done nothing. He merely told me what he was going to do: install an adjustable fan in the window to keep the bathroom cool. Then he said, "Come into my bedroom for a minute."

This wasn't a homosexual come-on. The man is as sexless as Barney Fife. As usual, he just wanted to brag about stuff and had no one to brag to.

"This is where it all happens." He pointed to his desk. Covered with papers, computer on. "I'm a financial expert. I understand international markets. I trade online all the time. I made thirty-one hundred dollars this morning. But don't tell anybody." I told him I wouldn't.

He added, "I'm working on a business plan. I'm gonna make a hundred million dollars in five years. Don't tell anyone about that either."

"Okay."

"You think I should buy a house?"

"I'd think with a hundred million dollars, you could buy at least two or three houses."

His room had the wood paneling that had been there since the last residents had abandoned the place decades ago. Then again, Clyde and Priscilla may be the apartment's original residents. One wall was nothing but notebooks and books on tape. Floor to ceiling. They had a full-size bed, no frame, suitable for two short people. Clyde and Priscilla aren't short.

The bedroom had no indication that a woman lived there. Not one.

In that vein, I want to make a point of mentioning that Clyde has lately made a point of mentioning how much sex he used to have with other women. He told me, and he told my neighbor, The Confidante, a nice, sane female neighbor who, like me, can't imagine why he'd be so compelled to go around telling everyone this—and, like me, is way out of his league. Whether all this alleged sex was before or after he got married is immaterial. The fact that he even claims as much proves either that he's delusional or that he ran across a lot of dumb, blind women in his day.

September 12

For the second night in a row, I've sat on my porch in the evening with both a beer and a glass of wine. I want to see if this will compel Clyde to come out of his apartment and tell me that he's barely touched alcohol since the '60s. You may call this alcoholic behavior. I call it Clyde-baiting.

Tonight, he came out to whistle for one of his cats to come home. Last night it was Priscilla's job; tonight it was Clyde's job. He and Priscilla come out every night and whistle for their cats repeatedly, apparently not realizing that the cats will come home when they're hungry. If I lived in Clyde and Priscilla's apartment, starvation is the only thing that would make me want to come back.

I held up both my beer and my glass of wine to make sure Clyde saw me. He did. And he muttered, "Damn cat's a pain in the fuckin' ass." Then he wheeled and went back inside.

For the second night in a row, the cats—the two that require calling, that is—came out of the bushes and walked up about two minutes after Clyde went in. The routine appeared to be so old that they didn't even look at each other and say "duh."

September 13

Pay dirt.

Once again, I sat out front, nursing a beer and my last glass of wine. Clyde trotted out. After our hellos, he said, "You got a beer there. That's good."

That's good? What have you done with Clyde? My Clyde?

"Say, Clyde, you know how you were telling me that you talked to a guy a couple of months ago and you said you had a revelation?"

"Yeah." His face contorted a little. He may have been confused, but more likely, he was thrown by the fact that someone was actually asking him something specific about himself. Usually, he doesn't need to be prompted.

"You said you were never happier. How's that going?"

"Aw, yeah, that. That didn't last."

"Oh? Why not?"

"It was unstable."

"The happiness was unstable?"

"Yeah. It's hard to explain to someone who's not a Scientologist. The mind plays tricks on you. The mind is its own universe. It's different from the brain. The mind and the brain are two completely different things. Anyone who thinks otherwise is a total fuckin' idiot."

Clyde calling other people idiots. I didn't even have time to love it.

"What kind of beer you drinking?" he asked.

"Whitbread. I found it at Trader Joe's."

"I bought a beer recently. One of those English beers. Whaddaya call them?"

"English beers."

"I can't remember the name. It tasted..." He made a face that matched his voice.

"Wait a minute. You bought a beer?"

"Yeah, I just felt like having one."

A moment later, he was off to get his cat, Misty. She likes to hang out by the pool, then likes to have Clyde carry her in. She's not crippled. Clyde's just codependent.

He reappeared. "Let me put Misty inside and put a shirt on."

Please.

He came back with a shirt—and a chair—and sat on my porch next to me, and did what he does best, what he's proven to me in these five years of being his neighbor is his greatest talent: He prattled incessantly and said nothing, most of it about the Church of Scientology. Occasionally he peppered it with, "It's hard to explain to someone who's not a Scientologist." The fact that he's been trying for five years and I still don't understand any of it was lost on him.

He reminded me about his ability to intuit people and situations, apparently unaware of the fact that he regularly proves the opposite. For instance, the other day, his upstairs neighbor told me that he called to thank her for being so quiet over Labor Day weekend. It didn't occur to him that she'd been out of town the whole time. This is also the same woman to whom he recently said, "I bet I can guess something about you. I bet you have a boyfriend." She replied, "You could not be more wrong."

In other words, nothing about Clyde has changed. Nothing. Happiness is as slippery to him as it is to the rest of us, and he hardly has all the answers to everything. But it's hell getting him to admit as much.

After an hour of this, I stopped him and asked him point blank what steps he's going to take to find happiness, to find his way out of this funk.

"There's this class I need to take. It's an objectivity course. It's called an objectivity course because it's objective, it's designed to get you out of your head."

"Clyde, you told me this exact same thing months ago."

"I know, I know."

"So why haven't you done it?"

"I don't know."

MEET OUR *REALLY* CRAZY PEOPLE

Saturday afternoon, I was minding my own business, driving down a residential street, below the posted speed limit, when I saw a guy throw a rock at a car. I played it cool and kept driving toward him. He pulled on the door handle, banged on the door, and displayed more general fury. Even as I drove right past him, he didn't seem to care that I—and who knows how many others—were watching this spectacle. That indicated to me that this was probably his car and he had locked his keys in and didn't have an auto club card, so he decided vandalism was the next best alternative.

Even if this was his car, his public display of rage was a disturbing sight, so I called the police. I described him and gave the location, just as the guy was storming away. So I followed him for a couple of blocks. Sure enough, a few minutes later, a police officer drove by, saw the guy, and stopped him to have a conversation. The guy's animated gestures suggested that he was stuck in some unfortunate situation and was going crazy trying to find the guy who had his keys or something. Whatever the case, the officer believed him. I was even close enough to hear the officer say, "Well, I hope you figure it out" or something. And the policeman left.

I bring this up because it reminded me that I hadn't seen such an open display of crazy in a while. True, there is a fine line between being crazy and being angry to the point of irrationality, and it can be hard to tell the difference. But the outward spectacle is often hard not to watch. Herewith, then, are a handful of brief tales of some of the more colorful characters I've seen here.

A few years ago, I was walking out of Cost Plus to my car, which was parked around the corner. Ahead of me, I saw an older woman sitting on a bench. She was mumbling to herself. When I passed her, she looked up at me, still mumbling. I couldn't make it out, so I leaned in.

Then her voice rose and she looked at me. "You're nothing! You're pathetic!" She had long whiskers growing out of her chin.

Instinctually, I kept walking—and didn't feel insulted, which was something of a personal victory. There was a time when I would have thought, "Is it that obvious?"

After I passed her, I saw a young woman walking my way. As she approached, I muttered to her, "Crazy person ahead. Crazy person ahead." I didn't make eye contact with her, so I couldn't tell if she heard me. And I didn't look back, so I don't know if she steered clear of the older woman or not. Looking back, I may have muttered it so incomprehensibly that she may have thought I was the crazy one.

In 1996, I started a new job in West Hollywood. I'd been there all of a week when I decided to have lunch at the Subway down the street. It was crowded. A few patrons ahead of me, a very angry black man angrily ordered a sandwich and angrily insisted that the sandwich maker not skimp on the ingredients, goddamnit. He made matching hand gestures as the employee worked, pantomiming piling on the meat and shaking the salt and pepper. He was making so much noise that it was impossible to ignore him, although the whole room seemed to be doing a good job. It may have been out of fear; despite his average build, he looked like he was one wrong word away from whipping ass on the next person who crossed him.

The customer in front of him, a nicely attired white woman, made a brisk attempt to grab her sandwich, pay for it, and get the hell out of there. She must have been a bit too brisk with one of her movements, because the man suddenly stuck his face into the back of her hairdo and barked something like, "Whatchoo say to me, you white bitch?" He yelled something else at her too. It may have included the word "cunt," but I don't want to accuse the guy of being dirty.

She paid for her food and got the hell out of there. I also recall him catching another black man eyeing him, to whom he yelled something like, "Whatchoo looking at me for? White man keeping you down. I ain't." Then he paid for his food—I think—and stomped out onto Sunset Boulevard.

At that time, I didn't like West Hollywood, and rarely visited it. My lunch that day did nothing to disabuse me of that feeling.

In 1999, I ran an art gallery in Santa Monica for a guy who was out of town for a long weekend. Since it was buried inside a shopping center, the gallery got very few window shoppers, so I had nothing to do for four days. The visitor who stayed the longest was the building's window washer. He came in and started chatting me up about politics, quickly segueing into why we should support the Republican Party. It was, he explained, because the Democrats were in league with the Communists to take over the world. After a few minutes, I realized he had a huge capacity for babbling. That's when I started timing him to see how long he could go. He went 26 minutes before stopping to ask me a question—plus the few minutes before I began timing him.

I was tempted to ask why a middle-aged guy who washed windows for a living would side with a political party that was generally indifferent to the country's window washers, but I had some sitting on my ass to do and didn't want any more distractions.

At a coffeehouse several years back, a young woman in a tennis outfit—white top, little white skirt, white tennis shoes—came in. She had crossed the street apparently without looking, nearly getting hit, someone later told me. When she got to the front of the line, she didn't order. Her eyelids fluttered and she kind of listed like a tall vase that got bumped and might or might not fall over. The guy behind her put his hands up to catch her, if need be. Then her two "friends" came by and said they'd take care of her. They escorted her out and disappeared.

When I was a teenager, I worked one day—and evening—at the Rose Bowl for some marathon concert featuring four bands. I carpooled with a friend who ended up working as an usher. Because I was a ticket-taker, I finished about three hours before he did, so I went to the car and just waited while the last band was performing.

Around 9:00, a slow-moving, skinny, marginally functional guy in his 20s came tottering out of the dark and right up to me.

"Hi, I'm Dave," he muttered.

"Hi, Dave. I'm Joe," I muttered back. We shook hands. I was happy to indulge him. There's not much to do in the Rose Bowl parking lot at night.

He stood there for a long silence as he tried to keep his eyes open. Then he said, "I'm fucked up." I told him I was sorry to hear that.

He asked me for a ride to his house. I told him I didn't have the keys to the car and my friend and I weren't going his direction anyway. I pointed him towards the front of the Rose Bowl where the buses and taxis congregated. He disappeared into the dark.

I knew a perpetually unemployed actor who lived out of his car and spent all his spare time at local coffeehouses with his dog, a Boston Terrier named Rebel. The guy, Michael, insisted that his dog was just misunderstood. The only person who misunderstood the dog was Michael. Everyone else quickly figured out that the dog was the reincarnation of Genghis Khan. It hated people on sight and growled at everything. Michael volunteered periodic stories about Rebel biting someone, but never acknowledged that his dog was dangerous. He would trot the dog out to say hello to people and let him sniff their pant legs. Every time Rebel sniffed me, he would get about two feet away and growl, while Michael stood behind him with a shit-eating grin on his face. I would always sit real still, try not to show fear, and murmur, "Michael, get that fucking dog away from me. Michael, get that fucking dog away from me."

As if Rebel weren't crazy enough, one night Michael gave him some leftover steamed carrots and Rebel scarfed them like they were slices of roast beef. I swear to God, I witnessed it with my own eyes.

One day, I saw Michael with a cast around his wrist. I asked him what happened. He explained that Rebel tried to lunge out of his car at a couple of people walking down the sidewalk, and when Michael tried to stop the dog, it attacked him.

"So where is Rebel now?" I asked.

"Oh, I had to put him down."

Meet Jezbo Vickers, Part Two: Drunk and Drunker

Oh, dear God.

You know, I'd like to think of myself as a civilized person. I don't comb my hair and I haven't used my steam iron in years and I don't shave every day, but seriously, I have manners. I don't think it's too much to ask the same in neighbors.

It is.

Just to give you his rap sheet—er, um, I mean his background—Jezbo Vickers, alias Drinko McThumblefuck, he of ageless liver via natural selection of centuries of devout Carolinian tosspots, alighted upon our heretofore generally peaceful complex about three years ago. No sooner did he arrive than I stopped getting hot water in my shower. In an effort to get hot water going in his flat, Jezbo had turned the knob down on my water heater.

Due to Jezbo's bad credit, Ken would only rent to Jezbo if he supplied triple the deposit in case he, by some shocking twist of implausibility, should be anything less than punctual with the rent. Naturally, Jezbo used this as a license not to pay rent for two months.

Ken still won't admit that he made a mistake by renting to Jezbo.

Now the only permanent visitor Jezbo has is Garth, who may or may not be his ex-brother-in-law. Since Jezbo disappears for weeks at a time—perhaps because he's lost, but that's just speculation on my part—Garth is the only permanent resident of the shared apartment. Garth, an out-of-shape, roll-with-the-punches kind of guy, is an overly polite and nice fellow, his choice in roommates and ex-relatives notwithstanding.

Even together, they have trouble with things as simple as mail. Flawed as their system is, it's elegant in its simplicity: Jezbo collects the mail and leaves it in a pile because most of the mail isn't for him. Garth doesn't look at it either. Then, one of them goes through it eventually. The only problem from the neighbors' standpoint is that the post office doesn't always deliver accurately. As a result, Jezbo and Garth might sit on someone else's mail for a while. Once, they went through their pile to discover that they had a piece of my mail. Two months after it had been originally delivered, they gave it to me with something resembling coffee stains on it. Not to worry. It was only a credit card bill.

I do have conversations with Jezbo, which are like little trips to a quieter, simpler place. His North Carolina drawl is reminiscent of, well, nothing. It is unlike any accent I've ever heard, even in *bad* southern movies where such accents stray all over the aural map. But our little chats carry me away to an oddly familiar place, a place where responsibility isn't even an afterthought. Where shiftlessness is a priority, where alcohol flows like braggadocio at a commercial audition, and where the conversation inevitably turns to trucks and barbecues. The man is the missing Duke of Hazzard.

One night, I was minding my beeswax on my front porch, enjoying a glass of wine, when Jezbo gimped through the darkness. He stopped when he saw me.

"What'cha' drinkin'?"

"It's a cabernet."

"Lemme have some of that." He was too drunk to remember that just because we're neighbors doesn't mean we're friends. Nonetheless, I went in, got another glass, and poured him a small drink-up-and-beat-it sip. He had a snort and said, "What's the name of this?"

"Charles Shaw."

"Who?"

"Charles Shaw. Haven't you heard of it?"

"Nuh-uh. Where you get it?"

"You can buy it by the case at any Trader Joe's in town." Food is something he picks up at a drive-through or pours out of E-Z aluminum dispensers marked "Tecate." Why should I be surprised that he's never heard of Charles Shaw or Trader Joe's?

He slugged the rest, demanded more ("Go ahead and fill it up all the way this time"), and proceeded to submit a tale about how he and one of his wives used to visit a local winery because of his fine palate for quality vintages. By the time the story and the glass were done, he asked, "What's this called again?"

"Charles Shaw. It's only two dollars a bottle at Trader Joe's."

"Two dollars? I could get fucked up on that shit."

Which leads us to the occasional visit by the police.

I'd like to reemphasize at this time that Garth is an unfailingly polite man. Every time I see him, he asks me how I'm doing in a way that indicates he may mean it. Whenever I pass him barbecuing out back, he always offers a serving of whatever he's broiling. That said, he also has a bit of congenital fuck-up in him.

One weeknight last month, Jezbo and Garth made their way to The Studio Suite to sing themselves some karaoke and have themselves a good old time. Garth met a woman who asked him to take her home, apparently because two other gentlemen were harassing her. So Garth took her home, then made the mistake of returning to the bar, whereupon the aforementioned gentlemen beat the hell out of him. To make the evening fancy, Jezbo came home early to entertain a woman who liked to be entertained, as evidenced by her howls of laughter—all goddamn night.

The thing that eventually woke me up for good was a calm conversation in the courtyard among several people. I peered out my venetian blinds to see Ken the landlord and six police officers talking down Jezbo and Garth after their fun evening. Garth's face had been pummeled to the point of puffiness. He had something wrapped around his head to stop the bleeding. I think it was a bandanna, but it may have been underwear. The whole thing was a bit of a blur. It was 4:30 in the morning.

I put on some pants and went out to listen. All I can remember were pieces. It should be noted that Jezbo was so drunk that he couldn't quite answer anyone or keep up with the conversation. He would just toss back whatever fact he could remember about the evening whether or not anyone had asked for it.

Officer: "The best thing you can do now is settle down and go to bed."

Jezbo: "That woman at the bar said she was a cop."

Officer: "You were making a lot of noise."

Jezbo: "We thought we was having a good time."

Ken: "Everyone in the building could hear you. See all the lights on in all the apartments?"

Jezbo (to me): "Could you hear us?"

Me: "Yes."

Jezbo: "You shoulda' said something. I didn't know you was sleepin.'"

Me: "It's 4:30 in the morning. I'm usually sleeping at this hour."

Jezbo: "I'm up there and Garth come in and he goes into the bathroom and he coughing up blood." If you haven't figured out by now why Jezbo continued to drink with his noisy tart instead of taking his friend to the hospital, you never will.

A moment later, Garth apologized to me and went upstairs, and the police apologized to me and left. Ken the landlord, for reasons I'll never understand, kept talking to Jezbo. Jezbo kept answering like a blind man trying to shoot ducks.

Ken: "You gotta stop doing things like this."

Jezbo: "We didn't go to The Studio Suite first. We went to The Foxfire Room."

Ken: "It's the whole bar scene. It attracts a bad element."

Jezbo: "Well, I guess I cain't go do karry-okie no more at all then, can I."

Ken: "That's not what I'm saying. It's the mentality of the people at places like that. Some of them are just violent and looking for a fight."

Jezbo: "They said Garth got hit with a shovel."

Ken: "Just go upstairs and go to bed. Those cops are out there sitting in their cruisers waiting for one of you to try to drive drunk somewhere and if you do, they're going to arrest you for DUI."

Jezbo: "They was just here. They coulda' arrested me then."

Ken gave up after a few minutes and left. Whenever I run into Ken anywhere, he always spends a moment to talk to me to tell me what's new. This time, he just walked away. He didn't say a word to me. He didn't even look at me.

The next afternoon, I happened to see Jezbo boot-heeling it down the stairs. I took a long look at him to see if there was any acknowledgment of the havoc he and Garth had wreaked the night before.

"How ya' doin'?"

He flashed his really false teeth at me. "I'm fine. I ain't the one who got beat up."

Meet Our Criminals

I don't know what it is about greater Los Angeles that encourages oblivious-ness and short-sightedness, but no matter how much bad news about our city that gets heaped upon us, most of us react either by building a tolerance for it or ignoring it. This helps us feel fortified against the awful fates that await us. For example, our geologists insist that, within the next 20 to 30 years, a major earthquake is likely to hit, bringing with it a series of problems of such enormity and general badness that they may dwarf those of any natural disaster that's ever struck the United States. Despite the plausibility of such horrors, we ignore them and figure—though don't articulate—that they can't happen, if for no other reason than that they're too inconceivable for us to comprehend.

While we wait for that bad news, however, there is always crime.

If you measure crime by what's reported on local TV, you'd think it's mostly murders, kidnappings, and car chases, and that they're mostly in South Los Angeles, a region that so many of us never visit that it might as well be Detroit. No one takes comfort in the crime or the reporting of it, but a diet of this kind of "journalism" gives those of us outside of South Los Angeles the false security that the rest of L.A. suffers far less crime, even though we all know there's plenty of crime to go around. And despite the plausibility of crime happening to us, we ignore it beyond ritualistic use of locks and alarms. Hell, if we can ignore an eventual earthquake of holocaustic proportions, we can certainly take our chances that criminals will hit other people instead of us.

That said, I'd like to introduce you to a few of the criminals I've encountered and chosen to ignore and hope they'll never show up again. Since they don't want to be caught, however, I'm afraid I don't have many names. At least you have to give the anonymous criminals props for the refreshing quality of not trying to promote themselves.

My apartment building's driveway is between my building and a large building next to mine. From the balconies next door, our driveway must look like a river in New Jersey, because someone next door likes to throw their cigarette butts into it. A few weeks ago, I heard a guy outside shouting into his phone. I went to the window and saw the shouter, a guy on a second floor balcony. He was also smoking. So I plopped into a chair to watch him until his cigarette was done. Sure enough, he flicked it into our driveway. He even pulled the very wienie maneuver of tossing it at an angle to make it look as if it had come from another balcony. I called the property manager and told her what I saw. I haven't seen a cigarette butt in our driveway since.

Maybe it's just a difference in styles, but Ken the landlord had his own way of solving the cigarette butt problem. He once collected all the butts in our driveway, put them in a plastic baggie, filled the bag with water to give it some heft, tied it closed, and chucked it hard into the scofflaw's balcony. He said it smashed into the sliding glass door and exploded all over the place. I don't think Ken knows better than I do. I just think Ken has been the landlord for a long, long time.

Ken isn't the only one who can technically be labeled a criminal. My neighbor Mac is not an out-and-out criminal. He's just a guy who wants his way all the time, and his way occasionally involves breaches of the law. Luckily for the rest of us, he doesn't have a yen for theft or recreational vandalism. He sticks to stuff that he's less likely to get nabbed for, things like noise pollution, public intoxication, and, when he feels it's necessary, hitting his girlfriend. And that's just the stuff I know about.

There is also the issue of his stolen Mercedes coupe. He used to park it in the back all the time. The one night he parked it on the street, it got stolen. I'm not saying he engineered anything, but he wasn't very discreet about the profit he made from the insurance settlement.

In fairness to Mac, there is some legitimate car crime here. Little piles of broken glass regularly materialize at random spots on the street, the unmistakable sign of an overnight car break-in. My neighbor Missy says that her car got broken into a week after she moved in here nine years ago. A former neighbor whose parking spot was next to mine had her car broken into last year. Of course, her car was a Mercedes, and mine wasn't. Some of the best theft insurance in Los Angeles is merely owning a car that isn't expensive or perpetually waxed and shiny.

My neighbor Katie says someone broke into her hatchback a couple of years ago, but the thief must have been some freezing cold homeless guy, she thinks, because all he took was some winter clothing she had in the back. (Yes, people can freeze in L.A.) She also thinks he was a meth addict who was tweaking at the time because a lot of her things had been taken out of her glove compartment and arranged neatly on her seat.

Then there are our taggers. We have plenty of them all over the area, and every few months or so, one of them drops by our apartment building for a showcase. But, like actors, taggers eventually give up because, like actors, most of them start to look the same after a while. The only difference is that it's easier for taggers to get arrested in this town.

Despite the competition and no discernible profit margin, a few of our taggers prosper. Someone named RHC seems to be doing well. In addition to nailing our wall last year, he's been hitting walls, curbs, and sidewalks all over the hood. His buddy, SPLIT, hit our wall on the same day as RHC last year. But I haven't seen SPLIT since then. Maybe he got discouraged because Ken painted over it right away. He shouldn't let one landlord's diligent graffiti clean-up get him down. Of course, SPLIT didn't help his chances by writing his name *on top* of the wall where no one could see it.

He should take a lesson from MTS. Here's another guy who nailed our wall once, but in big black letters like you're supposed to. But Ken the landlord painted over him immediately, too, which, to a tagger, is not unlike an actor's show getting cancelled after one episode. Haven't seen MTS since.

Getting back to the cigarette tosser, the recent events compelled me to keep sitting by my window to see how he would respond after having been tattled on. While I was at the window last week, some guy walked down our driveway. Understand, *nobody* walks down our driveway except a few of the tenants. But on this day, a squat Latino dude with baggy shorts and a shaved head waltzed on through. Not sure what he was looking for, but I doubt it was a shortcut to Pacoima.

I stuck my head out my back door and watched him head for our parking lot. He chatted away on a cell phone. Then he spun around and may have caught a glimpse of me. I ducked inside, then went out back the other way to "empty the trash." Didn't see him. Didn't see anyone. I'd never been so aware of how quiet it was back there. Even during the daytime. I walked across the lot to my car to see if he'd broken in. No signs. Then I heard the pedestrian gate clank open. I raced back to see the prowler running through the courtyard to the sidewalk. I followed him to watch him walk all the way down the street and disappear around the corner. I was hoping a police car would happen to drive by. No luck.

So I went in to call the police. On page one of the White Pages is a bunch of phone numbers for law enforcement, including, in big digits, 911. I couldn't figure out a way to justify a short, chubby Latino guy waddling down the sidewalk as an emergency, so I called the number for sheriff-slash-police in the San Fernando Valley. The number was out of service.

Then I flipped to the city agency pages and looked under police. There was a grand total of three phone numbers: 911, hearing-impaired, and Foothill Division. When I called the Foothill Division and explained that I only needed the phone number for the North Hollywood Division because it wasn't in the White Pages, the woman on the other end said she gets calls like mine all the time.

For the Recreation and Parks Department, the White Pages lists 17 goddamn phone numbers for your calling pleasure. But it lists only one police station.

Someone at the North Hollywood Division took my description of the prowler and said they'd send a patrol car around to look for him. She also asked me why I waited so long to call the police. I told her I had to follow the guy to see what he did and which way he went. I left out the part about how I would have called sooner if the North Hollywood Division weren't so obsessed with its privacy that it insisted on having an unlisted number.

The woman on the phone said she'd send a car around to look for the prowler. I haven't seen him again, and no one here has been broken into since then, but I haven't noticed an increase in police patrols either.

In order to get a better perspective on crime in L.A., I began asking people at random about their experiences. The very first guy I asked told me that his car got broken into four times and he got held up at gunpoint, all of which happened in otherwise nice neighborhoods not far from mine.

I decided not to ask anyone else.

WAIT

Meet Our Religious People

I was at a party last weekend where someone told me what happened to her and her husband when they moved to North Carolina. When the neighbors came over to visit, it was only minutes before the woman and her husband were asked, "So, what church do you attend?"

The story was told to illustrate how important religion is considered in North Carolina. I think it can be construed with equal fairness how unimportant religion is considered here. Of all the Angelenos I know, and I'd like to think that I know a nice cross-section of them, I don't know what religion most of them are, or if they even attend any kind of services. You'd think people living in a region where three of the valleys are named for saints would have a little more respect for God.

It's not that religion isn't cool to us. It just doesn't fit with many of us. Posers and materialists can't show off much in an environment as passive and conformist as church. Players can't find easy lays at church; not only is it difficult to hit on women in the daytime, but the scene is populated with too many ethically upright women. Entertainment industry types can't make connections at church. I've never, ever heard any story of an actor getting cast, a script getting sold, or any other show business success story that involved someone meeting someone at church. And anyone who's anyone in the music industry wouldn't be caught dead doing anything but throwing up on Sunday mornings.

I'm not a religious guy, essentially because I was not raised by particularly religious people. My mother and father were too busy being dissatisfied workaholics to let a little thing like religion influence them. They were married at an

Episcopalian church, only because, well, they had to get married somewhere. I never saw my father attend church, but I did see my mother start attending—not long after she divorced my father. She ended up going to Bel Air Presbyterian Church, a very nice church up on Mulholland Drive. For those of you who know nothing of Presbyterianism, it is the most, boring, vanilla, do-nothing religion ever invented. You show up, you sit down, you listen to the pastor, you put money in the basket, you get out. If they're feeling especially festive, everyone might get up and sing a hymn.

But for those of you who know nothing of Bel Air Presbyterian Church, it was the trendiest in town in its heyday. I didn't realize that pastor Donn Moomaw was something of a local celebrity until he was the top story on the news one day. Seems he was forced to resign due to some sort of indiscretion. Before his career ignominiously vanished, though, he was the personal pastor to Ronald Reagan. The Sunday after Reagan was elected president in 1980, I went to church just because he was going to be there. Somehow, my brother and I made it to the front of the receiving line to shake hands with him as he arrived. Yes, I was a starfucker at church. I was 11 at the time. Sue me.

I also found out that Bel Air Pres, as the locals called it, actually had a nice singles scene going on back then. Not to impugn the religious integrity of my mother, but she was single when she started going there. Unfortunately, she met a guy and married him, a particularly unreligious fellow who was not partial to children and who became my stepfather. Most people bring spiritual nourishment home with them after going to church. My mom brought home an asshole. And people wonder why I look down on organized religion.

Then there are the proselytizers, whom I suspect are everywhere anyway. Except for my neighbor Clyde's comedic ramblings about Scientology and how it's making him a higher life form, few people get in my face about my lack of religion. I'm not sure if it's because I'm too hermitic to cross paths with proselytizers or if the religious people in my life all know what an intractable old fart I can be about church. My religious credo: Do whatever you want; don't include me.

I also feel that just because the First Amendment allows a person to go to church every day of the week and twice on Sundays doesn't entitle them to nag the shit out of every straight gentile they meet. A few years ago, I went to a Catholic church—not to worship, but for the L.A. reason: to support a friend of mine who had the lead role in a play. The church cafeteria was converted into an auditorium for a production of *Joseph and the Amazing Technicolor Dreamcoat*. No sooner did I sit down next to some middle-aged woman than I got the sales pitch.

"Do you live around here?" she asked.

"I'm a little ways away, actually."

"Do you attend this church?"

"No."

"Why don't you come by here sometime for services? We're always looking for new parishioners."

"You have a billion worldwide. Isn't that enough?"

She said it wasn't. Andrew Lloyd Webber and religious zealotry at the same time. It was more than any human should be forced to endure. Fortunately, at that moment, I spied a friend and her gay Jewish acquaintance, so I ran over to sit with them. The proselytizer didn't follow.

We had a Jehovah's Witness here once. Several of them, actually. It was in 2004, right after Election Day. They scurried around the courtyard like munchkins just before the good witch arrived. They banged on doors in no particular order, even though it was late morning on a weekday when people aren't likely to be home.

Finally, my Witness knocked. She looked like Estelle Getty and spoke with a Spanish accent.

Witness: "Would you like to hear some scripture? We are living in the final days."

Considering how bad the news was, she was unnaturally happy about it.

Me: "Is it just a coincidence that you're knocking on doors right after George W. Bush got reelected?"

Witness: "No, no. We've been doing this for years."

I resisted the temptation to ask her at what point she plans on feeling foolish for warning of an immediate event that keeps not occurring. She offered me a copy of *The Watchtower* or some such. I declined, and she and her friends left. To this day, I regret not racing over to ask Clyde the Scientologist what he said to his Witness. Could you imagine that conversation? The absurd force meets the ridiculous object.

Actually, for all the proselytizing that the fringe religions do in this town, the most hair-raising episode happened with a pretty progressive religion, and the proselytizer was an old family friend.

I've known Bob since I was a kid. He was introduced to our family via, of all places, Bel Air Pres in the 1970s. He was the one, in fact, who talked my mother into attending The Pres. I suppose he figured the whole Dungan clan were a bunch of marks, because several years ago, he tried to get me to go to his new church.

He talked me into going to a Saturday morning sermon—for men only. I told him that I had to get back to the Valley by 10:00 A.M. for my religion: therapy. He told me it wouldn't be a problem. He and I and four of his friends piled into his Lincoln Continental and drove to a converted warehouse in Agoura Hills, about 20 minutes from his house.

Long story short, it was a problem. The thing started late, after an absurdly long parking lot breakfast. This being Los Angeles, the guest preacher was, of course, a celebrity: Meadowlark Lemon, the former Harlem Globetrotter who'd found religion and went around spreading the word. After about 500 men filed in, Lemon finally began around 9:20, which allowed me 15 minutes to stew in total silence as the fleeting minutes ticked away. Since Bob insisted we sit in the front row, Lemon's ass was about three feet away from my face when I turned to Bob and whispered, "I have to leave right now!"

Bob wasn't leaving, but he gave me his car keys and told me to drive myself back, that he and his four friends would make it back by catching rides with other people. I got up in the middle of Meadowlark Lemon's oratory, ran to Bob's giant car, and sped back to the valley. I just barely made my 10:00 appointment, where I yammered away to my therapist about how crazy everyone else was.

And then two days ago, I talked to Jessie, a casual acquaintance of mine. She is a sweet, polite, upbeat, bright, and attractive singer from the Midwest. She also attends church regularly. And I only know this because I overheard her mention it to someone else. Once.

I asked her about her religion and the apparent lack of religion in this town. She answered my questions in her sweet, polite, upbeat, bright, and attractive way. The conversation ended with her inviting me to her church. Not preaching, not badgering. It was a sincere invitation.

There is no punch line. There is no sad ending. From my elegant conversation with Jessie, I can only conclude that there are plenty more like her around town, engaged in ongoing religious odysseys and neither preaching nor bragging about them, proving that at least one thing, in one way, in L.A. is the way it should be.

Dare I say it gives me faith.

THIS IS THE ORANGE LINE

My friend Evans Webb, a retired scenic artist who now works in oils, told me once that he was advised by an art dealer never to create a painting with orange in it. The dealer complained that orange didn't sell well.

I think that art dealer should hang out a shingle as a public transportation consultant.

My fair city's latest incarnation of a good idea half a century too late is our Orange Line, a bunch of compressed natural gas buses that are trying desperately to look cool. They do look cool. They're large yet sleek, shiny and silvery, still so new that the local *vatos* haven't had time to autograph them yet. They run on their own busway, a freshly graded and paved street devoted entirely to the buses. But they strangely aren't cool. Perhaps the fact that they're buses has something to do with it. The consensus among us car-mongers is trains are cool and buses are not. Gee, if only they could have made this whole Orange Line thing a train instead.

Sit down.

Iterations of trolleys and interurbans existed well into the 1950s in Los Angeles, during those halcyon times when there was so much space and so few people that traffic congestion seemed like science fiction. Due to nonuse and/or payoffs from car and oil companies, depending on what you believe, the trolleys were discontinued and most of their railways paved over for street and freeway expansions. While all this expansion may have honored the reality that baby boomers were coming of driving age, the mystic phenomenon of new roads breeding congestion exploded throughout the city. This was so, in part, because the only public transportation that remained was in the form of buses, which occupied the same streets that car-users wished they could have had all to themselves.

Among the railways that fell into disuse was a line in the San Fernando Valley, shared by the Southern Pacific Railroad. It wasn't long before a fair argument was made that discontinuing the old Red Car that ran up to Van Nuys was a mistake, and studies were in the works to figure out the best solution for how to use the existing space for some kind of public transportation. Even though rails and crossing gates, decrepit as they were, existed along the chosen route (and had been used by freight trains as recently as the early 1980s), city planners ordered them all removed to pour a street onto it for a handful of buses.

As if the irony isn't thick enough, the Metro Transit Authority is trying to sell the bus to locals as a train. The open-air benches and glorified curbs are called "stations" and "platforms." Riders neither buy fares from the drivers nor are they obligated to enter through the front door; they buy tickets from machines on platforms and can enter through any of the *three* doors on each bus. And, of course, it's included on maps of the rail system; there, with the Red, Blue, Green, and Gold Lines, is the Orange Line, the bus, a Peter Lawford in a Rat Pack of trains.

During initial tests of the bus, there was one accident and a number of near misses. Now that it runs all day, accidents are more commonplace, primarily because Los Angeles drivers are devolving to the point where anything more than a standard four-way intersection is too confusing to navigate, particularly to those who have never visited busway intersections. To counteract the dangers, additional street signs will be posted soon and all busway drivers have been instructed to slow to 10 mph at intersections—all 36 of them—thus slowing what continues to be billed as a speedy alternative to the 101 freeway.

Still, the accidents that are occurring seem to happen with such disturbing frequency that it's hard not to imagine a more severe fix being in order. As long as the MTA wants to sell the Orange Line as a train, it may as well pile on the irony by installing crossing gates, not unlike the kind that are used in conjunction with actual trains, and that we used to have back when the busway was an active railway—on which rode... um... actual trains.

For people who think this is wisenheimery, consider that freight trains run on another east-west line in the Valley, on rails that, up close, hardly look in better shape than the rusted ones that were torn up for the busway. The MTA smartly plopped longer-range commuter trains on this line a decade ago in an effort to ease rush-hour traffic. It has worked, as have the standard-issue driver protection measures, except for the occasional suicide or super-devolved driver who doesn't understand the concept of flashing red lights and crossing gates.

On October 29, I went for a ride on the Orange Line during the everyone-rides-for-free weekend it opened. (I just love that new compressed natural gas bus smell.) I drove to the North Hollywood station, about five minutes from my apartment, to take a bus in a round trip. At six in the morning. On a Saturday. It's not that I wanted to save a dollar and a quarter. I just wanted to be first.

The ride out there was uneventful, save for the fact that I ended up on a bus full of MTA employees who were getting dropped off at each station to usher the predicted hordes. It was too bright inside to see outside, and too dark outside to see anything. I kept looking out the window and saw the reflection of a guy asking me why the hell I was up at 6 A.M. on a Saturday to ride a bus. I got off at Warner Center and promptly got on another bus heading back, wondering what all the to-do was for.

The ride back had a few odd ducks, including one guy who boasted being the first rider at previous MTA openings. What was most remarkable wasn't who I saw, but what I saw. It was getting light outside just as I was heading back. Unlike the ride east, I could now see outside the bus windows.

I saw the Valley from a different angle—for the first time since I can remember. I got to speed through Balboa Park on a route I'd never taken before, certainly not past a walking pace. Going over the L.A. River reminded me of the time my brother and I, years ago, walked the railroad where it narrowed over the river because we didn't feel like walking the long way around on streets to get back to Victory Boulevard. (This was back when the freight trains were still running on it. We weren't daredevils. Just dumb.) I got to follow the old rail line through the Sepulveda Dam Recreation Area, under the 405 freeway, a route I'd never walked as a kid because it wasn't on my way home and it looked scary anyway. I got to ride through the backsides of neighborhoods in Van Nuys via long, sweeping curves in an area where the surface streets are forever perpendicular and parallel and one only sees the fronts of houses. And I got to ride down the middle of Chandler Boulevard, like my mother did on the old Red Car when she was a little girl.

After feeling like I've taken every street in the Valley, I got to take another one, a unique one. There are *never* new roads in L.A. In the exurbs, yes, where they're always looking for new places to put houses. But never in the middle of a city. And for this to arrive in *my* city, the places that I walked as a child and have driven as an adult, it's a once-in-a-lifetime experience. There might never be a first time like this again, but there will be future times. It makes me want to take it again.

I've been seduced by this ridiculous monstrosity. The only question is, will enough of the other car drivers in the Valley feel similarly so as to justify the $330-million price tag. (Tack on another 10 million if they go for the crossing gates.)

When I visited my friend Evans the painter the other day to confirm the story about orange not selling, I asked him if he'd heard that from other art dealers.

"No, just the one time. But I hear 'no black' a lot."

Note to MTA rail line planners who are heading the light rail extension along Exposition Boulevard on the west side: Are you listening?

Meet Leon:
A Strange Enchanted Boy

In Studio City, along a charming stretch of Tujunga Avenue, is a coffeehouse called Aroma. In Aroma is a regular patron named Leon. Just know the following: He's about 5'7", somewhere in his 70s and walks like it, but is in excellent physical shape. He sounds like Katharine Hepburn but with more testosterone and less vibrato. He's not shy about talking to anyone who sits within earshot—particularly women—about philosophy, Buddhism, books, nutrition, or pretty much anything else. He's also not shy about dancing. He calls it dancing, anyway. He feels the rhythm of a song, he claims, and just lets his body react. Imagine a guy having a seizure but not falling over. That's the closest I can come to describing it.

He's also a lovable free spirit. He sometimes wears pants that he's decorated with chewed gum. He drives a Volvo that he painted himself—with paint and plaster.

Tuesday afternoon, I wandered into Aroma and Leon was there with Russ the writer and a few other regulars, just as he is nearly every day. After we exchanged hellos, I whipped out my portable audio recorder and began recording.

Me: All right, Leon. What would you like readers to know about you?

Leon: They should know I'm kind of a humanitarian—

Me: "Kind of a humanitarian"? You mean you skim money from the till when people aren't looking but you're giving the rest of the time?

Leon: No, no. Scratch that. I'm a kind humanitarian. I act with kindness as opposed to exploiting and raking money for my own purposes. Humanitarian actually doesn't describe me. Actually, I'm a humanist more than a humanitarian.

After getting on the subject of talking:

Leon: Well, I'm always prepared to talk. The reason why I'm prepared to talk is I'm totally unprepared. That makes it easier to communicate if you're not prepared, 'cause it's all spontaneous. 'Cause I'm not prepared to say anything, I'm capable of saying anything in a constant stream of words, because I'm not thinking about what I'm saying. So the words just come out. And I don't even know what's going to come out from one moment to the next.

Me: Do you ever worry about offending people because you don't know what you're going to say?

Leon: Oh, oh, yeah, but there's a quality... I wouldn't call it "censorship" exactly, but my motivation is to serve people and to make people laugh and to speak with compassion. That's an automatic censor. Words that are discompassionate don't come out. Words that are compassionate come out.

Me: That's a remarkable gift.

Leon: It's a gift from the giver.

Me: You must be the most compassionate person on Earth.

Leon: Well, you know the song, "There was a boy, strange... strange enchanted boy, traveled" here and there and so forth....

Me: I think I know the song.

Leon: The last line is, "The only thing you need to learn is just to love and be loved in return."

Me: Wasn't it "Nature Boy?"

Leon: "Nature Boy." That's "Nature Boy."

We start singing.

Me: "And then one day..."

Leon: "... one magic day..."

Me: "... that nature boy, he..."

Leon: "... he passed my way, and we talked of many things, of fools and kings. And this he said to me, [talking voice] 'The greatest thing you'll ever learn, is just to love and be loved in return.'" That's what he said to me.

Me: You sing like you dance.

We get on the subject of how he emerged from a depression to become the strange, enchanted boy he is today.

Me: Were you like this before as a younger man?

Leon: No, I was a bureaucrat.

Me: Oh, that's a little different.

Leon: A little different position. I was a director of juvenile hall and a probation officer.

Me: You slapped kids around, did you?

Leon: Well, I didn't slap them. I wouldn't do that. I wouldn't permit slapping them around. But there were times I would have liked to slap my staff around because they were not very insightful sometimes and they were kind of abrupt and sometimes even cruel with kids.

Me: Did you want to be a probation officer when you were younger?

Leon: Well, I never even thought about being a probation officer.

Me: What did you want to be as a kid?

Leon: [thinking hard] Um... I wanted to be an Indian.

Me: An Indian?

Leon: Yeah. (*He laughs.*) I remember telling my mother—I was running around half-naked in the house and she said, "What are you?" And I said, "Well, I'm an Indian." She said, "You want to be an Indian?" I said, "Yes, I'd like to be an Indian. Can you arrange that, Mom?"

Russ: He was 19 at the time.

After talking about his connection with trees:

Leon: And then I became a marine biologist. I was working quite the same thing as in the natural world. I mean you have these giant plants that grow from the ocean bottom. I forgot what you call them.

Me: Seaweed?

Leon: Kelp. Kelp, yeah. "Help! Help, the kelp needs help!" So I thought that I would help the kelp. I worked for the Department of Fish and Game, you know, for a period of time.

Me: Was this back in Massachusetts?

Leon: No, this was here in California. I had graduated UCLA, my graduate major was marine biology.

Me: And you were in some boxing matches when you were at UCLA.

Leon: Oh, I was on the boxing team.

Me: Got hit in the head a few times.

Leon: I got hit in the nose a lot. And that hurt so bad. 'Cause my nose was not designed to accept blows.

Me: So you're not supposed to blow your nose?

Leon: No, I had a high bridge on my nose. I still have. And it was an easy target for the other party. For my adversary.

Me: I see.

Leon: No you don't.

Me: What do you mean, no I don't?

Leon: You say you see. I'm not talking about my eyes. I'm talking about my nose.

Me: I know.

Leon: You should have said, "I smell." Not "I see."

We get on the subject of Abraham Lincoln.

Leon: But Lincoln is one of my great heroes, because he was an extraordinary man. Had a great sense of humor. He also was an Aquarian. He was born on February fifth, I think, and I was also born on February fifth.

Me: You ever think they may have switched babies in the hospital?

Leon: I could have been Lincoln. I could be a reincarnation of Lincoln.

Me: You could be 196 years old.

Leon: Well, it's possible, but not likely. Do you remember when I had the beard with no mustache?

Me: It's imprinted on my brain forever.

Leon: Remember people would say they saw me on the five-dollar bill? Is Lincoln on the five-dollar bill?

Me: Been so long since you've seen one?

Leon: I deal only with one-dollar bills. Well, Washington, also. He was a great president, I suppose. But he doesn't excite me or.... I don't feel the kind of relationship I have with Lincoln.

Me: You have a relationship with Abraham Lincoln?

Leon: I have a link with him. I'm linked to Lincoln because of my Aquarian... being both Aquarian.

By now, some of us are laughing, me included.

Me: I can't tell you how tragic it is that I have to leave. I should have done this a long time ago. All right, I have to go meet my friend for dinner.

Leon: All right. Is it female, the friend?

Me: Yes.

Leon: Mmm. Is she cute?

Wednesday.

He said he'd be at Aroma around 2:00 this afternoon. I arrived around 3:00. A couple of people from the day before showed up too. They didn't want to miss the show.

Leon wasn't there yet. As we sat around, along with a couple of other regulars, I started doing my Leon impersonation. By now it was close to 4:00, and Leon still hadn't arrived. It was agreed that I should record an interview with me as Leon, making up answers to questions I asked myself. I can't explain why this idea sounded so hilarious. You simply must hang out there sometime.

I was about to interview myself when that familiar leather jacket and rumpled shirt with fashion-defying stripes came in. He plopped his overstuffed document case down at my table.

Leon: I've been busy today.

Me: What were you busy with, Leon?

Leon: I can't tell you.

Me: We were talking about heroes yesterday. Do you have any other heroes besides Abe Lincoln? Or would you even use the word "hero?"

Leon: Hero... leads us to a definition of hero. And heroic. Heroic to my mind is just doing what you need to do every moment of the day. Or moment of the night. If you can do what is there to be done and you do it with the richness and fullness of experiencing whatever it is, then you are heroic. To be heroic is just to be in touch with the moment. Monks in a monastery are heroic when they're deeply in meditation because they're in touch with the spirit of who they are and how that spirit connects with the consciousness of others. So, that's being heroic. It's not climbing Mount Everest. It's climbing that mountain within each of us, not going just halfway—but being content with halfway, if that's how far you can go in intending to reach your spiritual peak. So there's a mountain within and there's a mountain out there. And the mountain out there is the mountain within. And if you can relate to the mountain out there in all your full consciousness, the likelihood is that you're relating to the mountain within in all its full consciousness.

He laughs his gentle, creaky laugh.

Me: That's really deep. I don't know if I can contain all that in one article.

Leon: I don't know how I came up with that. You have to tell me what I said. I don't exactly know sometimes what I'm saying. If it makes sense to anyone, there's probably a reason for me saying what I said.

Me: Let's not go into reasons.

Me: What do you think the city's biggest problem is?

Leon: I think—no, I know—it's the eighteen to twenty thousand homeless people on the streets in downtown Los Angeles. If you go east on 8th Street about five or six blocks, you'll see people living in boxes and wrapped up in newspaper and women and children living on the street.

Me: How would you go about correcting this problem?

Leon: Well, actually, it's quite simple. First you have to go to the people on the street and you have to begin to listen to them and talk to them and you have to get their proposals for correcting their condition, because no one is better informed on their situation than they are. And after you listen to them, and spend time living with them, then whoever represents the community in doing this—let's say it's me—I would live there for maybe two or three weeks, and at the end of the time, I would know exactly what needs to be done.

Me: You'd live on the street for two or three weeks?

Leon: Well, yeah.

Me: You wouldn't have a hard time with that?

Leon: No, not at all.

Me: Really?

Leon: Yeah. Not at all. In fact, it would be fascinating and interesting. I meet on the streets some of the most direct, honest, and down-to-earth people, you might say. That wouldn't be a new experience for me because I had that experience back in 1987.

Me: You were actually homeless for a little while?

Leon: Well, I was for a short time. I was on the beach in Venice. There was a loophole in the ordinances that did not allow the police or the sheriff to remove these people off the beach. Later, there was an ordinance that was legislated. That was in January in 1988. On January 17, it became effective and the people were to remove off the beach. But nature interceded. And there was a high tide that actually covered the entire beach, so the people had to leave the beach with all their possessions. So it wasn't necessary to kick 'em off. Nature took care of it.

Me: I know you met Harvey Keitel once.

Leon: Oh, right, I did, yes. That was at a coffeehouse called Nudie's. Jill... what's her name? Jill Gatsby. I was performing there that night.

Me: You were performing?

Leon: No, she was. But I was dancing. I got up to dance. And then Keitel was there and he looked across at me...

Me: You guys saw each other from across the room.

Leon: Something like that. He couldn't take his eyes off me.

Me: Really.

Leon: And then, after I finished, he just beckoned to me to come over and talk to him and then he said, "Well, what kind of job have you had in your life? What do you do?" He was curious about me. And I said, "Well, I was working for the county probation department. I was a director in a detention facility where people were locked up." And then he looked at me and he says, "Well, you know, you are certainly out of prison now. And you're a very, very free person." And that was his comment. And that was it.

Me: If there's one factoid about you that you want to live forever on the Internet, what would it be? The kind of thing you might want on your tombstone, for instance.

Leon: I hope you guys are having as much fun as I'm having. That would be on my tombstone. If you look at the tombstone, it would say I want everyone to have as much fun as I'm having at this time in my, in my, destiny, in my afterconsciousness, I don't know. And then, it would be "Leon." And you look at the tombstone and you would say, "Well, this guy is having all this—such a good time and he's under the ground. Maybe I'm not so bad off. Maybe I should be enjoying myself." So for the observer, this would be inspirational.

Me: I hadn't even thought about it that deeply. I just thought it was something clever.

Leon: Well, it wasn't.

Me: Well, you know what, I think that's enough for today.

Leon: I think that's enough for tomorrow and for the next week or month. I'll be glad to talk more.

Me: So you are still willing to chat.

Leon: To do what?

Me: Chat.

Leon: Oh. I thought you said, "shat."
Me: No, no, no, no, no, I said, "chat."
Leon: Oh. I'm willing to do both.

Author's footnote: Leon Siff died on September 26, 2006. He had a stroke while dancing. His friend and dancing partner said he looked completely at peace and unafraid the whole time it was happening.

Welcome to the Grove

You're going to hate me. You're going to think I'm a sellout, that I'm a no-talent shit-scribbler who doesn't even have the brains to write press releases for a pharmaceutical manufacturer. (That last part isn't true. I don't have the *stomach* to write press releases for a pharmaceutical manufacturer.)

I can honestly say I've never met a real estate developer I didn't like, only because I have never actually met any real estate developers. I'm inclined to distrust most people who push new things on us, not because of the things they make, but because of their motivation. They don't want to make something better; they just want to make a fortune—either by creating something no one needs and manipulating us into thinking it's necessary, or by fucking up something old that worked just fine.

But there is a real estate developer here in Los Angeles, who, by all accounts, is a nice guy, and has actually developed a relatively new large piece of real estate that is not a monstrosity. The nice guy of the moment, Rick Caruso, may have more of an impact on the direction of Los Angeles real estate in the next 30 years than anyone else. (Side bet: five bucks he gets a street named after him.) And his non-monstrous creation, The Grove, is not just a pleasant place to shop and eat. It is a pleasant place to be.

The first time I went to The Grove, it was about a year ago for what turned out to be a great first date with a woman with whom future dates did not uphold that promise. She was a fan of The Grove, primarily because it was near her apartment. After I stopped dating her, I didn't associate The Grove with that lovely first date. I associated it with her.

That all happened last Christmas season. When this Christmas season descended upon us, it reminded me of The Grove and the holiday spirit it displayed last year. I figured enough time had passed for it to deserve another chance. I was especially forgiving of The Grove because, unlike the woman, it never tried to manipulate me into coming back.

The lure of malls has always been convenience and safety. With The Grove, Caruso supplies both. Since he sees malls as town centers, there is no better place for The Grove than the unofficial center of Los Angeles. And it provides a sense of security that is anything but false. One wouldn't expect anything less from a former president of the Los Angeles Police Commission.

Not that we need to encourage consumption in the most materialistic city in America, but the amenities at this mall have raised the bar for malls everywhere. The parking structure features an LED board with a running tally of the number of open parking spaces on each level. Someday, such things will be no more amazing than retractable cupholders, but for me, that day hasn't arrived yet. Every time I drive in there, I still gawk at a machine that knows that there are exactly 138 available parking spaces on the level I'm circling, and 221 on the level above if I'm feeling finicky. And this is from one of those old-fashioned drivers who needs only one parking space at a time. (Now, if Caruso can come up with a machine that provides a live count of the number of people blocking traffic on an entire row because they're waiting for a close parking spot to open up, I'll name my first child after him.)

The Grove also has a concierge. It is a mall, people. There is no hotel on the grounds. But it has a concierge. This is no customer relations counter with staffers in matching polo shirts, either. It is a real concierge. How real? In 2002, a *Wall Street Journal* writer declared it the best in the country. Better than concierges at five-star hotels. *In the entire country.* To serve people who want to go to the movies and browse for sexy shoes.

There is a double-decker electric trolley that runs the length of the mall. I'm still not sure why, but it's a nice touch—like cell phones that take pictures. The décor is contemporary with neither that cheap ticky-tack feeling that developers love nor the art nouveau horseshit that everybody hates. The streets are unusually clean and the foliage is well manicured. At risk of insulting the place, it's vaguely reminiscent of Main Street at Disneyland.

And maybe I'm just imagining it, but on windy days, the wind doesn't blow in The Grove. And it's an open-air mall.

This wouldn't be Los Angeles if there weren't something to make fun of, however, and Christmas at The Grove provides an extra dash of unintentional cheer. Twice a night during Christmas season at The Grove, it sort of snows. At 7:00 and again at 8:00, the chimes ring, announcing to all that the snow will begin—

in seven or eight minutes. (Nothing in Los Angeles starts on time.) Then "Let It Snow" comes on over the outdoor speakers. Machines all over the mall rev up simultaneously and shower the assembled with... bubbles.

From a distance, it looks like a blizzard. Up close, it looks like soap. It makes bubbles when it lands in the pond. Street vendors have to clean it off their wares when the five-minute storm stops because it makes their stuff dirty, which would be hilarious if it were actually soap. Turns out, it's actually gelatin and water. And the snow machines are so loud that they have to turn up the music. And everybody cheers when it begins. For east-coasters looking to trash Los Angeles, it is a dream come true.

It also makes children happy. And nobody freezes their ass off. And chances are really, really good that the stuff is nontoxic. So suck it, east-coasters.

Then there is the Christmas tree. In the center of the mall is a white fir over 100 feet tall. According to a mall representative I talked to, in order to squeeze the tree into the mall, they had to cut another tree down.

It is also taller than the tree in Rockefeller Center. Suck it again.

Caruso's greatest trick with The Grove may have been something that was out of his hands entirely. My image of a land developer is someone who swoops down on the most expensive real estate he can afford, destroys whatever is on it, and builds whatever the hell he wants. I only think this because it happens all over Los Angeles all the damn time. Distant rumblings that my own apartment building will someday be torn down—for another apartment building—only fuel my cynicism.

A developer that arrogant might, say, take over Farmers Market—the generations-old open-air shopping and dining plaza and unofficial center of Los Angeles—and put, oh, a giant mall on it with high-end chain stores owned by corporations. Farmers Market is a tempting target. Except for one thing. The city declared it a cultural and historical landmark. It is no more available for development than Jupiter.

We may never know if Caruso Affiliated would have razed Farmers Market if the city hadn't played the "landmark status" card a decade earlier. But I'd like to think that even if Farmers Market were his for the razing, Caruso would have been too smart for that. Farmers Market is not only a city institution, it is not only a damn charming place to eat and shop, but it attracts huge business from locals and tourists alike. The smartest thing any mall developer could have done would have been to take advantage of all that foot traffic by placing a complementary shopping center next to it.

You tell me how to hate something enjoyable, convenient, and reveres what's left of our city history, and I'll be happy to do it. Until then, I'll be gawking at the parking space counter and taking a free trolley ride to Farmers Market.

Meet Laszlo Tabori:
There Is Only Running

Laszlo Tabori is my running coach. He is not a personal trainer. He was a world-class runner in the '50s, then he became a running coach. He meets a group of us at a local track and tells us to run. While he's at it, he tells us how to run, how much to run, what we're doing wrong, and sometimes what we're doing right. Before we run, though, we run, then stretch, followed by running, then the running begins. We cool down by doing a little more running, then some running.

We meet every Tuesday and Thursday at 5:30 in the afternoon. Laszlo heads another group every Wednesday and Friday at 5:45—in the morning. The man is 74.

Some people can't or won't follow his instructions. They usually quit before he exercises his right to refuse to serve them. Those of us who've stayed with it, though, end up knowing and perfecting the technique of proper running. And we're worked so hard that we're generally in the best shape of our lives.

And oh yeah, the man is an absolute riot.

I've known Laszlo for some time; his daughter has been a friend of mine since college. But I'd never talked to him much until one day about five years ago at an event at his daughter's house. So I sat down and chatted him up. It went like this.

Laszlo: "Hi, kid. Wot's nyew?" He's had a thick Hungarian accent ever since he came to the United States in the '50s.

Me: "I got a stress fracture in my foot. Doctor says I can't run for six weeks."

Laszlo: "You got the wrong shoes! Come to my store. I sell you a good pair a shoes."

It was true. I'd been running in these cheap pieces of crap I'd found at an outlet mall. When I showed them to him at his store a couple of weeks later, he made a face like he had gas. "Why you running in the stupid shoes?" It's never "some stupid shoes" or just "stupid shoes." There is always the direct article in front.

He sold me a good pair of running shoes. I know they were good shoes because I ran like hell in them and didn't get a stress fracture. I also know they were good shoes because Laszlo said they were. The man is always right.

Laszlo: "Why don't you come to the track over here someday on a Tuesday or a Turssday so you can run with the group?"

I told him I'd think about it.

I figured I must need a running coach since I was performing at such a high level that I couldn't go for a jog without breaking my goddamn foot. Two months later, my stress fracture's healed, and I decide to give his group a try. I wait at one end of the football field with a few of the others in his group. A minute later, he comes walking up. He gets about 30 yards away, stops, squints at me, and says loud enough for greater Burbank to hear, "I don't belieb it! Look who had da guts to show up finally!"

"Guts" Dungan has been running with him ever since. And collecting material.

He leads us through stretching and calisthenics every time, the same way, every time. The same 20 exercises. If you do any of them wrong, he threatens you with his boots. "Keep you knees on the ground else I step on it with my boots." Yesterday, during sit-ups, he told a guy, "Keep you hands behind you head else I tie them to you ears." The guy is 12 years old. He always finds this amusing. Laszlo, for all his bark, is basically harmless.

But there's logic to this rather harmless abuse. For instance, he'll only hit high school age kids over the head with his clipboard. When they reach college, he swats them on the shoulder—if he's not carrying a stick; if he is, he swats them on the ass. Rules. And he never swats women. He hugs them. Actually, they hug him. Women love the guy.

I didn't get the concept of hitting at first. I took his hitting me in the shoulder as license to hit his shoulder in return. When I ran a relatively fast lap early on, I exulted by smacking him on the shoulder.

He steered his granite face at me and said, "Don't do dat again."

I haven't done it since.

Corollary to "Laszlo is always right" is "everything is your fault." Even if you follow his instructions to the letter, it's your fault if something goes wrong. For instance, whenever I'm coming back from a sprain or something, he'll tell me to run easy on it. After each group of intervals, he'll ask how it's feeling. When I tell him it feels fine, he'll tell me to run a little harder. So I'll run harder, tell him it feels fine, he'll tell me to run even harder, and so on until I come back and tell him it's starting to hurt again. Then he says, "That's because you run too hard on it!"

Even if you do something well, he'll find fault. Once, when I set a personal record in the half-mile, I thought he was going to pat me on the back. Instead he yelled, "How come you don't do that every time!?"

Sometimes I'll walk by him and he'll say, "It's all you fault, Joe." For no particular reason.

Laszlo likes to tell me lots of things are *my* fault, which isn't a nice thing to do to a guy who's predisposed to believe such things in the first place. Sometimes he even walks past me and says, "It's all you fault, Joe." I just agree. I figure that if I argue, that'll get him mad and that would be my fault too.

He can be colorful in his criticism. For a while, he would tell me that my stride wasn't long enough. Variations of this have included, "Stop doing the Charlie Chaplin step" and "Why you running like a chicken?" My personal favorite has always been, "You running like you shidding in you pants." Lately though, he's simply said, "Take a longer step." I'm not sure if it's because I've graduated to a stage where I'm worthy of more constructive comments or if he's losing his sense of humor.

During one conversation, he was telling me about his coaching days back in the '70s. "You wouldn't like me back then. I was mean." The irony is completely lost on him.

Once, he was looking at all the "lousy" joggers on the track, then shook his head and said gravely, just loud enough for me to hear, "Lot of fet asses."

That last tale has reached legendary status.

I've been able to glean some wisdom from him, thanks to his rigid, unapologetic approach to life. One day a few years ago, he asked me "wot's nyew" and I told him that I was about to direct a short film and that I was a bit nervous, seeing as how I was going to be in charge of about 20 people the next day.

He suddenly looked up and set my fet ass straight. "Ven you see me on the track, do I say, 'Eh duh-duh-duh-duh-duh-duh....'" He scrunched his face up like he couldn't decide what to order at a restaurant. "Ah, fack! No! I go out dere, and I am in charge. You do vot I say or ged out! God it?!"

I got it. The film shoot went fine. And I didn't have to yell "Ah, fack" once.

There have been occasions when I'll miss too much running. If I go too long without seeing him, we have a chat like this:

Laszlo: "Who you?"

Me: "Hi, sir."

Laszlo: "Do I know you?"

Me: "Sorry, sir. I've been busy."

Laszlo: "Come here. Touch you toes."

This means bend over so he can swat you on the ass with his stick.

So he came back yesterday after a three-week vacation, and I lit into him the same way he lights into me when I skip running too much.

Me: "Who you? Do I know you?"

Laszlo held up his stick. "No, but if you touch you toes, I introduce myself."

A few weeks ago, one of the other runners asked me, "What are we going to do when he's gone?"

"I don't know," I said. "I try not to think about it."

THIS WAS THE TIME
I MET RAY BRADBURY

I am in tenth grade. Honors English. Mrs. Lobb wants us all to present oral reports about authors. Her spin: we pair off and present them as interviews. One of us as the interviewer; one of us as the author. My friend Ron Epstein and I ended up with Ray Bradbury because someone else beat us to Kurt Vonnegut.

It is Sunday, October 30, 2005, around 6:30 P.M. Two people are helping Ray Bradbury to the stage. The crowd goes quiet. In the interminable seconds it takes him to stand up and walk six feet to the chair, he says loud enough to fill the room, "You ever feel like everybody's looking at you?"

It is 1996. My friends Robban and Allison give me *Zen in the Art of Writing* by Ray Bradbury for my birthday. Robban had inscribed on the half-title page, "To Joe: The Writer! Enjoy and learn. Robban & Allison." What made them think I was a writer? At that time—and for a long time afterwards—I'd always thought of myself as a guy who'd written some stuff. But I was no writer. Surely not me, the guy who worked a low-paying crap-ass job and shared a house with four college kids. Then again, in those days, I did routinely have boilermakers for dinner.

The first movie Ray Bradbury saw was *The Hunchback of Notre Dame* when he was three. Between his vivid imagination and his permanent spine curvature, he came out of the theatre thinking he was a hunchback.

When Ray Bradbury came to Hollywood with his family during the Depression, he went to a movie studio one day and saw W.C. Fields standing outside. Bradbury, about 12 at the time, went up to him and asked for an autograph. Fields scribbled it, handed it to him, and barked, "There you are, you little son of a bitch."

It is late in the afternoon of Sunday, October 30. The Book Review section of *The Los Angeles Times* mentions that Ray Bradbury is speaking at the Studio City branch of the Los Angeles Public Library in about an hour. I have no plans. The library is not only close to my apartment, but it's about five minutes from the coffeehouse where I'm reading the paper. I keep my paperback copy of Ray Bradbury's *Zen in the Art of Writing* in my glove compartment, for reasons I can't remember.

The first time Ray Bradbury sold a story, he got a check for $14.

He eventually needed an office to write. The office he found was UCLA, in the basement of the library. Using coin-operated typewriters, he paid UCLA one dime after another so he could write, a half-hour at a time, and UCLA offered no classes to him in return. UCLA got $9.80 of Ray Bradbury's money. Ray Bradbury got a typewritten draft of *Fahrenheit 451*.

The Studio City Library sits on the site of what used to be another library. A massive bond measure was passed by city voters some years ago. The bond measure provided funds to tear down many of the existing libraries and their evocative period architecture for new libraries that have computer stations and overdone architecture. Just after this branch reopened several years ago, I remember reading a letter in the newspaper from a local citizen who was complaining that this expensive new library was noticeably lacking in books.

The library in Studio City is a favorite of homeless people. A small courtyard set off to the side attracts a squatter nearly every time I visit. Maybe it's the same squatter, maybe it's a different one. Sometimes it's more than one squatter.

Ray Bradbury: "The library is the center of our lives. And if it isn't, it should be."

I arrive early and park on the street right in front of the library, knowing how small the parking lot is. As I stand there and wait for the doors to open, I watch carefully to see just how many Ray Bradbury fans drive straight into the parking lot, long after it's filled up. Too many to count. I look down the block to see if anyone's parked on the street, about fifty yards away. The entire next block is vacant.

I notice an empty parking spot near a side door. A sign indicates that it is reserved for Ray Bradbury. I think to myself that I've known since researching Ray Bradbury in tenth grade that the man doesn't drive. I watch carefully to see if any of the cars herding themselves into the parking lot have Ray Bradbury riding shotgun.

While waiting, I troll for women, for hot, single, female Ray Bradbury fans. I can't find any.

When he was a young man, Ray Bradbury met a rich girl and asked her to marry him. Her friends told her not to marry him. He's going nowhere.

Bradbury: "I said to her, 'I'm going to Mars and the moon. Do you want to come with me?' She said yes. And that was the best 'yes' I ever got."

At first, they were so poor that he took his calls at a payphone outside their front door.

The event starts at 5:30 P.M. They open the doors late. We all file in and are handed fliers that tell us that Mr. Bradbury will sign autographs, but for no more than two books per customer and no inscriptions so as to speed the line along as quickly as possible.

At least 10 minutes after I take a seat, an event volunteer announces that Ray Bradbury will speak at about 6:30 P.M. In the meantime, he is in the next room signing autographs. Me and my copy of Zen in the Art of Writing head to the next room for an autograph.

Ray Bradbury and his stack of manuscripts took a train from Los Angeles to New York in search of literary success. He was met with total rejection by day and stayed at the YMCA at night. On his last night in New York, he met with an editor at Doubleday. The editor asked him if he had any novels. Bradbury didn't have any. Just short stories. The editor told him that his Martian stories were a novel of sorts, if he could find a way to tie them together.

Bradbury went back to the YMCA, spent all night typing up an outline, and showed it to the editor the next day. "By God, you've got it," said the editor. "Here's seven hundred dollars."

Bradbury had converted his Martian stories into what he described as Winesburg, Ohio on Mars. It was The Martian Chronicles.

When talk turned to other ideas for novels, Bradbury pitched another story. Said the editor, "Here's another seven hundred dollars."

While waiting in line for an autograph, a volunteer comes by with a bowl of Halloween candy. I take a little bag of candy corn and scarf it. Another volunteer, a middle-aged gay man, comes up to me—no one else in line, just me—and volunteers another bag of candy corn. "You went through the first one so fast!" he said. I go to this library all the time. I never knew it was so cruisy.

I finally get up to Ray Bradbury to have him sign my book. I slide my copy of Zen in the Art of Writing across the table, open, just as one of the volunteers had asked us to do. I had it opened to the title page, the next page after the half-title page where my friends Robban and Allison had inscribed it so long ago.

Bradbury looks down at my book and stops abruptly to look up at me. He squints a bit and turns his head to one side. He must have had a reaction to the book, I think. Here everyone else is getting autographs for *Fahrenheit 451* and his latest book, *Bradbury Speaks*, and then I come along with this truly insightful book. Not just anyone reads *Zen in the Art of Writing*.

He studies my face for a long pause. I conclude exactly one thing from this: *The man knows I'm a writer. He's thinking of a clever inscription.* This, in spite of the fact that the flier clearly states that due to time constraints, Mr. Bradbury cannot personalize books for people. But he's making an exception for me, because I'm a writer. He's so old and wise that he can tell I'm a writer. He knows just by looking at me that I'm a writer, and here in my cruisy library he's thinking of just the right kernel of wisdom that I need at this moment in time so that Joe the writer can go on to boundless success and can tell everyone the tale when he's 85. And he divined all this without either of us saying a word.

He finally breaks the silence with this pearl of wisdom:

"Can you speak up? I don't hear so well anymore."

He was looking curiously at me because, in the din of the room, he thought I'd said something to him.

"I didn't say anything."

Then he puts his head back down and writes "Ray Bradbury" on the title page, just above the part that reads "Ray Bradbury." He doesn't say anything else.

"The answer to everything is to keep being in love."

"Stay in love and go back to your loves constantly, again and again and again."

"Just do it! Find the love and stick with it!"

Ray Bradbury is done talking. I pull my car away from the curb and make a left into a residential neighborhood to get away from the madding crowd. I find another madding crowd. Right there by the street are two local news vans. I didn't realize a Ray Bradbury signing was such an event. Then I see the crowd lining up. This is across the street from the library. I drive the length of the block before I find the end of the line, where I yell from my car window, "What's going on?"

"Haunted house up the street."

Haunted houses draw big crowds every year. People love them. More people want to walk through a stranger's house than hear Ray Bradbury tell them to go fall in love and stay in love.

Television stations will provide news coverage of what amounts to temporary home decor, but no reporter would walk across the street to chat up a literary legend.

"It's been a great pleasure to talk to you. I hope you come back here another time. Take care and God bless."

This Is How We
Deal With Terrorism

As a large, high-profile city, Los Angeles is, no doubt, being scouted by terrorists. We have not only a large population, but a density per square mile that, in some areas, rivals that of Manhattan. We have plenty of well-known icons that, if destroyed, wouldn't just hurt us. It would shock us. If we see anyone acting suspiciously, we ignore them, regardless of their nationality. There's just one thing, however.

There will never be a terrorist attack in Los Angeles.

First of all, our traffic ruins everyone's plans every day, all the time. There are people who have been commuting on the same route for years who are still unable to predict how long their ride to work will take on any given day. A bunch of terrorists all relying on each other to show up someplace at the same time would be foolish to try it in a city whose transportation system is as constipated as ours.

Even if terrorists could somehow utilize chaos theory and hypothetical calculus to figure out exactly how long any car ride will take before they take it, they do not have the patience to put up with the traffic. In order to tolerate our gridlock, you turn into an automaton. One day, you try to remember why you want to go from here to there so badly and you can't. If you're lucky, you can merely philosophize as to why you tolerate such a stressful, colossal waste of time. Your urge to make the pain stop eventually becomes so overwhelming that you don't have the patience to integrate it into a plan for mass murder. You either kill yourself quickly and privately or you take the high road and quietly move to Oregon or Las Vegas or Rancho Cucamonga. No terrorist organization can afford such defeatism or entropy.

I also think that terrorists get lost and frustrated easily. It's not based on anything scientific. It's just a little something I cling to. Street addresses here make huge jumps whenever a street leaves one city and enters another. Along part of Robertson Boulevard, the addresses jump around from block to block. We have multiple Main Streets, 3rd Streets, Santa these, Dona those.... We have two San Vicente Boulevards. Two San Vicente Boulevards, for crissakes. I'd like to think terrorists just couldn't put up with this.

There is also the question of how to attack. Ever since 9/11, hijacking a plane is basically out. Biological attacks won't have a large-scale effect, either. Poisoning the air won't do any good because the wind doesn't blow here. Our tap water is famously undrinkable already, thanks in part to the high levels of chlorine, which could kill anything terrorists dump into our aqueducts. I suppose if you put enough of anything in our aqueducts, you could neutralize all that chlorine. Heck, if that happened, people might start drinking the water again.

With or without those options, terrorists are up against the fear factor too. Say what you want about us being wimps, but most of us were here for the Northridge earthquake, which caused billions of dollars in structural damage all over the city, killed 51 people, and injured 9,000 more. Some of that was due to the fires caused by the quake, but most of it was done by the quake itself, which came with no warning and took less than a minute. Furthermore, we know another one is coming and we're preparing for it by not moving. If that doesn't scare us, how the hell are jihadists going to come up with something that does?

This being the show business capital, there is also the ignorance factor. As someone in the industry once observed, nobody knows anything. (Nobody knows who the hell said it.) He was talking about how ignorant everyone in show business is, particularly about their own business. There's something about that hollow know-it-all-ism that rubs off on other people in this city. No matter how fixated on the task, any group of people trying to accomplish anything in this town will eventually get caught up in arguments and power plays, to the detriment of the common goal. The higher-profile and more delusionally induced the project is, the more vulnerable it is. A terrorist plot carried out by fringe religious maniacs is no match for such foolishness.

The ignorance extends even to the *alleged* terrorist attack. Take this famous quote from President Bush, telling us in February 2006 about a plot his administration had broken up four years earlier: "We believe the intended target was Liberty Tower in Los Angeles, California." Here in L.A., we can't say we weren't relieved to hear that this plan had been thwarted. We would have felt even more relieved if we actually *had* a "Liberty Tower." What we *do* have is something the locals call the "Library Building," which, to a suicidal terrorist in charge of a plane, must look pretty tempting. Still, few of us believed the president. Being a city full of Democrats, we have a hard time believing anything President Bush says, particularly when he can't get the name of a goddamn building right. For all we know, terrorists might have been planning to ram a Dodge Dart into Pink's Hot Dogs.

Luckily, we now do have an institution into which we can put more faith. It's called the Joint Regional Intelligence Center, or J-Rick amongst friends. Its main feature is search software that shares information from federal, state, and local law enforcement databases to catch terrorists and follow up on potential threats to our national security. It is the first such information clearinghouse of its kind in the country, and it is in Los Angeles. Bad-ass.

Which leads to the biggest reason there will never be a terrorist attack here. Not only can we stop terrorism before it happens, but we already have. It happened last year, before J-Rick was even set up. Four men were caught plotting a large-scale attack on multiple points throughout the L.A. area. They were part of a radical Islamic organization called Jam'iyyat Ul-Islam As-Saheeh, or JIS for short, which sounds like jizz, which is what these four men will likely be felching for life thanks to our law enforcement officers.

Los Angeles is a dream factory. Everyone, it seems, comes here sooner or later, to pursue their dreams or at least consider it when they see everyone else doing it. However, the only thing we do better than make dreams come true is crush them. For once, that dispiriting skill is useful for something besides making screenwriters drink and actresses cry.

In other words, terrorists, keep dreaming.

Meet Clyde Langtry, Part Nine

Clyde hasn't been so talkative lately. Oh, sure, he'll stop to chat me up about things I don't need to hear about, like his penis. "I don't mind saying mine used to be an eight, but now it's about a five," he volunteered to me a few months ago. I wasn't sure if he was talking about length or some Scientology genitalia scoring system.

And he was nice and nosy a month or so ago when a couple of plainclothes police officers knocked at my door.

"What was that all about?" Clyde asked.

"Oh, they wanted me to look at some photos of homeless guys to see if I could identify the one who peed on our driveway and yelled at us a while back."

"I don't trust police. I never get involved in anything like that."

This is the same man who's asked me to keep an eye out for riffraff when he's out of town. Nice to know he's sticking his neck out for me as well.

But also, I've been avoiding him. I'm losing tolerance for indulging crazy people—or maybe only the ones who are most bothersome. One might say Clyde Langtry has a bothersome streak.

However, on Sunday, he was in rarest of rare form. He raced out of his apartment when he saw my girlfriend and I walking up.

"I've uncovered the most amazing conspiracy." He regularly skips greetings and gets straight to the reason he's accosting you. "Now, I know, you're going to think I'm crazy," (you put in your own punch line here; I've run out of them) "but I found something on Google that is the biggest violation of the First Amendment in history. But I can't tell you about it."

He rambled on about how he couldn't tell me about it, whereupon I let my girlfriend off the hook by telling her she could go in to take care of whatever it was that she had to take care of, which was nothing, but I'm sure she wanted an escape.

"Yeah, yeah, good, you go in," Clyde said to her. "I don't know how much I can trust you." It's not that Nicole isn't trustworthy. It's that Clyde is paranoid.

Now it was just Clyde and me in our courtyard, in broad daylight, talking about this big, big discovery he's made that he couldn't tell me about—followed by him telling me all about it. "Just type in _____, _____, and _____. And click on the first site that comes up. You won't believe it."

I repeated the three words back to make sure I got it.

"Google is just amazing. I hit return, and the results came back in, like, zero-point-twelve seconds or something." He's floored by the conspiracy and by a search engine. If he had an Xbox, he might never leave his apartment again.

"Have you told your wife about this?"

"I can trust her, but only to an extent." Naturally, he's sharing his secret with me instead.

Because he'd made his point, he continued talking for another 10 minutes, slowly getting to the core of his real problem, which was him being bothered by how screwed up he is, and how he was programmed so poorly in his upbringing. It was not unlike the sort of thing one does in therapy, which he's been programmed to abhor yet doomed to practice without even realizing it. Clyde Langtry is hilarious.

"When I was eight or nine years old," Clyde said, "my mother would take me into the bathroom and turn on the faucet so I would be ready to take a leak. How screwed up is that?"

"Very."

It took me a while to get him to shut up long enough for me to say goodbye and shut the door in his face. This is also routine with him: I get to my door, I open it, I step in, lean on the door, inch it less and less ajar so that he can barely see my face. Hint after hint that I'm done and he doesn't even have the courtesy to ask if he's boring me to death. Either he's extremely unaware of social cues or he's writing his own column somewhere. ("That obliging dumbshit neighbor Joe let me talk for 12 minutes again today. Man, why doesn't he just slam the door on me like everyone else?")

About four minutes later, there was a knock at the door. Clyde was standing there with his laptop, showing me the first Google entry when one types in the three magic words. I told him he was a raving loon, annoying as flies at a picnic, and if he didn't leave me alone then I would call the FBI. But the words I used were, "Thanks, man. I'll check it out when I get a chance."

A short while later, I stepped out the back way to take out the trash. When I got back, Nicole was at the door talking to him. He was asking her if she knew of any computer security experts, just in case the feds or the Martians or someone were hacking into his computer and checking up on his Internet searches.

The conspiracy Clyde is onto is, essentially, that one extremely powerful U.S. organization owns another extremely powerful U.S. organization that's in a completely different line of work. It isn't much of a conspiracy, I figure, because both organizations are widely despised by most Americans and who gives a shit anyway; consolidation is so 1990s.

But the reason I omitted the search items above is just in case Clyde is onto something. I don't need the extremely powerful, many-tentacled beasts behind this possible conspiracy to render me to Syria for interrogation. And, in fact, the Web site he told me to read didn't make much sense anyway. That said, I've never seen Clyde so worked up. He was a bit unhinged, even for Clyde.

Last night, I tried to find him for some follow-up on this issue, mainly regarding the fact that I didn't think it was a conspiracy.

I knock at his door. He isn't home, yet his car is in the driveway. How is it that a man who's mastered the art of showing up to talk one's ear off can disappear during that rare moment when one actually wants to talk to him? Has he mastered irony too?

A little while later, his wife, Priscilla, comes home. I wander out to talk to her and she tells me they planned on going to dinner soon and that they might be turning in early.

A little while later, I catch a couple of other neighbors outside chatting. I join them for as extended of a conversation as I can, knowing that the sound of chatting neighbors attracts Clyde like the electric can opener draws the family dog.

Nothing. His lights are on but no one's home.

I leave for a spell. When I come back, his car's gone.

Now what? Has he been rendered?

A little while later, I hear his crappy blue car roar up the driveway. (He had two and a half dinners that night, he'd tell me later.)

I pour a glass of wine and go out to wait for him. Priscilla is whistling for the cats to come in. She gives up and goes back in, leaving the door open. One of the cats comes in. She keeps whistling. The cat leaves.

Clyde walks up.

I hate living life with regrets, but one of the greatest regrets of my life is, on this night, not having the ability to recite things from memory having heard them only once. For tonight, Clyde Langtry, he of questionable mental status, flew the coop—or at least taxied for take-off.

He talked for an hour. I barely got a word in. He digressed on tangent upon tangent upon tangent. He barely talked about the conspiracy. He just jettisoned himself from one story to another, none of which had anything to do with his discovery. He kept admitting that he was digressing, then just kept staying off track and interrupted me when I tried to steer him back. I decided that Crispin Glover will play him if this column ever becomes a movie.

"You're never going to meet a more perceptive person than me," he said at one point. "That's a fact. I can tell what a person's thinking just by looking at them and reading them." This explains why he's entrusting his secret discovery to a satirist.

Priscilla came out. "Don't talk too long," she said to him.

I was able to squeeze in one question. "You know, I went to that site you pointed out. So just for the hell of it, I typed [the two organizations' names] into Google. It came back with 380,000 hits. So if you're onto something that hardly anyone else knows about, why is it that there are so many pages with [the two organizations] on them?"

It took 10 minutes for him to say what he could have said in one: The real sites, the ones with the real conspiratorial information, are what Clyde called "nanny" sites. That is, they're hidden from searches that children could make. And most of the hits I got probably had the two organizations in contexts that were unrelated to the conspiracy. I had one question for the guy and it elicited the most uninteresting thing he said all night.

Other Clyde comments included:

"I'm a fuckin' genius. I don't care what you think."

"I'm an organizational genius."

"I'm great at research."

"Lemme tell you something. There are two ways to live life: being reasonable and being unreasonable. And I'm here to tell you that being unreasonable is the only way to go."

"I almost died several times in the past year. Not for real, but spiritually."

He reached into his crotch to adjust his hernia belt a few times. He ripped a big fart too. Didn't apologize for any of it. The man has ass meat in his head.

Remember, all this was coming at night, in the dark, with no one else around, from a man who looks almost exactly like President Bush. It's a good thing I wasn't on drugs or else I would have shit my pants right there in the courtyard.

"Lemme take you inside to show you something."

By now it was nearly 11:00, and Priscilla was about ready for bed. I was barely inside the door when Clyde shouted to her, "Put something on because I wanna show Joe something in the bedroom." This whole thing really begs for context.

He took me into his bedroom. It was just as I remembered it from the time before. Dreary and unchanged since about the 1970s, I'd guess. Not one sign that a woman lived there. And one wall was floor to ceiling with notebooks, most of them from Scientology. He thoughtfully pointed out which ones were rip-offs and which ones weren't.

He fired up his laptop computer and showed me something on the desktop. "That link, that's the one I wanted to show you. Don't pay any attention to these others." We didn't actually visit the Web site. He just wanted to show me the icon.

We retired back into the dining room, which has no dining table. It has his drafting table instead, on which was one of many notebooks that happened to be open to a page about arguments. "All arguments between two people are explained right here," he said. "They all have to do with a third person." He laid out two glasses cases and a cassette tape to illustrate the two arguers and the third person, proving that he's a spatial genius too.

By now, his manifesto had degenerated into a speech about how he thought I'd benefit from Scientology classes. I farted just to see if he'd acknowledge it. He didn't. But he did tell me to leave my wine glass outside because he hated the smell of wine.

He pointed out framed certificates and more notebooks, and then opened up a side closet to show me something else. It was at about this moment that I realized something I'd never thought about before: His apartment has the exact same floor plan as mine. There but for the grace of God....

He pulled out something that looked like a typewriter case and opened it to reveal a Scientology meter of some kind. The idea is that the subject holds a cylinder that's connected to the machine, which, from the looks of things, can measure no more than the pulse of the subject. The operator asks the subject questions and the machine registers changes it detects in the subject. Back on Earth, I think they call these lie detectors.

Clyde the genius thinks the invention is brilliant. The thing had a grand total of three LCD displays. "It has a clock on it too. I guess this is the clock." He pointed to the one that displayed the time.

It happens to all humans who talk to Clyde, but I never thought I'd see the day. We'd been talking too long, and we crossed the tipping point, the moment where one's capacity for hearing Clyde talk had been reached. For at that moment, Priscilla, the easygoing woman who always has time to chat with any neighbor about anything, *came out and got mad at him.*

She opened the hallway door and just stood there in her robe. How is it that they have a hall door and I don't, I wondered.

"I'm just showing Joe something," Clyde said. "Joe's cool."

"It's time for you to go to bed."

"Joe's asking questions and I'm answering them. He's cool." I hadn't asked a question in half an hour.

"I should go," I said. I felt like a cassette tape near two glasses cases.

"No, you stay. We're having a discussion."

"Just remember..." Priscilla stammered, "...what we talked about at dinner tonight!"

Holy damn, they were having a fight, right there in front of me. It was like watching ugly dogs fuck.

"Yeah, yeah, I know, I know!"

She went back into the bedroom. Clyde closed the door. It opened again.

"No," she said. "I just want to hear it."

She *wants* to hear us talk about this claptrap?

"Just go to bed!"

"Leave the door open!"

"Will you get in there already?"

"I can get out of here, really," I said.

Clyde insisted that I stay. Priscilla finally disappeared into the bedroom and he finished his show and tell of the Scientology meter.

"Ain't that cool?"

"Yeah." It wasn't.

We exited back into the courtyard. I apologized for not leaving earlier. He said his wife was crazy.

Then he told me that he was all alone with his thoughts about this whole conspiracy business, as well as the feeling that he wasn't able to talk about any of it to anyone.

So I did what I should have done years ago.

I walked away.

MEET THE AUTHOR

I know where Paris Hilton lives.

Knowing things like this against our will is one of the side effects of living here. As much as I present myself as a detached outside observer, I'm infected with Angelitis. Angelitis is a condition that afflicts residents of Los Angeles, and its symptoms include misplaced priorities, self-importance, ethical vacuity, uncontrollable materialism, and falsity in relationships. Then again, I don't obsess over my car or my appearance, I'd like to think I'm not a self-important phony, and when people ask me what's new, my answer never involves a screenplay or an agent. And, in fact, people sometimes mistake me for an east coaster. So maybe I'm merely a carrier of the disease.

The reality is that I'm not only a native, but I've lived here my whole life, which means I don't have a frame of reference for what a normal city should be like. All I can do is look at the people and realities of my city with my own sense of irony and bullshit detection. And as cities go, L.A. has a mind-boggling amount of irony and bullshit.

Any sane person would move out, right?

I know where Paris Hilton lives.

I can't help not forgetting things like that. I try to forget them, but I can't. Try not thinking about pink elephants. See what I mean?

I think about a lot of things. I think about all the failed food experiments before people figured out sublime combinations like chocolate and red wine. I wonder how fish wash themselves. I wonder who's in charge of naming the streets. I think about how if gold is just another element, why scientists can't somehow slightly fuck with a neighboring element, like lead, and turn it into gold. When you consider that the only thing separating one element from another is its number of electrons, neutrons, and protons, and that lead has more of each than gold does, gold is kind of already in lead. All you have to do is take away a few electrons, neutrons, and protons from a lead atom, and then you have a gold atom. Who says this can't be done?

I'm fascinated with parking enforcement laws, commercial airplanes, and small towns in Nevada. I couldn't begin to tell you why.

I used to get angry more often. A lot of it was just walking-around bluster, the kind that only alienated people—which only made me angrier. But sometimes I got creative about it. Like when I was working at this dotcom in 2001. There were some people in my department whom I wouldn't trust to water my plants and they were making more money than I was for doing far less work. The injustice was so infuriating that I exacted a little revenge when I left the company. As a relatively early hire, I qualified to buy as many as 2,500 shares in the company at a strike price of 15 cents per share. This was a great deal except for the fact that the company wasn't yet listed on the stock exchange and was in the process of going down the shitter. Still, this seemed like a good chance to take a piss on the doormat on my way out. So, at my exit interview, I slid a dime and a nickel across the desk of the human resources manager and requested to purchase one share, please.

The woman took the money and put it in her desk drawer, then led me down the hall to a lawyer to make sure I could make a cash purchase of so few shares. The lawyer was a little uptight woman who had picked her hairdo out of *Librarians Monthly*.

"I—I—I think it's okay," she said. "I—I know you can't buy partial shares. I'm pretty sure you can buy any number of shares. But I—I—I know you can't purchase fractions of shares, like quarter shares or half shares."

"Well of course not. I'm not cheap."

I eventually got my stock certificate in the mail, no doubt at great legal and administrative expense to the company.

If I heard correctly, a rule later got passed that prohibited anyone from trafficking in fewer than 100 shares at a time so as to keep anyone from pulling such an annoying stunt again.

I went to California State University, Northridge, for my bachelor's degree at a time when I was so dumb to life that it would be years before I even knew my head was up my ass. I was a business major because the college was close to my house—or I went to that college because I wanted to be a business major. I don't even remember anymore. I changed my major to TV-Film because television and film were more interesting.

I know where Paris Hilton lives because someone told me. Sometimes people mention stuff to me and it sticks. Someone told me that grapefruit has fewer calories than it takes to digest it. Someone told me that 3 percent of the population bites their toenails. Someone told me that pubic hair toupees were invented during the black plague because the plague made one's pubic hair fall out and pubic hair had aesthetic value back then. I've remembered all those things too. Does that make me crazy? I just remember a lot of stuff. Sue me.

When you think about it, knowing Paris Hilton's address is really not such a strange thing to know or admit. It was just something I heard. I'm not obsessed with celebrities, really. I see them once in a while and then forget about them—until I think of them again. Did someone say, "Pink elephants"? Damnit!

Okay, there was the time I saw Quentin Tarantino in a movie theater and I asked him for a job. What was I supposed to ask for? His autograph? I was unemployed. Fat lot of good that would have done me. And besides, he was there to see one of his own movies. Paid money and sat in the third row. And you think *I'm* weird?

I also remember my first day of fourth grade at a new school right after our family had moved. A girl named Cathy asked me to lead the class in the morning flag salute. I didn't know how to lead the class in the flag salute, and I thought it was ridiculous of her to ask the one person in the room who hadn't seen it done before. So I whispered to the first kid nearby, Donald, what to say. He whispered back, "Put your right hand over your heart, begin." I repeated it and led the class in the flag salute, then sat back down in my seat that had been occupied by a girl named Donna who, a week earlier, had been killed in a car accident.

I don't remember Donald's last name, but I remember he had a little round bandage on his cheek to cover his ringworm. There was also a kid named Tim who I rather liked. I heard a few years later that he'd tried to set his mother on fire.

I might be crazy. I don't think I am. Then again, whenever someone fears they might be crazy, that's good sign that they're sane. I'm pretty sure I'm sane. My shrink tells me so. But I keep seeing her once a month anyway. That's not exactly a sign of a Zen Buddhist.

I'm positive I used to be crazy. Let me take that back. Not because I'm a liar, but because I'm too impulsive about my word choice. I used to call myself crazy all the time. But I wasn't crazy. I was aware enough to start seeing a shrink voluntarily, wasn't I?

I'm positive I used to be depressed. That's when I started seeing my shrink. Twice a week. I really wasn't doing well back then.

I know where Paris Hilton lives. I live in Los Angeles in spite of that fact.

I live here because I was born here and despite the city's flaws, I've gotten used to them. Maybe it's made me discontent on a level that I'm not even aware of, but until I become aware of it, I'm staying.

Most of my friends and family are here, despite how crazy they may be. My brother once visited all 58 counties in California within a span of four months—

while keeping a full-time job here in L.A. I have another friend who, at one time, only wanted two books: one about the actress who played Ethel Mertz, and another about the whole "two Darrins" thing on *Bewitched*. I'm friends with two people who are the only two people I know who have volunteered stories to me about times they've crapped their pants as adults. As coincidence would have it, they're a couple. I'm friends with a woman who's a pack rat. She married a man who's a neat freak. I point to them as proof that God has a sense of humor.

I have one friend who cries at Paul Giamatti movies, draws R.I.P. pictures of celebrities when they die, and not only knows exactly how many times he's seen *Jackass: The Movie* (it's gotta be over 40 by now), but he laughs his ass off every time he sees it. He also occasionally sends scary and/or embarrassing fan emails to an actress friend of his, signs fake names to them, and attaches random Internet photos of males who are either physically deformed or incredibly ugly.

I'm friends with people who were afraid they'd be mentioned in my column because they think they're weird. They're among the more normal people I know.

And that's just the stuff off the top of my head.

Then there are the people I don't know. I get tailgated by them. I had my car broken into by one of them. They make noise when I'm trying to sleep. They put junk mail on my doorstep. At least one of them leaves his dog's shit in front of my apartment building all the time. So many work in the entertainment industry. Tens of thousands of crazy, crazy people. I shouldn't say that. There are actually some sane people in show business. His name is Dennis Franz.

I'm here in spite of the fact that nearly every quality of life in Los Angeles continues to worsen. Traffic is murderously bad, the air is brown, the houses are impossibly expensive, and we're running out of water and what little we have is full of chlorine. We don't have enough police. Our public school system sucks. We don't have enough hospitals *and* some of them suck. In recent years, my city has been nurturing two seemingly contradictory qualities at once: The cost of living is approaching extortion levels while the city is turning to shit. And people keep moving here. And there's no end in sight.

While working on this column, I can remember thinking that maybe I was writing this column because it would compel us all to make Los Angeles better. Then I decided that was crap. I hope my city can do better, and I wish to hell it would. But I doubt it will. Fact is, the reason I wrote this column is because Los Angeles is easy to make fun of.

As it turns out, I did *not* know where Paris Hilton lives. I was a little less shallow than I thought I was all this time. I was told it was at the north end of Fairfax Avenue. But I just discovered that that is not true. I know this because I just did a little research and found out the exact address.

Now I know where Paris Hilton lives.

Like the book? Please join the OFFICIAL L.A. NUTS BOOK FAN SITE on facebook. Get updates on the book and related events—and even FREE stuff.

Also, please review or discuss it on any of these book networking sites:

goodreads.com
shelfari.com
librarything.com

And check trincopublishing.com for future titles.

Questions? Thoughts? Comments?
Any of your own "nuts" stories to share?

joe@lanutsbook.com